$35⁰⁰ ̲

THE HOUSE OF COLLINS

William Collins, 1789-1853

THE HOUSE OF
COLLINS

*The Story of a Scottish Family
of Publishers from 1789 to the
Present Day*

By

DAVID KEIR

COLLINS

ST JAMES'S PLACE, LONDON

1952

*This book is set in Fontana, a type face
specially designed for the exclusive use of
the Publishers*

PRINTED IN GREAT BRITAIN
COLLINS CLEAR-TYPE PRESS : LONDON AND GLASGOW

TO
THE PRESENT UPHOLDERS
OF THE TRADITION
WHICH THIS BOOK RECORDS

Contents

7

Illustrations

The portrait of Dr. Chalmers by Sir John Watson Gordon, P.R.S.A., is reproduced by kind permission of the Board of Trustees of the National Galleries of Scotland.

The photograph of Bridewell Place is reproduced by kind permission of Fox Photos, Ltd.

The photograph of W. A. R. Collins was taken by Walter Bird and that of W. Hope Collins by the Carlyle Studios, New York.

Author's Foreword

It is natural that the early characters in this book should be strong and rugged men, for they were born and bred among the high-lights and deep shadows of eighteenth-century Scotland. But some were also figures of unusual energy and power, notably William Collins I and his close friend and mentor, Dr. Thomas Chalmers. Chalmers requires here a word or two of preface.

In the first half of last century that redoubtable divine shook the whole social and ecclesiastical fabric of Scotland, and startled more than one Prime Minister in England. A great many books have therefore been written about him, most of them following the pious approach of his first biographer (and son-in-law), Dr. Hanna, and dealing chiefly with his remarkable gifts as preacher and teacher. But Chalmers was also a prolific author. He had a keen eye for a publisher's contract and an ardent, impulsive temperament which often whetted his business as well as his spiritual sense. For this reason and because I have been able to excavate a great deal of unpublished material about him from the Chalmers' MS. Collection in the University of Edinburgh's New College Library, the Chalmers of this book differs in some respects from the many portraits drawn by Church authorities. The other sources upon which I have relied will be found in the bibliography at the end of the book.

D. K.

CHAPTER I

High Summer in Scotland
1789-1813

I

SCOTLAND IN 1789 was a country of bewildering contrasts. A traveller, crossing the Border for the first time in the Glasgow stage coach, would have been reassured by the sight of well-enclosed fields and good husbandry. A few hours later, as the horses struggled up the Dumfriesshire hills, he might have recalled Dr. Johnson's jibe that the country was naked and its hedges of stone, only to doubt the Doctor's imperious wisdom in the rich pastures and plantations of Lanarkshire. But his strangest sight was still to come—in the outskirts of Glasgow where he must have noticed how oddly the black and grey reek from cotton mills and iron works mingled with the blue smoke of ancient gables. For Clydeside was already in the grip of industrial change; and the northern kingdom was pursuing her destiny, as all nations do, by creating new problems in the solving of the old.

Of this new Scotland in the making there were many miniatures for our traveller to study. Close at hand he might have visited Eastwood, a Renfrewshire parish older even than the thirteenth-century papal Bull which first gave it honourable mention. But if the parish wore the mellow look of a long lineage which hangs as surely as lichen over ancient communities, it

13

had none the less moved with the times. In its main village, Pollokshaws, a cluster of cloth mills and a dyeworks mirrored both the swift encroachment of industry on the pastoral life of the west, and the humble lot of its thousand spinners and weavers. Their cost of living was low, since a pound of cod could be had for a penny and of beef or mutton for under threepence. On the other hand, as wages sometimes fell to 1s. 2d. a day, their savings and spendings were equally meagre. Yet there was an air of vitality about the place. Many of the weavers were studious, and although the purchase of books and sevenpenny newspapers was out of the question, the Bible, in almost every cottage, rubbed cloth with well-thumbed circulating volumes like Boston's *Fourfold State* or the latest penny chap-book.

Eastwood's land-workers on the whole seem to have been a contented lot. By 1789 the ploughmen and orramen, who before mid-century had lain on mattresses of heather and bracken and studied the stars through gaping chinks in their shed roof, were living in stone cottages. Most of them still wore rags or rough plaiding in the fields. But on the Sabbath the better-placed ploughman was likely to sport a blue coat, velveret waistcoat, corduroy breeches and white cotton stockings, perhaps even breast-ruffles and a muslin cravat; while his wife and daughters, after a joyful discard of their old-time blanket-gowns, went to church in pleasing cotton dresses, scarlet plaids and duffle-cloaks.

There is a pleasant savour about this, but after all despite the march of industry, the folk of Eastwood and their kindly laird, Sir John Maxwell of Pollok still lived in Arcadian surroundings. "The little hills rejoicing on every side have their brows adorned with plantations or natural woods. A number of small rivers wander among the vallies," wrote the parish minister, Stevenson MacGill, in Sir John Sinclair's contemporary *Statistical Account of Scotland*. "The parish seems well adapted to manufactures; and in general, the people are more healthy than those usually are who follow such occupations. This may be owing in part to the fresh currents of air which blow frequently with considerable strength between the surrounding heights; and very much to the tradesman mingling sometimes with his sedentary employment the exhilarating and healthful exercises of the garden and the field." Apart from providing health and exercise, the fields of Eastwood also gave pasture to cows and horses, and produced "plentiful potatoes." So the people of this cheerful parish were evidently douce and diligent folk. Indeed the Kirk Session records for 1789 acquit them of any serious offences; and a year or two was to pass before the parish's recurring profligate lapses disturbed the Church authorities. But this, like original sin, was an old, old story. In the 1730's the Kirk Session in strong protest against "the profane swearing and hideous execration, the drunkenness and excessive tippling, the idle rioting and debauchery, the profanation of the Lord's Day, and other heinous immoralities," had pledged itself to "restrain the practice of those vices and all other crimes that are prejudicial to the trade and morals of the inhabitants of the village of Pollokshaws and this neighbourhood."

Half a century later the Pollokshavians were enjoying a modest lustrum; and it was among a law-abiding community on the 12th October 1789 that a child was born who was one day to found not only a great publishing house, but a family with a long record of service to Scotland and the British Commonwealth. His name was William Collins.

Though many efforts have been made to trace William's parents among the incomplete registers of the eighteenth century, their circumstances and place of origin are still unknown. Several members of the family last century entertained the suggestion, based on remote hearsay, that they hailed from Ireland. Another belief, held by the well-known family of paper-makers, is that they and the publishers had a common progenitor in Edward Collins, an Englishman—supposedly from either Shropshire or Suffolk—who arrived in Glasgow for the first time in 1746. But this, too, seems to be only ancestral rumour. Edward Collins, a picturesque figure suspected of Jacobitism, is reported to have told his family that before Culloden he was conscripted against his will by the Duke of Cumberland near Edinburgh, and beyond question, he founded the Glasgow paper-mill at Dalmuir which bears his name. There is no sure evidence that he was also a forebear of the Eastwood family.

Whatever their origin and vocation, we know for certain that by the time he was four or five years of age the boy's parents could afford to have him taught at the parish school—a privilege which many of their poorer neighbours had to forgo, since, in the country's old parochial fashion, the school fees were 5s. a quarter for mathematics, 4s. for Latin, 3s. for arithmetic, 2s. 6d. for writing, 2s. for English, and one guinea for a special course in book-keeping.

But here, as there is a long way to travel with William Collins, we must study more closely the profound influences at work on eighteenth-century Scotland, since these conditioned the whole of his remarkable career.

When the "auld sang" ended with the 1707 Treaty of Union, most Scots were furious at their below-stairs betrayal by a supple nobility. They were also numbed and bewildered. Yet, long tutored in a stubborn school, they still had the knowledge—or instinct—that infinite variations can be played on the oldest tune; so that poetry continued to be a flame of the spirit, and soon the nation was singing again in the bright unbitter tradition of Dunbar and Barbour, and of the ballads. With resilience born of long poverty, the Scots also began to reap good merks from their reluctant association with England, and finally they carved out a new and momentous intellectual life, not least within the Kirk.

The terrors of the eighteenth-century pulpit, we know, have often been caricatured, and little enough justice done to the loving, parochial sense of the average minister. There can, however, be little doubt about the zest with which he wrangled over what now seem to us the lesser points of the law, or about his "lang three-mile prayers and half-mile graces." There is certainly none about the majestic awe with which he pondered the fact of, and detailed the nature of, the wrath to come. He

believed with the celebrated Thomas Boston, above all things, that
man's innate wickedness, unless corrected, would be visited
by a Miltonic drama of flaming torment to be avoided only by
an agonising wrestling-match with a terrible Jehovah. "'Twixt
sermons," wrote Boston once, "I went into a barn by the kirk
much dissatisfied with myself: saw how I had brought on myself
that heavy altercation, went to God taking shame to myself,
wrestled with him for pity, laying all oars to the water. . . ."
It was Boston, too, who wrote that shuddering description of his
sick wife, "struggling to hold fast to Christ like a bird on the
side of the wall, gripping with its claws." But Boston's sombre
approach to divine love was in keeping with his environment.
In the vast mosaic of human sadness there can be few more
joyless monochromes than that of Boston's Ettrick manse, set in
a lovely countryside but cheerless even when the sun lit up the
rolling hills behind it, and dripping in a shroud of melancholy
when the rain fell, or a Scotch mist gloomed for days on Ettrick
Water and its minister.

The grim doctrinal theology of the Bostons was sustained
almost of necessity by quasi-judicial sanctions.   Kirk Sessions
had the power to levy fines for such petty delinquencies as digging
potatoes or hoeing a row of turnips on the Sabbath. Adultery,
real or suspect, meant an inquisition by ruling elders who were
often out of tune with the Sermon on the Mount; for if some
were assuredly fighting in its external shapes the enemy that was
within, there were others who had a horror of sin which overcame their humanity; or they were men like Burns' Holy Willie
who gloried in supporting the long nose of the prying elder
with the long arm of the Church. Whatever the elders' driving
force, the *guilty* Susannahs of Scotland were often doomed to sit
on the "cutty stool "[1] of repentance in face of the congregation
and endure on successive Sundays the appalling ignominy of
pulpit admonition.

Equally intemperate were Penny Weddings, which had become
riotous, and the Holy Fairs—those convivial open-air Com-

[1]The phrase evidently comes from *cutty* or *kittie*, a light woman.

munions satirised by Burns. In 1789 old men in Eastwood could recall how thousands of people had poured into the parish for the Sacrament, how they listened a while to the preachers of note, but gladly went in search of twopenny ale during the duller discourses. Fortunately, these saturnalia and the iniquity of the "cutty stool" were dying away in the Lowlands as the century closed, and ministers of the Kirk could even visit a theatre without undue fear of Presbytery arraignment.

In literature and the arts, the stirrings of the century's spring were followed by a midsummer blaze which even the Forty-Five could not darken. For if Scotland had lost her constitutional sovereignty in 1707, she quickly established a compensating sovereignty of intellect unchallenged in the world at the time.

Some of the northern kingdom's most able sons sought their fortune across the Border. Mansfield adorned the English judiciary. James Thomson's poem *The Seasons*, as the first natural, or perhaps semi-natural, challenge to outworn classicisms, paved the way for Cowper and Wordsworth. Tobias Smollett, another exile, gave the novel humanity, if only by his boisterous flavour of wits and wenches in taverns and at street-corners. Eastwood's own stone mason, James Tassie, made his exquisite portrait medallions the rage in London during the 70's and 80's. Nevertheless, these achievements, being expatriate, must have seemed a somewhat unheady cup to the stay-at-home Scot who was himself living in both an old and a young-masterish environment. By 1789 Henry Raeburn the painter had opened a studio in Edinburgh, where already Robert Adam the architect was leaving memorials of his genius in the grave beauty of the New Town and the towering monoliths and classic quadrangle of the University's Old College, then being rebuilt. Earlier still, Adam Smith of Glasgow, David Hume and Principal Robertson of Edinburgh, and many others had cast a reviving influence on European economics, philosophy and history as surely as Cullen, Black and their fellow scientists had stimulated the sciences; the *Encyclopædia Britannica* itself was issuing from an Edinburgh close; and scholars could recall the comely print with which the Foulis brothers of Glasgow had clothed the Greek and Latin classics.

During such an intellectual summer, creative literature was bound to flower in the sun. James Boswell with his great book carved out a new biographical tradition. Allan Ramsay, the Edinburgh periwig-maker who founded the first circulating library, and after him Robert Fergusson, gave poetry, even before Wordsworth, a natural singing voice; while Scotland's ancient balladry, on whose collection young Walter Scott was beginning to brood in 1789, burgeoned again in such magic minstrelsy as Jean Elliot's:

> I've heard the lilting at our yowe-milking,
> Lasses a-lilting before the dawn o' day;
> But now they are moaning on ilka green loaning:
> The Flowers o' the Forest are a' wede away.

Such poetry, even on its simple folk-song plane, would alone have been a brilliant efflorescence. But the long light that fell on eighteenth-century Scotland burst suddenly into an even brighter flame above the cottage-roof of a major singer, Robert Burns. For here was a voice of genius, speaking out of the very soul of man's sadness or his joy with such humanity and passion that the patrician, long frozen among his classical folios, was as deeply stirred as the poor man whose reading of Burns brought him, for the first time, a new sense of human rights and social injustice. That light was not to die. It influenced poetry so far beyond the Cheviot Hills, and radical politics so long after the flames of the French Revolution had faded, that to-day, as we explore the individual richness of his time, it is clearer than ever that Burns was one of the makers of modern Scotland.

But there was still a sterner field for Scotland to explore—that of formal education. Here by the same questing urge she revived her venerable University tradition to enduring purpose. Year by year in the century's closing decades and well into the nineteenth century, England's Whig aristocracy—seeking an escape from the contemporary prejudice and patronage of Oxford and Cambridge—sent its scions up the Great North Road to sit in the ancient classrooms of Scots professors. Lord Melbourne went to Glasgow. Two other future Prime Ministers—Palmerston and Lord John Russell—sat at Edinburgh under Dugald Stewart (whose homilies on moral philosophy reminded Lord Cockburn of the "opening of the heavens "), along with the great Marquis of Lansdowne and that engaging wit Sydney Smith, who despite his initial view that Scotland must be the "garret of the world," stayed on to help found Francis Jeffrey's *Edinburgh Review*. From the homeland Stewart attracted a similar pilgrimage: Francis Jeffrey (who also studied at Glasgow and Oxford); Henry Brougham (a future Lord Chancellor); Sir Walter Scott and Cockburn himself.[1]

Though most of these men came, as a matter of course, from families of means and merit, the universities were as powerful a magnet for the rustic poor. It was characteristic of the age that hundreds of lads in their visions saw the four University cities of Scotland shining through peat flames as hopefully as their shepherd fathers scanned a red sky at night among the sheep-hills. Of such were young Thomas Carlyle, who left Ecclefechan to walk to Edinburgh, some eighty miles away, on a dark frosty November morning; or the four Gaels from the Western Isles who sailed up the Clyde in a fishing-boat, lived on board during their University classes, and sailed away to the west again at the end of term; and above all the great exemplar, Alexander Murray. Murray was a Galloway shepherd's boy who learned to write with a blackened heather root, attended the village school for only sixty-six weeks, and then, at the age of eighteen, tramped across the moors to the University of Edinburgh—master already of French, German, Latin, Greek, Hebrew, Arabic, Abyssinian, Anglo-Saxon and Welsh. Murray admittedly had genius; but there were many others around him, less gifted perhaps but burning with the same enthusiasm for study.

Outstanding among these was William Collins, a typical, forceful product of his age—passionate to learn, eager to apply

[1]Oliver Goldsmith and James Boswell (who also studied at Glasgow) were earlier Edinburgh students. Lord Brougham's mother was an Edinburgh hotel-keeper; his father was English.

his learning, and endowed with certain moral qualities which raised him far above the level of his schoolmates.

His schooldays were happy. By lucky chance he had the greatest affection for his schoolmaster Alexander Loudon, a young and much-loved teacher whose salary from the Kirk Session—for instructing a hundred children (including twenty boarders who eked out his income)—was £8 a year, with a free house and garden. It was fortunate also that he venerated the parish minister whose frequent appearances in the crowded schoolhouse he described fifty years later as "visits of kindness." They assuredly influenced his destiny, as Stevenson MacGill was quick to notice the eager bird-like child on his wooden bench, encouraged him in boyhood and adolescence, and gave him assistance and advice in the critical years of his young manhood. So the school years passed. The boy became Loudon's star pupil of whom it was said many years later by a contemporary that his "diligence and ability" were quite as remarkable as "the uniform propriety of his conduct."

Occasionally he trod the few miles to Glasgow, where his fortune was to lie, to stare at the busy sights of a city in transition. At the start of the eighteenth century, Glasgow with an ancient University, had been a jewel among the academic cities of Europe. Its Cathedral, preserved from the wilder furies of the Reformation, lay over the wynds and corbelled gables like a mitre on a tranquil head. Nor was there any greater bustle in the city's commerce. On most evenings the merchants who had chaffered earlier over the Scandinavian timber which had come up the Clyde from Dumbarton in broad-beamed gabbarts repaired to their friendly wynds, walked on summer evenings among the golden fields of broom near the Broomielaw, or gazed from the top of their climbing streets at the peak of Ben Lomond in the blue distance.

As the century wore on this medieval calm was lessened. When the Treaty of Union gave Scotland the right to trade in English colonies, a handful of Glasgow traders—known to history as the Tobacco Lords—built merchantmen to take linen and other textiles to the West Indies and America. In exchange they brought back tobacco, rum, sugar, West Indian names for Glasgow streets, and an arrogance so worthy of the proudest hidalgo in Toledo that nemesis was almost inevitable. Yet in the end this came from without rather than within. After years of swaggering on the Trongate Plainstanes—in scarlet cloaks, cocked hats, powdered wigs, silver-buckled shoes, and gold-headed canes with tassels—the mushroom majesty of these Plainstane Princes collapsed with the ruin of Glasgow's tobacco trade during the American War, and "the dark sea-born city" had perforce to forge a new destiny out of iron and cotton.

By 1789 there were thus fourteen thousand looms within thirty miles of Glasgow Cross. With the deepening of the Clyde the Broomielaw had begun to bristle with masts. The Forth and Clyde Canal was almost completed. The steam engine had already been made possible by a device which occurred to James Watt whilst taking the air on Glasgow Green. And it was only four years since Mr. Vincent Lunardi had stupefied the burghers by making a balloon ascent from St. Andrew's Square. Glasgow had not taken long to become the vortex of Scotland's industrial revolution.

II

Soon after 1800 William Collins, with less time to study the city attractions, is believed to have left school and gone to work at the loom in Pollokshaws. If so he must have worked long hours by day. Evening, we know, was a candlelight time for books (first among them the Bible), and occasionally perhaps for a few wistful reflections on the poverty which had barred his way to Glasgow College. Yet he could not have been a dreamer of idle dreams: his mind was intensely active and ambitious; and at the age of either seventeen or eighteen he became a clerk in John Monteith's cotton-mill.

Here, finding his fellow-workers once again engulfed in one of Eastwood's periodical falls from grace, he pondered how to save them. But junior clerks do not usually set the moral tone of a factory. It is proof of William's courage and force of character as well as of his burning religious conviction that he immediately started a crusade in the Monteith Mill to pluck his mates from the burning. On Sundays he offered religious instruction; on week-nights he gave secular lessons in English, writing and arithmetic after the mills had closed. And soon, as the scheme caught on and the number of his pupils grew, the character and reputation of the mill so improved that the buoyant and impulsive young clerk became the special protégé of Stevenson MacGill, now ministering to the wealthy merchants in Glasgow's famous Tron Church. It was partly due to Stevenson MacGill that in 1813 William Collins put the mill behind him for ever and, with a nucleus of twenty boarders, opened a private school in Campbell Street, Glasgow. He had also by that time married Jane Barclay, daughter of a well-to-do Paisley engineer.

The Collins seminary, ambitious from the start, had three divisions—a day school and two separate evening schools. At all three the young schoolmaster taught English for fees varying between 10s. 6d. to 15s. a quarter: writing and arithmetic cost half a crown less. His school accounts, carefully kept in a clerkly hand, show that the tools of his new trade, which cost £25 during the first year, included 171 copybooks (£3 9s. 11d.), multiplication-tables (9s.), slate-pencils (2s.), quill pens (6s.), instruments (£4 5s. 0d.); and that his text-books included Walkinghame's *Arithmetic*, Lindley Murray's *Grammar* (which stayed in circulation for more than a century), and fifteen copies of a book quaintly named *Tyro's Guide*. He had of course house-rent to pay, but his total income for the first year topped £250. And he had somehow found time to begin the second of his many moral missions.

Glasgow, transformed in two decades, had a swift missionary appeal to the young enthusiast. The city's population, more than one hundred thousand including surburban dwellers, was mounting every year as fresh incursions of Irish immigrants and destitute Highlanders invaded the city. Looms had spread, it would seem, almost at shuttle-speed, though the weavers of Scotland were suffering such bitter distress that forty thousand of them came out on strike while William Collins was setting up his schoolrooms. Footpads haunted the roads on the city's outskirts. As a final scourge, the city was also being invaded by whisky in a form so cheap and noxious that it soon became as big a curse to Glasgow as cheap gin had been to Hogarth's London. In such unkindly soil lawlessness took easy root, and the magistrates had only too often to repeat their familiar proclamation:

"As many acts of violence and outrage have been committed for some years past, during the evening of His Majesty's Birthday (*George III*), the Lord Provost and Magistrates think it proper, in this manner, publicly to express their determination to punish with the utmost severity of the Law, any person or persons who may be found engaged in such unwarrantable and disgraceful proceedings on any future Anniversary of the King's Birth."

Truly, a dismal change had overtaken the graceful city which had delighted Daniel Defoe and even evoked gruff praise from Dr. Johnson. But William Collins was so alight with the reformer's authentic flame that the darkening city slums appealed to him as a new and thrilling world to conquer. Within a year his enthusiasm had so impressed the greybeards of the Tron Church that they made him an elder of the Kirk—at the phenomenal age of twenty-five.

It was an outstanding tribute. But by this time William Collins was recognised as a personality and a vivid one; for if his whole soul was aflame for religion, his friends were also aware that his volatile evangelism was accompanied by the kind of determination which brings material success. His other qualities are less easy to denote, though the sensitive lineaments of the only known likeness of him, particularly the penetrating half-humorous eyes and resolute mouth, speak reliably enough. Less transparent in the picture are his other traits: the spiritual fire destined to be still alight in old age; a generosity, often far beyond his means; the emotion roused in him by vice and

illiteracy; verbosity—so often a mark of the enthusiast—
which he may have over-nourished by absorbing too many of the
long-winded orotund eighteenth-century sermons; his high and
nervous mettle; and always his unfailing energy. These were
probably his most patent characteristics. But he had also the
stubborn simplicity of a man of faith, a Scottish love of dialectic,
and a deep-rooted sentimentalism which found natural expression
in veneration of martyrs, in hero-worship of Chalmers and later
Wilberforce, and a rose-coloured focus of his own prospects.

Although religious he was by no means a sobersides: his eyes
were much too quizzical for that; and we know that when he took
to the platform his speeches contained amusing asides of which
he allowed only one to appear in published form—a reference to
a London newspaper advertisement for a "snug house to let in a
good gin-drinking neighbourhood." But while he was not a dull
dog, his tingling passion for religion and good works was too
great ever to allow him to be tempted into a life of comfortable
good humour. For no successful crusader even if he has a playful
side can devote himself merely to personal enjoyment; and above
all things, Collins had tremendous faith and sustained zeal. When
he was caustic, as he could be, it was only to those who had, he
felt, betrayed a worthy cause. His errors of judgment were
usually the result of carrying his volatile enthusiasm at the
point of too impulsive a sword. Above all, when he got a clear
impetus to travel faster along the path of righteousness his self-
sacrificial instincts overflowed in noble deeds.

Such an impetus was provided in the first year of his eldership
by a visit to the Fife village of Kilmany. There he heard Thomas
Chalmers, a preacher of such passionate genius that Collins could
not rest until he had persuaded his fellow-elders to have him
translated to his own kirk in Glasgow. From that event strange
and turbulent results were to flow, none perhaps more unexpected
than William Collins' sudden adoption of a new career. But in
1814 that venture was still five years away; and in the meantime
many storms were to blow round preacher and teacher alike.

CHAPTER II

Comrades in Arms

1813-1819

I

AT THE time of his arrival in Glasgow, Thomas Chalmers was ten years older than William Collins. For some years he had been pursuing what he called "the dull and unvaried course of a clergyman's life" at Kilmany. But despite this lack-lustre pose his pulpit fame grew steadily. His style was original and luxuriant, and he shunned such sleepy sermon conventions as preaching from the same text over a dreary waste of successive Sundays, like Henry Grey Graham's Shetland minister who preached for eighteen months on the text:

> "And they came to Elim where were twelve wells of water, and three-score and ten palm trees: and they encamped there by the waters."

So did the worthy minister, and abode there rather longer than the Biblical bedouins. For each tree and each well was made the subject of a sermon—a process of over-cultivation which must have reduced the oasis to desert and the congregation to slumber. Young Chalmers' pulpit in the year of Trafalgar rang with more stirring words:

> "May that day when Bonaparte ascends the throne of Britain be the last of my existence; may I be the first to ascend the scaffold

26

he erects to extinguish the worth and spirit of the country; may my blood mingle with the blood of patriots; and may I die at the foot of that altar on which British independence is to be the victim."

The Kirk Session might well have felt that such defiance was more suited to the fencible's red coat than to the black Geneva gown. Their anxieties were soon set at rest. A near-fatal illness and the reading of William Wilberforce's *Practical View of Christianity* swept Chalmers into the "High-Flying" Evangelical movement, which in Scotland had begun to thaw the bleak glacier created by the cold, exhausted deism of the Kirk's Moderates in the preceding century. The Moderates had much to their credit. In the early part of the eighteenth century especially, the Church of Scotland had been strangely compounded of compassion and cruelty, as we have seen. But as the century wore on, its Moderate party loosened many of the restraints which extreme Calvinist interpretations had rendered intolerable, and wove the cloth of religion in the pattern of a wider culture: hence the disappearance of the "cutty stool" and of the more fanatical, fatalistic kind of "brimstone" preaching. But that task was over, and the Moderates were now facing a revolt against their very tranquillity, led by men like William Collins and Thomas Chalmers who had a keen Evangelical awareness of death and judgment and an intense desire for the religious life, and therefore poured their passion on the glacier in a warm, turbulent stream. Chalmers in particular was a supreme rhetorician, with an effect so magical, even in Kilmany, that not only the ploughmen there but a growing number of curious listeners from distant places assembled in the little church Sunday by Sunday to hear the kindling of his genius in all its early fire. This career, unusual for a country parson, ended in the year of Waterloo.

In the previous year (1814), when Stevenson MacGill accepted a professorship at Glasgow University, young William Collins, himself a convinced High-Flyer, had become the spearhead of a movement to make the Kilmany minister MacGill's successor. He had been especially and profoundly impressed by a Chalmers article on the evidences of Christianity in the *Edinburgh Encyclo-pædia*, and after making the long journey by coach to hear him, had fallen completely under the Chalmers spell. The choice of the Tron Kirk minister, however, lay within the patronage of the Glasgow Town Council into whose ears the Duke of Montrose, the Lord Provost and other influential figures were already dinning the cry, "Chalmers is mad." William Collins at once organised a petition, signed by two hundred leading members of the congregation, in favour of the "madman." This convinced the wavering City Fathers. Chalmers was duly chosen; and in jubilation the twenty-five-year-old organiser of victory sent him a letter on behalf of the Kirk Session which ended with the true Collins touch:

> "Accept then, Reverend Sir, of the best affections and the cordial invitation of a People whose arms and whose hearts are open to receive you."

By the autumn of 1815 Chalmers was established in Glasgow, and the whole city was alight. From the very start of his ministry dense crowds thronged into his church. Though designed to hold fourteen hundred people, usually half as many again stormed its pews to hear the young Fifer's torrent of metaphors, so rich and glittering and clothed in such sustained splendour that for thirty years, though his voice was unmelodious, Chalmers kept his power of making audiences, as a fellow-minister put it, "intensely excited, leaning forward in the pews like a forest bending under the power of a hurricane."

The most striking feature of this unusual eloquence was undoubtedly its wealth of imagery. From many examples of this, the following passage, reproduced solely as an example of his oratorical style, illustrates best perhaps its range. It is taken from an address on Catholic Emancipation—delivered, said the *Caledonian Mercury*, with "prodigious force" and eliciting "a burst of applause so deafening and enthusiastic that the effect was altogether sublime":

> "It is not by our fears and our false alarms that we do honour to Protestantism. A far more befitting honour to the great cause is

the homage of our confidence; for what Sheridan said of the liberty of the Press admits of most emphatic application to this religion of truth and liberty. ' Give,' says that great orator, ' give to the Ministers a corrupt House of Commons; give them a pliant and servile House of Lords; give them the keys of the Treasury and the patronage of the Crown; and give me the liberty of the Press, and with this mighty engine I will overthrow the fabric of corruption, and establish upon its ruins the rights and privileges of the people.' In like manner, give the Catholics of Ireland their emancipation; give them a seat in the Parliament of their country; give them a free and equal participation in the politics of the realm; give them a place at the right ear of Majesty, and a voice in his counsels; and give me the circulation of the Bible, and with this mighty engine I will overthrow the tyranny of Antichrist, and establish the fair and original form of Christianity on its ruins."

"Here," said Lord Rosebery, who had himself a notably silvered tongue, "we have the striking effect produced by quoting a fine passage of eloquence from Sheridan, and overtopping it by his own."

Here also, for he was not always fettered to the grand manner, is an example of the Chalmers style at its most lapidary:

"A Moderate sermon is like a winter's day, short and clear and cold. The brevity is good; the clarity is better; the coldness is fatal. Moonlight preaching ripens no harvest."

With such eloquence ringing in his ears, William Collins sat every Sunday under the large cupola of the Tron Church among the wealthy merchants and their feather-flaunting wives, gazing with boundless admiration at the great barbican of Chalmers' brow and his heavy Lutheran face. He also, in a short time, became one of the divine's closest friends, as Dr. Chalmers' *Private Journal* shows.[1]

"Mr. Collins came in after supper, and we had a great deal of worthy conversation " is a typical entry about this time, and again: "Took a step to my worthy friend, and along with Mr. Collins had another visitation." Hardly a day in fact passed

[1] Dr. Chalmers received his Doctorate of Divinity from the University of Glasgow early in 1816.

without cordial meetings between the two men, and soon the friendly young teacher was even able to influence the direction of his minister's prophetic shafts. "I was proceeding to finish off my preparation for to-morrow," remarked the minister on one occasion, "when in came Mr. Collins, and beseeched me, as the town was choke full of strangers, that I would preach my sermon on dissipation."

But passive reverence of an idol was never one of the young man's qualities. Within a few weeks of Chalmers' arrival in Glasgow, William Collins opened in his own house the first of a chain of Sunday schools. He persuaded thirteen children to attend on the first day. Within two years, by immense labour, he secured the attendance of twelve hundred children in similar schools throughout the parish. Yet despite his religious fervour, the young teacher did not neglect his profession. By 1817—birth year of his first-born, William the second—the annual income from his school had leaped up to £750, an extraordinary revenue in those days for a private dominie. But in many ways Collins was quite as remarkable as the divine he hero-worshipped, a fact which his hero was soon to recognise.

II

The chief bookselling family in Glasgow at this time was that of John Smith, an old man with two sons—John Smith the Youngest, as he was styled while his grandfather and father of the same name were both living, and Thomas, a young man aged twenty-two of fine character and great personal charm. Within a short time of his arrival in Glasgow, Thomas Smith became to Chalmers what Arthur Hallam was to Tennyson. Together they walked several times a week along the banks of the new Forth and Clyde Canal. They dined together daily, and corresponded faithfully when either was absent from Glasgow, till this strange, near-romantic friendship almost overpowered the temperamental divine. "O my God," he once wrote in his *Private Journal*, "save

me from all that is idolatrous in my regard for him." To Thomas
Smith himself he wrote: "O my dearest of all earthly associates,
had the happiness of our friendship been without alloy, it would
have been too much for earth."

Unhappily Thomas Smith died within a year of these utterances, and we find the Doctor cherishing a lock of his friend's
hair and praying earnestly in his correspondence for "the
temporal and everlasting good " of the Smith family.

In the sharing of a common grief the friendship between the
two families so deepened that Dr. Chalmers and John Smith the
Youngest, who was in charge of the business, soon arranged with
complete mutual trust for publication of a series of week-day
sermons delivered by Chalmers in the Tron Church during 1816.
These sermons, which became famous as the *Astronomical
Discourses*, had had an almost bewitching effect. The moment
the Tron bell sounded, the merchants poured out of their
counting-houses into the church, to become entranced for an
hour as the Doctor transported them to the heavens

> "where the Divinity reigns in all the grandeur of his high attributes
> —where he peoples immensity with his wonders; and travels in
> the greatness of his strength through the dominions of one vast
> and unlimited monarchy."

The merchants then returned to work. John Smith, too, went
back to his bookshop convinced that such spoken pomp—in that
high noon of sermon tasting—deserved wider attention. His
overtures to Chalmers were promptly met; and in January 1817
he published, jointly with William Whyte of Edinburgh, the
Astronomical Discourses as a 12s. volume. With this enterprise he
scaled the very summit of success. Six thousand copies were sold
within ten weeks, and twenty thousand within a year. Hazlitt,
who read the sermons under an apple-tree at Burford Bridge,
noted that they "ran like wild-fire through the country, were the
darlings of watering-places, were laid in the windows of inns,
and were to be met with in all places of public resort," while
Robert Chambers, the Edinburgh publisher, recalled almost

twenty years later in a letter to Dr. Chalmers that the *Discourses* had "stretched my mind to the very verge of rapture."

This furore was naturally gratifying both to author and publisher. For if the publisher had secured a best-seller, the author had been paid £1,800—two favourable circumstances which encouraged them to pass more intimately than ever through each other's gates. Within a few months, indeed, we hear of them setting out together in a chaise for London where the Doctor was to preach. On their way they made a preliminary holiday tour of the English counties as far south as Gloucestershire, where Smith, who was to visit Paris, parted company. Thither the Doctor sent him the following affectionate, and, in the light of later events, noteworthy message: "Mrs. Chalmers and I are both anxious to hear of you and we both love you."

After a short interval author and publisher met again in London where Smith witnessed the emotional scenes—when Chalmers preached—which prompted Canning to say: "The tartan beats us all," and Wilberforce to enter in his diary: "All the world wild about Dr. Chalmers." And assuredly Chalmers had exceeded his friends' most sanguine expectations. The cream of London society—in hundreds of carriages—flocked to hear him. At one of his appearances the building was so crammed with expectant listeners that young ladies of fashion were hauled in through the vestry windows in hope of finding a seat; while the pressure of the congregation against even the church windows destroyed some thirty panes of glass.

The loyal Smith was affected by these scenes, and by Chalmers' eloquence which he described in a rapturous letter home as "the most astonishing display of human talent that perhaps ever commanded sight or hearing." But also, since the stars in their Discourses seemed fixed and favourable, he naturally hoped for a second volume of sermons as soon as possible. Optimistically, he returned to his bookshop, leaving his author to rest and study at a Lanarkshire inn with another faithful friend. "My elder, Mr. Collins," Chalmers wrote in his *Journal*, "has come out to spend the time with me, and I am living in great comfort and retirement."

In due course John Smith offered Chalmers one thousand guineas for a 7,000-copy edition of a second 12s. volume of sermons, unwitting that the Doctor while in London had also been star-gazing—at a London publisher's imprint—and was about to plunge into a correspondence which, though it led to a most unecclesiastical quarrel, had at least the advantage of giving William Collins the dominie a new and spacious outlet for his talents.

Strange events followed Smith's offer. In May 1818, Chalmers informed Longmans that he would have a 500-page volume of sermons ready by the summer: would Longmans publish it at 12s. conjointly with his former publishers, and what should he " secure for each edition? " Longmans, delighted to add such a celebrated name to their list, suggested half the profits on each edition, and £800 for a first edition of 6,000 copies. They also disclosed the Doctor's overtures to Smith, who in turn confided his " surprise " to Whyte that neither of them had been consulted.

After much swallowing of pride, it was agreed that the three publishers in equal shares of £350 should give Chalmers £1,050 for an edition of 7,000 copies, and by the end of February 1819, after many hold-ups, the volume was ready: 4,600 copies were bundled on to the Glasgow-Edinburgh post wagon, of which half were to be subscribed[1] by William Whyte among the Edinburgh booksellers; the remainder—for Longmans who had spent £45 on advertising the volume in England—were put on board a Leith smack bound for London.

Presently it became evident that the volume—popularly known as the *Tron Church Sermons*—was selling badly, being overloaded with elaborations more suitable for the pulpit than the printed page. When this became clear beyond doubt Chalmers,

[1]In booksellers' terminology the word "subscribe " had then two meanings. In Whyte's case the bookseller would agree to take (i.e. "subscribe " for) so many copies. The other form of "subscription " was that followed by Robert Burns and his friends who secured an advance list of 350 pledged "private subscribers " for the Kilmarnock edition of his poems.

unknown to his publishers, began to brood on the reasons for the only too obvious recession of public favour; and soon, to his own satisfaction at least, he found a good commercial one in a rumour that the booksellers were grumbling about the publishers' allowances. By-passing the Smith family, he took the Prince Regent coach for Edinburgh in the second week of June (1819) to vent his indignation on William Whyte.

Whyte was loyal in his defence, but the Tron Church tornado was so irresistible that within a fortnight, while John Smith was travelling in the Austrian Tyrol, an imperious philippic—from which the following extracts are taken—hurtled out of the Tron Church manse on to the hoary head of Smith Senior:

"I have very recently learned your proceedings with the Trade of Glasgow respecting my last volume, and have obtained the most satisfactory assurance that by deviating from the usual terms you have stirred up a just and proper resistance on the part of many respectable Booksellers and have done what was highly fitted to alienate them.

"My belief is the proposal for exacting a higher price than is customary from the Trade originated with you, and was only concurred in by the other Publishers. I mean also to write them on the subject, and if I am wrong in the supposition, I am subject to your correction, and to theirs. But in the meantime I do not hesitate to say that I can have no comfort in having any further correspondence with you in the business of authorship.

"I will not disguise it that reviewing my past intercourse with you and your family since I first fell into your hands, I feel myself affected by very powerful emotions. There was one period of that intercourse in which I fondly thought that I had found in the bosom of an affectionate friendship some compensation for the intimacy of the Country Parish I had abandoned. The enchantment has now fled, but when I think of the changes that are past, and those that are soon to follow, I trust by the spirit of God I shall be calmed by the solemn contemplation, both into charity and into peace."

Though the friendliness of the old man was shattered by this unexpected polemic, he acknowledged its receipt with "much surprise," and promised an immediate reply on his son's return.

Pending that event, the Doctor diverted his spleen to his other publishers.

To Whyte he wrote:

"I make free to advise you that a liberal and magnanimous policy is the line most conducive to your interests as a man in Trade, and certainly by far the most suitable to your profession as a Christian."

His letter to Longmans, almost as peremptory, produced the spirited reply:

"The terms upon which your book was sold to the Trade were the common subscription price, or the sale price (the price at which books are offered to the Trade at Coffee House sales) on taking over 100 copies. Be assured we could never be influenced to act in any irregular manner to the prejudice of any Author or of his work under our care."

By this time, however, irreparable damage had been done. John Smith the Youngest had returned from his foreign tour, and the Doctor was to find him a mettlesome antagonist.

"The charge you have made," wrote Smith in a letter much too long for quotation in full,

"is that there has been a connivance to defraud you of reputation and profit. Before admitting such a suspicion, charity might have suggested that even had the allegation been true of a deviation from the customary allowance to the trade, there might have been sufficient cause for it known only to those who had acted so, or, that considering their situation and character in life it must have been the result of an unwitting error altogether unconnected with the baseness you allege. . . . In justice, however, to ourselves we state that sentiments towards you, which may now be nameless, did prompt us originally to take your works on unusual terms for authorship, and also to take labour for them never expected from publishers. As you imagine them to have been so great an object of profit to us we may now without restraint of delicacy assert our belief, and we believe Mr. Whyte will coincide in it, that no edition of your Discourses realised to us 12½% on our outlay or an eighth of the retail price."

Within two years Dr. Chalmers had in fact received from his

publishers, who also published several remunerative single sermons, the very large sum for those days of £3,000. But the Smith family claimed that their total profit out of their author's works was only £470. It is hardly surprising—if this figure is accurate—that feeling aggrieved they rose strongly in their own defence.

III

During this turmoil William Collins was preparing for Dr. Chalmers' translation to the new parish church of St. John's—in the heart of Glasgow's poorest population—where he was to have that restless romantic, the Rev. Edward Irving, as his assistant. Though his appearance was marred by a squint, Irving, with folds of thick black hair over his youthful shoulders, was tall, handsome and swarthy as a Romany. His intentions, as remarkable as his appearance, had been to learn modern languages, wander round Europe for a time, and then convert Persia to Christianity. Instead, he accepted an invitation to assist Dr. Chalmers in Glasgow. Irving had not yet arrived in the city when Chalmers was balancing the St. John's project against the offer of a University chair at Edinburgh.

After earnest consultation with the Glasgow Town Council in which William Collins took a leading part, Chalmers, stirred deeply by the sordid twilight of the Gallowgate slums and the tragic ratio of one pauper for every twenty-seven persons in the city, agreed to take up his pastorate among them on condition that the cumbrous system of poor relief should be administered by the new church. He stipulated only that the necessary funds, provided solely by the church collection plate, should be administered by an " agency " composed of his church office-bearers, who would visit all applicants, scrutinise their applications for relief, inquire whether relatives with means had been invited to assist them, and whether they had applied for work where work was known to be available. For a time the adoption of the scheme hung in the balance. The Town Council, which had to create the new parish of 10,000 people out of other parishes, was not only nervous about the plan, but had to obtain legal sanction for it. Inevitably, therefore, the impetuous Doctor was soon so quickly on edge that he even doubted the fidelity of his loyal lieutenant. "The keeping up of this mysterious silence on the part of Mr. Collins disturbs me greatly," he wrote on 22nd August. Fortunately for his peace of mind, the much-desired letter from William Collins duly arrived, conveying "the united assurances of the most zealous and influential members of his agency, that their attachment and confidence remained wholly unshaken, and that their only regret was that he should have suffered any apprehensions as to their fidelity to prey upon his spirits." Much comforted, Chalmers returned from holiday within a few days, to make public a lengthy dissertation on his plan for the new parish. And this time, by an abrupt turn of fortune's wheel, his publisher (and future printer) was William Collins.

The exact steps by which the young man exchanged the schoolroom for the bookshop and the printing office are not quite clear, but it certainly was an astonishing decision. Right up to the end of 1818 he was immersed in teaching and preaching. In that year he raised the annual revenue from his school to just over £1,000, and his mettle was such that a further expansion was inevitable. Yet, by 1819 he had decided on a leap into the unknown and had mastered sufficient of the mysteries of the trade to justify the risk. He had also mustered his tools and raw material. Why?

Probably in view of his environment he had felt the lure of printer's ink for some time. At this period Glasgow had as many printers and booksellers per head of its population as any other city of the United Kingdom. The numerous Glasgow newspapers of the time ran columns of book advertisements in every issue. There were circulating libraries and literary clubs all over the city, and the bookshops sold not only classical works in plenty, but the books of every contemporary author of note in Great Britain. Glasgow was in fact a literary centre despite Lockhart's tilt at its "counting-house *blood*, dressed in a box-coat. Belcher

handkerchief, and top-boots, or leather gaiters, discoursing
(Ædepol!) about brown sugar and genseng." But this alone would
not have tempted him. There can be little doubt, from our
knowledge of his character, that as he surveyed the flood of books
around him he saw that the printing press was the best vehicle
for spiritual teaching, as Chalmers had realised. Probably, too, it
was Chalmers who, after the break with Smith, impelled him into
publishing by the offer of both moral and material support. It
is certainly a tribute to Collins' dynamic power that the celebrated
Doctor, with easy access to John Murray or Constable or any of
the other great publishers, should have been willing to entrust
his manuscripts to a humble unknown.

At any rate, by July 1819 the plan was far advanced on the
assumption that the business would be solely a Collins concern.
But early in August there was a new development when in
William Collins' abounding energy and ability Chalmers
suddenly saw salvation at last for his problem brother Charles.

Charles was a strange apparition on the Glasgow scene. A
decade after his famous brother he had left the University of St.
Andrews, after developing mild tuberculosis, and drifted idly
into the Kilmany manse with no occupation. Dr. Chalmers'
energetic mind was repelled by his brother's obstinate fecklessness.
"He wants accommodating manners," he recorded in his *Journal*,
"is noisy and impetuous and wilful to such a degree that I do
not feel myself at liberty to offer him a single direction or
request." None the less, when Thomas went to Glasgow in 1815,
Charles went too—for a stay which lasted more than two years.
It was a period of continued indecision. For a short time, despite
his then inadequate knowledge of the subject, he advertised
himself as a teacher of mathematics. When this exploit failed,
most members of the Chalmers' circle tried to assist him. John
Smith, explaining that Charles' object was "literary employment
—Editorship—the charge of a public library—amanuensis—or to
have a teaching or travelling tutor's charge of one person," even
recommended him to William Blackwood as an Editor for
Blackwood's Magazine. On the self-same day Charles was writing

to Smith that he had a chance of a clerkship in the Court of Session, but unfortunately his sponsor for the job was a man of dissipated habits who was also "anxious that I should become a member of his debauched club." "I resisted," he explained, "and retreated with the appellation of a country greenhorn, from his society."

To shorten a long story, this toiling and moiling was suddenly ended by the unpredictable Charles himself who wrote to Smith: "I am extremely sorry you did not consult me before pronouncing on my literary merits to Mr. Blackwood, for I assure you I do not know a single rule of the art of writing, and so far from possessing habits of composition I never composed above four times in my life in the least connected with literature." It was fortunate that within a week of this last effusion the tireless Smith secured a place for him in William Whyte's Edinburgh bookshop at a salary of £36 a year, in acknowledgment of which Charles wrote gratefully: "I assure you, my dear sir, I consider this situation which you propose as a godsend to me, for I was just upon the point of engaging with an inspector of roads to break stanes for him at so much the cartload."

But Charles was still not to be relied upon. Having impulsively decided that thirteen shillings a week was a sufficient competence for matrimony, he married an Anstruther girl without the knowledge of his family. The subsequent convulsion in the family circle need not be recorded here. Suffice it to say that by the summer of 1819, again spitting blood and suffering from tubercular fatigue, he returned with his wife to Glasgow, and at Chalmers' request William Collins accepted him as a partner.

By 27th August the preparations for the new publishing house were so ripe that the Doctor put on paper his intention to publish a pamphlet about his "connexion" with St. John's Parish. "I want my brother and Mr. Collins to be the sole publishers," he wrote. "It will form part of a series of papers which, if God spare me, I mean to publish from time to time on the Civic and Christian Economy of our Large Towns."

These August plans went forward swiftly in September. It was arranged that Charles in view of his Edinburgh experience should superintend the bookselling and stationery side of the business; William Collins the publishing, printing and binding. Collins as senior partner had by far the largest share in the business, since not only his entire savings but loans from his wife's family had been employed in the purchase of printing presses, printer's ink, paper, and the leasing of premises. He also received an advance of £800 from Dr. Chalmers for the printing works which were kept distinct from the retail side of the business as William Collins & Company, Printers. Charles, too, received a similar loan to ensure him an adequate stake in the associated company of Chalmers & Collins, Booksellers and Stationers. The interest on both loans was payable in half-yearly instalments.

Collins' late-summer activity became feverish as he worked night and day on his first book in an atmosphere of mingled gaiety and gloom. On Glasgow Green the inhabitants of the city were pouring in to see Mrs. Cook, the eighteen-year-old giantess (she was 7 ft. high), and her rival "Mr. Thomson, the Scottish giant measuring eight feet high, who fought at the Battle of Waterloo, and afterwards in Paris measured heights with Buonaparte's celebrated Drum-Major, when he proved to be Two Inches Taller and received from Field-Marshal Blücher a Silver Medal." Elsewhere on the Green were George Wombwell's "Rare and Wonderful Animal the One-horned Rhinoceros, or Real Unicorn of Scripture, which cost the Proprietor 800 Guineas, and is the only one living in Europe." "This monstrous creature," proclaimed Mr. Wombwell's bills, "will impress the minds of the rising generation with the most sublime idea of the Deity." Unfortunately by September, when Madame Sacqui arrived from Covent Garden to dance on the tight-rope at the local theatre, hungry weavers had begun to riot in the streets, Glasgow was in a state of emergency, and William Collins' enterprise could hardly have started under more forbidding auspices. While he was printing his first book, for example, many of Glasgow's new gas lamps and hundreds of shop windows were broken all over the city. Magistrates read the Riot Act from the Black Bull Inn. Troops cleared the streets of thousands of demonstrators, many of whom had assembled near the printing office. Even the first Collins' newspaper advertisement was overshadowed by a magisterial announcement that further riots, tumults, pillage and plunder would be put down by force; shops were to shut early; and all well-disposed persons were to keep off the streets. Under the grinding rub of low wages, high prices and unemployment the temper of the Clydeside weavers and iron workers had become frenetic.

In spite of all these hazards, Collins' preparations went on apace. The bookshop, flanked by shops selling grain, ham, butter and cheese, lay at the east end of Wilson Street. The small printing works with its flat-bed printing press opened at No. 28 Candleriggs Court, in the ancient Candleriggs where Glasgow's candlemakers had once gone through the riggs (or cornfields) to boil and purify their tallow in the "Crackling House." And by good luck there were so few delays that by mid-September the printers—with some outside help—were sufficiently well ahead to justify a preliminary advertisement of the first Collins publication in the Glasgow newspapers. Nine days later—on Thursday 23rd September 1819—the *Glasgow Courier* announced:

TOMORROW WILL BE PUBLISHED
BY CHALMERS AND COLLINS
Booksellers and Stationers—68, Wilson Street

PRICE 1/-

THE CHRISTIAN AND CIVIC ECONOMY
OF LARGE TOWNS

BY THE REV. DR. CHALMERS

No. 1

Remarks applicable to the outset of Dr. Chalmers'
connection with the Parish of St. John

On the following day scores of people thronged through the

polished stone entrance into the low-ceilinged shop where the book lay among the works of more famous publishers: the *Waverley Novels*, the poems of Cowper and Burns, Macpherson's *Ossian*, Malthus' works on Political Economy, the works of Hannah More, and many periodicals including *Blackwood's Magazine*, the *Edinburgh Review*, and the *Eclectic*. Twenty-four hours later the two partners, their shopman Mr. Scott, and their first author Dr. Chalmers, were reading in the *Glasgow Courier* the first review of the first Collins publication.

CHAPTER III

The Hazard Begins

1819-1822

I

THE ALMANAC of history is medallioned now and then by climacteric years when the world's fortune seems to hang in the balance. In such a year William Collins was born—during the glare of the French Revolution in the Old World and, as now appears, the no less significant election of America's first President in the New. By odd chance, too, his business was born in a year which, despite its more sober aspect, was none the less as formative a twelve-months as any in the nineteenth century.

The year 1819 marked the birth of a most varied collection of authors—George Eliot, Arthur Hugh Clough, John Ruskin, Walt Whitman and Queen Victoria.[1] It saw the publication of the first cantos of Byron's *Don Juan*, Wordsworth's *Peter Bell* and *The Waggoner*, Walter Scott's *Ivanhoe*, Lockhart's *Peter's Letters to his Kinsfolk* and the first Trade Union newspaper *The Gorgon*. It was the year when Keats was writing *Hyperion*, Shelley *Prometheus Unbound* and *The Cenci*, and Charles Lamb many of his most enduring letters and essays.

In such a brilliant period William Collins must have felt

---

[1] "We authors, ma'am," Disraeli is supposed to have murmured when the Queen presented him with a copy of her *Leaves from the Journal of Our Life in the Highlands.*

encouraged by the literary fertility and reading habits of the time. Moreover, two-thirds of the books sold in Scotland were religious. His nearest market was a University-Cathedral city with a rising population. His star author in a neighbouring street was the best-known preacher of his day, though this was to prove a mixed blessing. Tongues wagged so freely in Glasgow that soon Dr. Chalmers was forced to send a tactful message to a lady who had desired publication of an essay dedicated to himself:

"I do not know whether Mr. Collins has written you in regard to the dedication; but you must really permit us both to say that there are many serious and weighty objections against the appearance of it. I have already been made the subject in print of most gross and ungenerous imputations, on the score of the interested connexion which is alleged to subsist between myself and that house; and anything so very eulogistical printed by them would, I am sure, give a colour to these imputations, and altogether form such an exhibition as might revolt even many who at present entertain no suspicion of that kind."

More troublesome than gossip was the Smith controversy. John Smith, now a man with a grievance, was growling unwisely about the Doctor to his friends. In any event, Dr. Chalmers' change of publisher had raised intricate problems. Both Smith and Whyte possessed considerable unsold stocks of the Doctor's works, and Collins to his chagrin was therefore precluded from printing them himself and driving up their sales unless he bought them at unwarranted expense. It was certain, too, that their very existence—in view of Chalmers' inflammable temperament—was likely to involve William Collins more directly in the old quarrel. In the meantime, while John Smith was fanning its embers, the Doctor was as prolific as ever. Early in the New Year (1820) the Candleriggs imprint appeared on Part II of his *Economy*, and on an educational pamphlet, printed by an outside printer. But 1820 soon brought serious troubles. When Part III of the *Economy* appeared, Glasgow citizens were reading a poster on their walls, urging redress of the people's grievances at the hazard of arms "by order of the Committee of Organisation for forming a Provisional Government." Five thousand troops, as the result, were billeted in the city; shots were fired in the streets; sixty thousand Glasgow workers came out on strike; and a handful of weavers who took up arms at Bonnymuir were executed. In these conditions business almost came to a standstill. Shops shut early, strangers were ordered to withdraw every night from the city by 7 p.m., and the townsmen were told by the magistrates that if rioters broke the cherished municipal gas-lamps, now eighteen months old, they were to illuminate their front windows.

Yet somehow William Collins continued to popularise his imprint. In the fashion of the time he allied himself with other publishers in joint publications such as Cleland's *Rise and Progress of Glasgow* (still an invaluable source book), and an edition of Macpherson's *Ossian* (intended to "bring forward every proof of the authenticity of the wild strains of the Celtic bard "). In May he published at 1s. 6d. a volume of two lengthy Chalmers' sermons on the *Importance of Civil Government to Society* which quickly sold 6,000 copies in the first two editions. He also advertised: "At the request of several Gentlemen a Cheap Edition of the Sermon will be published, price 9d. each "—the first Collins cheap edition.

Throughout the summer he was busy as well with his first major volume—an eight-shilling book of *Commercial Sermons* by Dr. Chalmers in the lineage of the *Astronomical* and *Tron Church* volumes. This book reached its third edition by the end of December, but had to be printed by a Trongate printer named James Starke owing to prior calls on his own presses. To cap a most successful year, he published—on Christmas Day—a new instalment of the *Christian and Civic Economy*.

In other respects the year had been disquieting. During the autumn the Smith storm had been revived. John Smith, a strong unambiguous character, had noticed these signs of progress with an aggrieved eye and a growing conviction that he had been treated harshly by the Doctor, and that William Collins and Charles Chalmers were achieving success on the basis of a literary goodwill which he had helped to establish. He began to criticise Dr. Chalmers within the circle of his friends, and soon his criticisms became audible enough to cause a volcanic disturbance in the St. John's manse. It was at this point that the fine gold in Chalmers became so dim that to understand his attitude with any sympathy we must again take into account the fiery nature of his genius, and remember that a big engine needs a big exhaust.

Since the great divine's death more than a century ago there has been unanimous praise for his *benignity* and *good humour*, his *thoughtfulness* and *lack of vanity*. It is clear, however, from his *Private Journal* (never published in full), his correspondence with his publishers, and from the vast anecdotage about him, that Chalmers' temper was always uncertain despite an incessant and moving struggle against the deep-seated choler from which it sprang. It was an outburst of rage which cost him a mathematical assistantship at the University of St. Andrews when mathematics was his passion. At Kilmany he once recorded in his all-revealing *Private Journal*:

> "I must be particularly careful as to the quantity of food and wine that I indulge myself in. An excess of either adds to my physical irritability and exposes me to those delinquencies of conduct and temper which I mourn over afterwards. Let me be strong and decided on this subject and adhere invariably to the rule of never exceeding three glasses of any intoxicating beverage whatever." (May, 1810.)

Nor was this an isolated instance. A hundred times and more, the *Journal* records his unending fight against irritability and anger; and as many times it prays for "deliverance" from the use of immoderate language.

There is another gentler side to the portrait. Chalmers *could* be most benevolent and broadminded, and very modest despite the adulation which surrounded him. Although his family sometimes winced under his lash, as their unpublished correspondence shows, they were devoted to him and he could be playful with them. He was obviously the sort of friendly family

man to whom his daughter Ann could easily write in the
contemporary mode of more serious invitations:

> "REV. SIR,
> The honour of your presence on Friday the 8th current at
> 2 o'clock afternoon to accompany the funeral of my chicken will
> much oblige
> Sir
> Your most obedient Servant
> ANN CHALMERS "

On such an occasion he would play manfully. And indeed, over
the wider field of humanity's afflictions, the sympathies of few
men could be more easily aroused. The news of a friend's death
produced tears, and tears frequently rained down on his sermon
notes in the pulpit, though a few minutes later his declamations
would be robust and vehement, and often as misleading to others
as to himself. Thus in the General Assembly of the Church of
Scotland, a layman's complaint that he was "excited" brought
the amazed reply: "Excited! Does the gentleman say that I am
excited? I am as cool as an algebraic problem."

What, then, is the explanation of his complex character?
Firstly, if one side of him was keen and hard, and the other warm
and generous, he must have been an extreme instance of the
blend of opposites which makes the Scottish character, and which
finds in his native Fife as delicate a poise as anywhere. But Fife
is not over-populated by men of elemental, emotional genius,
and it is in the very fact of his genius that we find the key to
his character. Such a man is nearly always an easy prey to
mankind's lesser weaknesses—to impatience, irritability, and the
flight of reason over trifles. In Chalmers' affairs seeming neglect
or inattention, even a sparrow-wing touch of mental discomfort,
affected his impulsive mind with a sense of being trammelled:
the result was only too often querulousness, asperity or open
anger.

Thus it must have been with the John Smith affair. Here was
an obstacle, a new and trammelling threat to his pride. As swiftly
therefore as John Smith's hints of "roguery" and "villainy"

came in through his front door, the Sermon on the Mount flew out at the back. In a fit of passion he suddenly widened the scope of the quarrel, and this time William Collins was more directly embraced by its fury.

The immediate cause of battle was *Scripture References*, a slim paper-covered volume which Chalmers at Kilmany had compiled in 1814 for Edward Lesslie, a Dundee bookseller. Little had been heard of this fifteen-page booklet till Chalmers' Glasgow fame stimulated for it a demand which Smith satisfied by purchasing, as he imagined, the copyright from Lesslie, and thereafter publishing several editions with his own imprint. By 1820, when the booklet had reached its fifth edition, William Collins resolved to print a sixth. To his surprise, however, on offering to buy all the unsold copies as a necessary preliminary, he found Smith convinced that his Lesslie purchase included the copyright. Here indeed was an obstacle sufficiently galling to wake the tiger in Chalmers' blood. The upshot was that early in December, Smith received a warning from a firm of Glasgow solicitors that Dr. Chalmers had instructed them to institute legal proceedings unless the booklet was turned over to the firm of Chalmers and Collins forthwith. To make matters worse, the lawyer's letter was not confined to the *Scripture References*. Dr. Chalmers, in high temper and seeing a chance to crystallise his differences with Smith, revived the entire controversy from the beginning.

"It is required," wrote his lawyers, "that you should at the same time subscribe a letter addressed to Dr. Chalmers acknowledging in unequivocal terms, that in all your transactions with that Gentleman, you found him to be most fair and most honourable, and that if you ever said or insinuated the reverse you were guilty of gross falsehood and defamation."

Smith, on receiving this threatening missive, at once offered to submit the *Scripture References* issue to arbiters. His offer was as quickly rejected; but when court proceedings were again threatened he bowed to the gale, and by Christmas Eve had sold all the copies in his possession to the Chalmers and Collins bookshop. There remained the grand controversy—now more than two years old.

On 21st December 1820, Dr. Chalmers, accompanied by his lawyer and by William Collins whose loyalty must have overcome his doubts about the wisdom of these proceedings, met Smith round a table. Smith, hoping to end the affray forever, produced the following certificate:

"I hereby declare that I never had just cause to say or to insinuate that Dr. Chalmers conducted himself otherwise than uprightly and honourably respecting the publication of the Tron Church volume of Sermons or in any other of his transactions with me or with Messrs. John Smith & Son."

In retrospect, this seems a sufficient apology. The Doctor, however, refused to accept it unless the word "handsomely" was inserted after "honourably"—a proud quibble which condemned both parties to a further wearying struggle. Smith, who had admitted his fulminations against the Doctor, refused the condition point-blank. "I stated," he wrote in a record of the meeting,

"that while I could acknowledge that he acted uprightly and honourably in his *transactions* with us, that I would not acknowledge his *conduct* to have been handsome, chiefly in consequence of a letter addressed by him to our house during my absence last year on the Continent, which had occasioned great distress at the time to my father and sister and that I would not insert the word in the certificate. After some further conversation with his agent and Mr. Collins and on their return, Dr. Chalmers said that he would accept of the certificate as proposed if I would allow the question of whether or not he was entitled to insist on our inserting the word 'handsome' to be decided by Referees."

This was agreed. Arbiters were appointed, and the issue was simplified thus: firstly, should the word "handsomely" be inserted; and secondly, was Dr. Chalmers right in his allegations that Smith had jeopardised the *Tron Church Sermons* by inadequate allowances to the booksellers—which brings us back to the original cause of the quarrel, and its next round.

Smith at once asked the leading publishers and booksellers for their opinion of his trade allowances. Three Glasgow booksellers declared in reply that they had disapproved of Smith's original proposal to charge 9s. 0d. each for under 12 copies and 8s. 9d. from 12 to 25, but that this "did not prevent them from subscribing for as many copies as they thought they might have a demand for." Archibald Constable, at the height of his Edinburgh fame, thought that Smith's terms were quite proper. Byron's publisher, John Murray, less helpfully observed that he never stinted the trade who were his most liberal supporters, and the only customers whom he desired, in their allowances of the most *popular* work. "Neither," he added, "do I make any difference if they have taken 6 or 600, for each man I know does not or might not (and I don't wish him) to take more copies than his business requires."

By May 1821, when the quarrel seemed to be nearing its end, the gladiators prepared for the final effort. Each submitted an immensely long document to the arbiters. Smith emphasised that he had voluntarily handed over the copyright of the *Scripture References* to Mr. Collins, although he was amply protected by the Copyright Act. The demand for the insertion of the word "handsomely," he considered to be "exceedingly extravagant," and added: "When parties have quarrelled, for one of them to insist that the other shall make an acknowledgment that he had in all circumstances in regard to the cause of the quarrel acted handsomely, is surely demanding more than it can at all be supposed that the other with any degree of truth with any reference to his own feelings could concede." He then rebutted Dr. Chalmers' figures for his allowances to the trade, on the ground that he had never received more than 8s. 6d. for the 12s. book from any bookseller,[1] and added that Dr. Chalmers' publishers had always been most liberal to him as an author. Dr. Chalmers had, for example, received £150 for his Sermon on the death of the Princess Charlotte: 8,000 copies of the Sermon were printed, but more than a fourth were still unsold; "so that

---

[1] This seems true. His original allowances to the trade undoubtedly raised protests which he seems to have met by restoring a more generous rate.

Dr. Chalmers has obtained the fat and the publishers the feculence of this speculation." With some justification he also complained of the language used by Dr. Chalmers in his paper—a thunderous piece of invective amounting to thirty-two pages of closely written foolscap, which is too long to be quoted here except in a few extracts. After recapitulating his belief that Smith's allowances, which he set out in great and perplexing detail, had done his book irreparable injury the Doctor declared:

> "Dr. Chalmers has no other desire and never had than just to be quit of Mr. Smith and to bury all the past in silence. He for eighteen months refrained from a subject that pained him and disgusted him till roused by the insolent and outrageous calumnies of his quondam publisher and by whom he was charged with rascality and villainy in consequence of these very transactions which ought to have covered himself with confusion."

Next, the Doctor declared his conviction "that if Mr. Smith is left in possession of a single charge he will turn it to every purpose of mischief that an active and unquenchable spirit of malignity can devise." He concluded:

> "That irrepressible tongue which ever works and never wearies has, Dr. Chalmers understands, again been busily employed and there is reason to fear that its foul articulations have fallen with a withering influence on the hearts of men whom Dr. Chalmers once conceived to be his friends but who may think better of it when they shall come to perceive that they have been listening all along to ex parte statements which may also require the apology of delirium to account for them."

In July 1821 this two-year quarrel over a few pence, a booklet and a word was still unfinished, and its outcome remains a mystery. It is unfortunate and perhaps significant that many pages of Dr. Chalmers' *Journal* for 1821 have been excised; and that no mention of the quarrel has been found in any of the Collins-Chalmers correspondence still in existence. It is clear, however, from the following *Journal* entries that the quarrel was either still an issue or was somehow revived as late as 1822:

5th Jan. Reply to John Smith. Bilious partly from the (——) return of the subject. Parochial visits. Mr. Collins' strength and support—and settled our accounts.

12th Jan. Mr. Smith's matter is coming more urgently upon me and altogether affairs are thickening towards another great discomfort or great decision which I pray God may be finished in the believing view of immortality.

4th April Have been variously exercised by the great (topic) but let me restrain all enjoyment in the evident discomfort of him who has been the great instrument of my distress. He at the same time has been the instrument of salutary discipline to my soul I trust. O God, give me the right and charitable treatment of him.

This last extract may show either a temporary triumph for Chalmers or a final decision in his favour. Whatever the outcome, the controversy sheds a blaze of light on contemporary publishing methods, on Dr. Chalmers' surging temperament, and on the Scot's character under provocation. For if the quarrel was clearly a petty one, the participants were strong, and in every other respect, unblubbery men. They had inherited not only what Sir Walter Scott called "the old Scotch causticity," but the sturdy ascendant atmosphere of eighteenth-century Scotland. Feeling keenly, as Scotsmen can when touched on the raw, they spoke as they felt, each according to the light of his own logic; and thus, since Scotsmen are perhaps most formidable when their logic is gilded with passion, both Chalmers and Smith became harsh and astringent while the quarrel lasted. Certainly to both men, "Blessed are the meek," was a fading trumpet-sound on a distant horizon.

II

While these violent tides were raging round the Tron Church manse, William Collins seems to have acted mainly as a trusty breakwater. After six years' almost daily intercourse with Dr.

Chalmers he had become both faithful disciple and intimate friend. Primarily the secret of this friendship lay in a community of religious interest. For if Lord David Cecil is right that religion is the most sublime emotion known to man, Collins' state of sustained emotion, sublime at least in its sincerity, could hardly fail to attract the older man's admiration. But since there are bores among the devout as well as the profane, and religious sincerity alone would not have sufficed to keep their friendship alive, we must assume that the Doctor was also magnetised by the vitality which radiated from the young man's wafer-like physique, by his refusal to accept the most convoluted problems as insoluble or the most stubborn opponent as unconvertible, and above all, by his general enthusiasm. In 1821 it was inevitable that such a man, if religious at all, should be an Evangelical.

By this time the Evangelical movement had given Britain a new conscience. Its English leaders were men of great repute—Charles Simeon, Wilberforce, Lord Macaulay's father Zachary, and Babington—who had the common aim, in Wilberforce's words, of correcting society's "utter forgetfulness of its being the great business of life to secure our admission into heaven and to prepare our heart for its service and enjoyment." To this end they lived, for the most part, exemplary happy lives in sparkling contrast to the sombre piety of Thomas Boston a century before. Yet they all had a certain constriction of outlook. They were seldom to be seen in the theatre. Sunday they made into a day of steely austerity. Zachary Macaulay, and here was a happy man, compared novel-reading during the day with "drinking drams in the morning" and forbade his son the habit; while Dr. Chalmers, according to his lively daughter Ann, "cruelly prohibited" his family from reading Byron.[1]

Nevertheless, they were powerful enough to quench much of the libertinism which had lapped over from the eighteenth century. In England, as the result of their influence, divine service began to be attended by men who in the not-so-distant

[1]From Ann Chalmers' privately printed Diary for 1830, a document full of such charming, un-Byronic naïvetés as—"I am partial to English clergymen. They are very agreeable, though generally of short stature. They have such amiable smiles."

age of Boswell and Wilkes would have been happier round a faro table or in a bagnio in Covent Garden.

Of equal importance to the nation's social life, this religious revival brought with it a new humanitarianism. The struggle against bull- or bear-baiting, cock-fighting, duelling, flogging in the Army, and slavery—William Collins displayed an anti-slavery petition in his bookshop—was led in the main by Evangelicals, as challenging figures in an age of mingled restlessness and elegance as Cobbett, Orator Hunt and the Glasgow weavers. It is clear, then, that by 1821 they had performed great services to the State; and certainly in William Wilberforce they had a lay leader whose Bill abolishing the slave trade had not only brought him world renown, but had created a turning point in the world's history.[1] More intimately he was the idolised, almost legendary centre of a devoted circle of friends which William Collins was about to join.

Before meeting his Christian namesake, the Scottish William was to encourage one or two distinctive if not very distinguished Scottish contributions to Evangelical literature. Like most Scotsmen in 1821, he found no flaws in the halo with which public reverence for their sufferings had crowned the Covenanters. They were martyrs who had died for the same non-Erastian faith which he himself professed, and their graves "on the vacant wine-red moor" had inspired him from boyhood with a deep, romantic veneration.

His most picturesque effort to glorify the Covenanters was *Helen of the Glen*, a 1s. 6d. novel for children written in five days by Robert Pollok, a young consumptive divinity student.[2] Pollok in sore need of money for his University class fees, persuaded Collins, sensitive both to his poverty and his saintliness, to give

---

[1] The debate (1807) and the tremendous ovation which Wilberforce received when the Bill passed is movingly described in Professor Sir Reginald Coupland's *Wilberforce*, published by the Oxford University Press in 1923 and re-published by Collins in 1944.

[2] Pollok followed *Helen of the Glen* with *Ralph Gemmell* (of which Collins was joint publisher) and *The Persecuted Family*. After his death, Oliphant the Edinburgh publisher purchased the Collins copyright of *Helen of the Glen* and brought out the three stories in a single best-selling volume, *Tales of the Covenanters*, which also appeared for many years in the Collins list.

him £15 for the copyright. He then sat down with his publisher to revise the manuscript. "At present I am engaged with Mr. Collins," he wrote to his brother early in 1823. "The correction goes on pleasantly. . . . I esteem Mr. Collins more, both in talents and manners, the more I am acquainted with him."

Pollok's book has now little intrinsic value. It does, however, reflect the contemporary aura round the Covenant and the kind of literature which publishers of the period considered suitable for the lusty taste of Scottish children:

> "As they (Claverhouse's dragoons) approached with their prancing steeds and gleaming armour, uttering 'strange oaths,' Helen turned pale and seized her mother's hand. The soldiers appeared rather intoxicated, and their whole aspect was fierce and cruel. . . . 'Her blood be upon her own head,' cried the brutal dragoon (after Helen's mother had been killed by a carabine shot) as he turned his horse and galloped away, unmoved by the expiring agonies of the mother, or her little daughter, that swooned by her bloody corpse."

Here indeed was strong red meat. But Collins also leaped forthrightly to the defence of his spiritual ancestors in the *Sabbath School Magazine for Scotland*, his own sixpenny monthly journal for teachers. No critic of the Covenanters was safe from his forthright pen, not even Scotland's idol, Sir Walter Scott, who had dared to characterise some of the Covenanters' excesses in *Old Mortality*. "Among those who have wantonly attacked the character and conduct of the Covenanters," said the magazine, "the 'Great Unknown,' author of the Scottish Novels, has secured for himself a place which will hand his name down to posterity as the advocate of despotism, persecution, cruelty and oppression."

This apart, the magazine is an interesting mirror of the Evangelical's intense awareness (or fear) of another world. In it, reports of "sudden deaths" culled from the newspapers, and book reviews of William Collins' rather frightening children's novels, are invariably embellished with solemn reminders of life's transience and the inevitability of judgment before a great white throne. Preparation for eternity, as the all-absorbing

Evangelical passion, was clearly to govern William Collins' career for a long time to come.

III

In May 1821 Collins issued his first schoolbook—*A System of Commercial Arithmetic for Use In Schools and Private Families*. Two months later, he hurried round one afternoon to the coach office in Nelson Street, paid down £4 13s. for an outside seat in the London mail, stowed a valise crammed with his early publications and samples of stationery in the coach's boot, and set off for the south.

Imagination travels easily with the ardent young publisher on his first journey to England. The coachman and the scarlet-liveried guard, armed against highwaymen with cutlass and blunderbuss, would doubtless point out the sights on the way. But the animated eye of this unusual passenger would miss nothing as the coach-and-four climbed slowly up the moors to Beattock, dropped quickly down to the spacious features of eastern Dumfriesshire, and clattered into Carlisle. We can picture him stretching his cramped legs at coaching inns, follow him through the shires of the old pastoral England where yoked oxen still worked in the fields and friendly Jane Austen houses lay on the borders of splendid, ducal parks. We can guess, too, his exhilaration when the coach plunged into the sudden astonishing bustle of London.

His early days in the Capital were wholly devoted to business. He called on his agent, George Whittaker, a bookseller who distributed Collins books in London and supplied the Wilson Street bookshop in exchange with most of its English volumes. He also visited Mr. Smith of Smith Elder and Company, a Scotsman born in the same year as himself, with whom he was frequently to co-publish. But his chief quarry, Wilberforce, lay in Kensington Gore to which he quickly repaired. No full record of this first meeting exists, but, like everyone else, Collins must have

been charmed by his idol's warm-hearted friendliness and drollery.
Wilberforce, for his part, was impressed by the slender young
Scotsman's answering enthusiasm, for within a year he was
praising him to the skies in Evangelical circles, and four years
later wrote to Collins himself:

> "I cannot conclude without assuring you that it has given me real
> pleasure to form a personal connection with you. I could not but
> entertain a sort of ready-made respect and goodwill for you on
> Dr. Chalmers' account, when you presented yourself to me as his
> friend, but though that is a character of which no man could wish
> to divest himself, you now want no intermediate link of connection,
> but I feel real esteem and regard for you for your own sake."

The other members of the Wilberforce circle also opened
their doors. In August he explained the pauper situation in
Glasgow and his own publishing intentions to Zachary Macaulay,
who had worked in a Glasgow merchant's office at the age of
fourteen and was a product like himself of Scotland's eighteenth-
century upsurge. To William Collins, such a man was valuable
if only for his influence in the counsels of the widely-circulated
Christian Observer. But if Zachary Macaulay was thus to prove
not only a lovable friend but an important ally, William Collins
also appealed forthrightly to Macaulay. "You have done me a
great kindness in affording me an opportunity of knowing Mr.
Collins," he wrote to Dr. Chalmers, "and I wish it had been in
my power to mark my obligation in some more effectual manner.
However, he has produced an impression on my own mind which
I trust I shall not forget and which I trust also that I may be
enabled to communicate to others." It was wholehearted praise;
but Collins by this time had sped on to Macaulay's brother-in-
law, Babington, and then, by a winding turn, to Harrow where
he visited the Rev. J. W. Cunningham, that enlightened clergyman
who sanctioned the burial of Byron's natural child Allegra in
Harrow Church, only to discover, when his churchwardens
objected to a memorial tablet above her grave, that the child
had to be buried anonymously under the doormat. At Harrow
the flying Scotsman left a new impression:

"I found Mr. Collins full of zeal, of intelligence and, I doubt not, of piety," Cunningham wrote to Dr. Chalmers, "and was delighted to find so ardent a champion of your plans and friend to your honour and interests in an individual so thoroughly acquainted with both. It has been very amusing to us here to find that your influence upon those coming into contact with you extends even to phraseology and I could again imagine when I listened to Mr. Collins that I heard a sort of echo of your own emphatic and peculiar dialect. It behoves you, Dear Sir, to take care of your words and actions if you are thus to inoculate your followers and friends."

From Harrow—it seems a natural journey—Collins went on to Cambridge where he cajoled substantial orders for his publications out of the local booksellers. But Cambridge also enshrined for him a more personal objective—the great Charles Simeon, than whom there have been few more remarkable figures in the long history of Anglicanism. When he first began to preach at Cambridge, undergraduates hurled stones through the windows of his church and his parishioners complained to their bishop of his "alarming and terrifying" preaching; but he remained there for fifty-four years. Being wealthy by inheritance, it was his custom to buy advowsons for young clergymen whom he had personally trained not only in Evangelicalism but in pulpit delivery for which he had a passion. "How did I speak this evening?" a fellow cleric asked him once. "Why, my dear brother," came the reply, "I am sure you will pardon me—you know it is all love, my brother—but indeed it was just as if you were knocking on a warming-pan—tin, tin, tin, tin, without any intermission." But despite his eccentricities, his fame and influence were vast—far greater than that of any primate, said Lord Macaulay during Simeon's lifetime; or in the words of a later historian, G. M. Trevelyan: "Had it not been for Simeon, the Evangelical clergy would have continued to drift into Dissent, as the easier method of conducting a peripatetic mission after the manner of Wesley, athwart the bounds of the parish system and in defiance of Church order." No publisher of religious books, by these tokens, could have had a more influential friend, especially as Simeon was later to become a Collins contributor. But here we must leave our roving publisher, steadily working his way north among the booksellers of England's industrial cities. By November he was back in Glasgow.

Although Charles Chalmers was a somewhat feckless partner, the business had not suffered from William Collins' long absence. From start to finish of his long journey, he had kept in touch by letter with the Candleriggs. He had also secured such encouraging orders that by the end of the year he was able to pay Dr. Chalmers £665 in literary fees and £20 as the half-yearly interest on his £800 loan. Needless to say, he also resumed his public work with customary zest, snatching an hour or two daily to move about among the poor and needy in the Gallowgate and the surrounding wynds, where visitors incessantly besieged him or were diverted to him for information about Chalmers' famous schemes. Thus, one day he is reported as being Lord Elgin's guide around his Sunday schools. On another, he is engaged in a skirmish with Robert Southey's strange friend, Dr. Andrew Bell.

Bell, commemorated now by a plaque in Westminster Abbey, by Madras College at St. Andrews which he founded, and by several other schools and scholarships, was the son of a St. Andrews barber. As a young man he had gone out to India where he invented, much to Collins' disgust, the Madras system of education by which prefects chosen for monitoring purposes became in essence boy-teachers as well. On his return—with a fortune in his pocket—he decided to campaign for his pet theories, and chose Glasgow as an early hunting-ground. The hunter was soon disillusioned, however, judging by Chalmers' recital of the chase to Edward Irving:

> *Dr. Chalmers:* I had a call from Dr. Bell this morning. I was lying awake in my old woman's room, cogitating whether I should get up or not, when I heard a heavy step in the kitchen and the door opening, and the speaker entering, a rough voice exclaimed, "Can this be the chamber of the great Dr. Chalmers?"
> *Irving:* And what did you say?

Chalmers: I even told him that it was, and I invited him to stay and breakfast with me. I knew that Mr. Collins was to be out with a proof, and was glad to think that the discussion between the merits of his school system and the Scottish, which I knew was soon to follow, would be supported by one who, I suspected, was more than a match for him.

Irving: Well, and how did it turn up?

Chalmers: Mr. Collins arrived as I expected, and to it they set tooth and nail.

Irving: And the result?

Chalmers: Collins was too many for him.

But the heavy-jowled, thick-bespectacled, lightning-tempered Bell was an obstinate campaigner. He hung on later, said Dr. Chalmers, " with great vehemence and volubility in behalf of his method. He spoke himself hoarse to me about it on my walk from the church to the bath: and on the Monday morning at breakfast I got him and Mr. Collins to have a further engagement thereanent: I believe he has left us in some degree of dudgeon."[1]

[1]From Hanna's *Memoirs of Dr. Chalmers.*

CHAPTER IV

New Horizons

1822-1825

I

IN 1822 William Collins launched an ambitious new venture. He had been keenly aware for some time that the scattered theology of the past two centuries had become dusty and often inaccessible. Now he planned to bring it together in a uniform series. Each volume was to carry a steel-engraved frontispiece and a preface by a distinguished contemporary writer; and, dependent on their size, the volumes, bound at first in grey paper-boards with paper label title, were to sell at prices varying between 3s. and 10s. 6d. Thus began the *Select Library of Christian Authors*—a pioneering enterprise whose imitation by other publishers soon led to a wide re-publication of ecclesiastical literature.

The first volumes to appear were Romaine's *Treatises upon the Life, Walk and Triumph of Faith* and *The Imitation of Christ* by Thomas à Kempis, with Introductory Essays by—but by whom else?—Thomas Chalmers, D.D.[1] Chalmers was eventually to contribute nearly a score of the seventy essays in the series—a composite task for which he was paid more than £600. But at this stage other well-known contributors were essential. To find

[1]Collins issued them in cloth binding and also in a Pocket Edition after 1825. *The Imitation of Christ* with Chalmers' Essay was still on the Collins' list seventy years after its first publication and was later included in the *Pocket Classics*.

61

them, Collins again took his place in the London coach in the late summer of 1822; and again it is possible to piece together from scattered fragments of evidence the high-lights of his trip.

He seems to have travelled down the west side of England, calling on booksellers in Liverpool, Manchester, Birmingham and other large industrial towns. In Bristol he visited John Foster, whose now-forgotten *Essay on the Evils of Popular Ignorance* (1820) had quickly run into a sufficient number of editions to establish his reputation. Foster, sprung from sturdy intelligent weaver stock, was an ex-Baptist preacher who had turned to letters as a permanent profession, though he wrote with immense labour. His tardiness was happily unknown to William Collins when he invited him to write the preface to Doddridge's *Rise and Progress.*

The fate of this preface is perhaps best told in its author's own account, written to a friend three years later when it was still unfinished:

"Not without some reluctance on my part, Mr. Collins fixed Doddridge's *Rise and Progress* on me. . . . He did his part with a despatch not at all pleasing to me, and actually the whole large edition has been lying as dead stock in the warehouse for two years, in default of my task being performed. Again and again he has written, and I have been too much ashamed even to answer his letters, though expressed in the most mild and friendly spirit. Bad health, to which I find that mental labour is *just* poison (to use a Scotch adverb), has been in alliance with my horror of composition —and so the procrastination has gone on, one six months after another, while I have felt ashamed, and mortified, and self-reproached at being thus the cause of a very serious loss, in the plain trade sense, to Chalmers and Collins. At last, however, these feelings together with the excellent man's expostulations and remonstrances, have had the effect of driving me to try an attempt at the unwelcome service."

Two months later the good Foster wrote again to his correspondent that his "master from Glasgow" had just visited him, and "seemed to be content to put the cudgel in the corner on finding that the thing was *bona fide*, almost done." But this was no ordinary preface. When finished, at the end of September 1825, it was revealed as a book in itself with no less than one hundred and sixty printed octavo pages, and Foster was writing to his correspondent in modest triumph that the work was at last completed. He added the modest aside: "I do not know whether I shall be induced to do, on a much more confined scale of extent, another thing or two for the same employers. But indeed, I shall have to see whether they will ask me." His last doubt seems to have been borne out by events. Despite the chorus of praise for Foster's mammoth preface, considered by most reviewers to be his best work, Collins evidently decided that his printing press must be served by authors who suffered from less prolonged phases of inertia.

But this vexation lay ahead. In 1822 the worthy Collins, happily unaware of the coming war of attrition with Foster, coached cheerfully from Bristol to London to canvass the next contributors on his list—Wilberforce as a matter of course, and Edward Irving who earlier in the year had been translated from Glasgow to London. The image of Foster was still radiant in his mind. "Mr. Collins seems to have enjoyed his journey much and to have thriven on it," wrote Irving to Dr. Chalmers. "He is in the clouds or rather above them about Foster ' the great man '—that is his *nom de guerre* with the worthy father of your session."

For his own part, Irving willingly promised a preface—to the *Life of Bernard Gilpin* (the saintly sixteenth-century divine who travelled on preaching missions about the North of England, where he died after being knocked down by an ox in Durham market-place). An even greater prize was Wilberforce's pledge to write a foreword to Witherspoon's *Essay on Regeneration*. But imps of mischief clustered round this trip. Though Collins wanted the Witherspoon essay at the earliest possible date, six months later, on 6th January 1823, Wilberforce noted in his diary: "I heard Macaulay's paper on East India sugar, and tried to finish my long-promised Preface to Witherspoon." Wilberforce, though far from well, was fortunately of sterner metal than

Foster. He completed the Preface two days after his diary entry; and within a few weeks the book was published.

To return to the summer of 1822, Collins' last act in London was to arrange a meeting in Suffolk between members of the Wilberforce circle and Dr. Chalmers. "I really think you ought to come thus far to meet them especially for the sake of the good and venerable Wilberforce," he urged the Doctor by letter—a plea to which Chalmers amiably assented, keeping luckily a record of the meeting. "Then in came Mr. Wilberforce," he wrote, "who really looks a great deal better than when I saw him last; but nothing can exceed the singularity of his movements. He positively danced and whisked about like a squirrel. He insisted on taking some packages with his own hand to the carriage that was waiting us at the door, and skipped before us in such a way that I could not refrain from laughing outright. I have the utmost love for him, at the same time, and the utmost reverence. He spoke highly of Mr. Collins, and was friendly and kind to the uttermost."

While Wilberforce was thus praising Mr. Collins in Suffolk, the *Sentinel* was lambasting him in Scotland. This splenetic journal was the Glasgow counterpart of the Edinburgh *Beacon*, a high-Tory scandal sheet of such spleen that even the true-blue Sir Walter Scott had to disown his support for it. The *Sentinel*, hardly less rancorous, copied the *Beacon's* rashness with literally fatal results: an internal quarrel between its editors and printers revealed Sir Alexander Boswell of Auchinleck (James Boswell's son) as the author of what Lockhart called "certain truculent enough pasquinades" against a well-known Scottish Whig, James Stuart of Dunearn. Stuart challenged Boswell to a duel, and the baronet, in Lockhart's words, "fell in as miserable a quarrel as ever cost the blood of a high-spirited gentleman." There could be no duel over the *Sentinel's* attacks on Dr. Chalmers and William Collins, though they, too, were "truculent enough." As witness: "The last two numbers of the *Civic Economy* happily contain a few sentences that are intelligible"—a fair sample of its spring style in 1822. By the late summer the *Sentinel*, more daringly, was advising Chalmers to "keep above the tricks of the book business," and also "to set a much higher value upon his literary character than to attempt to edit such works as THOMAS À'KEMPIS, either to furnish work for his co-partners, or for the gain that can accrue from them, especially when his time is so much occupied, that he is obliged to introduce a slice of one of his old sermons as part of the "introductory essay." Not surprisingly, the journal also picked on several of Collins' novels for children—those deservedly forgotten works which appeared in the spring and summer of this busy year under such enervating titles as *Fanny Fairfield, the Farmer's Daughter*, by a Lady; and *Tommy Welwood, Or a Few Days Of Incident and Instruction*.

Fortunately the *Sentinel's* vigilance was soon to flag. In any event, William Collins by the end of 1822 had not only thrown up a formidable rampart with the first three volumes of his *Select Library*, but Dr. Chalmers as a target was about to fall below the horizon of his Glasgow critics.

II

At the beginning of 1823, Chalmers announced his acceptance of the Chair of Moral Philosophy at St. Andrews University. In the complex of life to-day, when the Church has lost some of the social ascendancy it enjoyed over a smaller population, it is perhaps difficult to imagine the sensational effect of such an announcement. That the greatest pulpit orator of the day should —as the gossip went—tuck himself away in University precincts seemed incredible. The city of Glasgow, which had taken a special pride in its ornament's sway over the multitude, was preternaturally shocked. Many criticisms were hurled at him: he was on the retreat; he was running away from a task which had proved beyond his powers; he was betraying his system of poor relief which only his own drive and persistence could maintain. But the Doctor was deaf to these roaring winds. For the time being he had had enough of crowds, of what, in sudden revolt, he once described as

"the popularity of stare, and pressure, and animal heat . . . a popularity which, with its head among storms and its feet on the treacherous quicksands, has nothing to lull the agonies of its tottering existence but the hosannahs of a drivelling generation."

At a hastily summoned meeting of his "agency," Collins explained that Dr. Chalmers' reasons for his impending move were ill-health, his conviction that he could now serve the Church best by training its ministers, and his wish to have time and leisure to prosecute his "other favourite pursuits." The same night (20th January 1823), the disciple reported to his master:

"Your resignation as soon as known produced a very great sensation in town. Every person was thunderstruck and though the most positive assurances of its truth were given yet the utmost scepticism prevailed on the subject. Your agency came in great numbers to be satisfied, and everywhere the deepest regret was felt and manifested. . . ."

Eventually the criticism became so noisy that Chalmers had recourse to his elder for the publication, in February, of a *Defence by DR. CHALMERS, addressed to the Thinking and Unprejudiced part of the Inhabitants of Glasgow.* This allayed the storm. A banquet, at which Collins was one of the stewards, was held in his honour; and at his farewell sermon in November the crowd scenes were compared by a Glasgow newspaper with the storming of Badajos. In fact, the un-robust Collins, who organised the Doctor's "agency" into guides and sentries to control the crowds, risked life and limb, for dense crowds rushed the doors and the military were summoned from an adjoining barracks to keep order. It was a timely end. Weary of the clamour, Chalmers departed as quickly as he could for the cloisters of St. Andrews, and Glasgow grew colder and darker.

Yet if the leader himself had gone, an active disciple was still left in the Candleriggs. Not only did William Collins throw himself with increased fervour into the affairs of the parish, but, being no longer in the Doctor's daily thrall, he became so self-reliant and venturesome, and published so many new books, that soon he was forced to acquire an extra warehouse at 37 Wilson Street. He also got his name on to the title page of the *Eclectic Review* (a famous religious journal of the time) as one of its chief distributors in Scotland. His book sales increased. As the result of his journeyings, orders for his own publications increased rapidly, while many of his friends in England even ordered books from his bookshop which they could as easily have purchased in their neighbourhood. We find Edward Irving, for example, sending an order for psalm-books for his London church, accompanied by an earnest prayer that they should be "not quite so ornate as the last." In Scotland, James Douglas of Cavers, a well-known laird, once wrote to Dr. Chalmers: "Would you order books to the amount of Forty Pounds from Mr. Collins and have them distributed throughout your parish. Mr. Collins' bill will be a treasure showing what works and in what proportion you order for the spiritual wants of your parishioners."

Not all the volumes published during these feverish years were theological in the strict sense. They included *The History of the House of Rowallan Written in Year Prior to 1657 by Sir William Mure, Knight of Rowallan* (though even this was pietistic); an *Oratorical Class-Book* for School Elocution Classes (the second Collins schoolbook); and a travel-book by a ship's surgeon, issued jointly with Underwood, the Fleet Street publisher. But in the main his output consisted of sermons; ephemeral religious novels with such damping titles as *No Enthusiasm: a Tale of the Present Times*, and *No Fiction: a Narrative founded on Recent and Interesting Facts;* odd volumes like the *Memoir of a Clergyman's Wife in St. Petersburg;* and an anonymous *Essay on the Objects of Taste*. Some of these must have been unprofitable. There is certainly no hint of a best-seller in John Campbell of Carbrook's heavy tractarian title: *Observations on the Anti-Christian Tendency of Modern Education*.

Fortunately for the firm the torrent threw up in 1823 a best-

seller, *The Christian Philosopher* by Thomas Dick. As a lad Dick
had worked at the loom with books on astronomy propped up
before him, until at the age of sixteen he got himself to the
University of Edinburgh, became a teacher, and finally persuaded
William Collins to publish his work. Few books can have been
more successful. It ran at once into edition after edition, reached
its tenth by 1846, and continued to be reprinted with regularity
until the twentieth century cast Dick's works into oblivion.

III

William Collins was soon to have another best-seller author on
his list—the raven-haired romantic, Edward Irving. This
visionary was now on the crest of popular success. Wilberforce,
who thought his writing affected and bombastic, told Hannah
More that his language in the pulpit was "remarkably and even
felicitously forcible and impressive," and quoted Collins—"a very
sensible inhabitant of Glasgow "—to the effect that Irving was
a "truly good man and active pastor, particularly attentive to
the poor." Cunningham of Harrow, in a letter to Chalmers,
thought of him as a "clever and good man who has been seduced
into drinking two bottles of champagne." Charles Lamb on the
other hand called him a "Boanerges of the temple," and Canning
praised him in the House of Commons. Not surprisingly, in the
light of such praise, the dense crowds that invaded his church so
speeded Irving's Byronic rise to fame that every Sunday morning
for a year or two Holborn was thronged with crowds and with
carriages bringing Princes of the Blood, Cabinet Ministers, the
nobility, and such celebrated literary figures as Carlyle, Lamb
and Coleridge to hear his poetical glow and glitter.

The Irving bubble was soon to collapse, but not before
William Collins had profited from its iridescence. His first Irving
publication—in May 1822—was that preacher's flowery farewell
sermon in Glasgow, an utterance so eulogistic of his former
chief that Dr. Chalmers was embarrassed. Not so William

Collins. "I had almost resolved to refuse flatly the flattering requests of my friends to publish that poor discourse," wrote Irving to a friend, "but yesterday there came such a letter from Mr. Collins, full of argument and the kindest encouragement, that I have resolved to comply, and shall signify my resolution to him by this post." It was perhaps fortunate that before Collins set his press in motion, Dr. Chalmers' wife laid determined hands on the manuscript, deleted the more florid parts of the panegyric, and remained unperturbed by Irving's expressions of "astonishment and indignation" when he returned to Glasgow and noticed the liberties she had taken. However, this rift was quickly mended, and towards the end of 1823 Irving was struggling, almost in the Foster manner, to finish his long-promised preface to *The Life of Bernard Gilpin*.

"My Dear Mr. Collins," he wrote from London on 24th February 1824:

> "I pray you not for a moment to imagine that I have any other intention, so long as God gives me strength, than to fulfil my promise faithfully. I am at present worked beyond my strength and you know that is not inconsiderable. My head! My head! I may say with the Shunamite's child. If I care not for it the world will soon cease to care for me and I for the world. . . ."

Within a few months William Collins again crossed the Border—primarily to seek authors for the *Select Library* but also to improve his struggling sales organisation. Behind him he left his compositors at work on the printing of Andrew Crichton's *The Life and Diary of Lt.-Col. J. Blackader*, a lively religious book by one of the Duke of Marlborough's commanders. At the time the effect of this book's re-publication was probably slight. A century later this very edition, with its Collins imprint, was to prove a valuable source-book for Dr. G. M. Trevelyan's major work, *England under Queen Anne*.

On arrival in London the young publisher went straight to Wilberforce, as he always did, and to Irving who was now in constant touch with Thomas Carlyle. Carlyle, who thought Irving the "freest, brotherliest, bravest human soul mine eyes ever came into contact with," had less sympathy with the voluble Christianity of Irving's Scottish publisher.

"One day," he wrote in his *Reminiscences*, "Irving took me with him on a curious little errand he had. . . . A certain loquacious extensive Glasgow publisher was in London for several weeks on business, and often came to Irving, wasting (as I used to think) a good deal of his time in zealous discourse about many vague things: in particular about the villainy of common publishers, how for example, on their ' half profits ' system they would show the poor authors a printer's account pretending to be paid in full, printer's signature visibly appended, printer having really touched a sum *less* by 25 per cent. . . . Irving could not believe it; denied stoutly on behalf of his own printer, one Bensley, a noted man in his craft, and getting nothing but negatory smiles and kindly but inexorable contradictions, said he would go next morning and see."

The "extensive loquacious" Collins was vindicated the next morning, as Carlyle was forced to admit. Of greater moment was Irving's promise that his next major volume should be published in Glasgow; for such a promise in the conditions of the time meant a best-seller. Blithely the thirty-five-year-old publisher then turned north to seek in Sheffield a new hero— James Montgomery.

Montgomery, then editor of the *Sheffield Iris*, was a saintly man whose work is still known to millions of people all over the world though only a small proportion of them could name its author. Yet Montgomery should be well known. He is represented in almost every hymnal by some of the best-known hymns in the English language: notably by *Go to dark Gethsemane* and *Prayer is the Soul's sincere desire* which William Collins published for the first time, and by the still more famous *For ever with the Lord* with those haunting lines:

> *Here in the body pent,*
> *Absent from Him I roam,*
> *Yet nightly pitch my moving tent*
> *A day's march nearer home.*

Montgomery was yet another product of Scotland's eighteenth-century ferment. Born at Irvine in Ayrshire in 1771, he left the town as a child, served later in a baker's shop, tried unsuccessfully to sell his adolescent poems in London, took up journalism as a career—in days when free critical expression was treated by the government as sedition or criminal libel—and went to prison for printing a Belfast clergyman's enthusiastic ballad on the fall of the Bastille. But he also wrote a number of long poems such as *The Pelican Island* and the *Wanderer in Switzerland* which pleased Scott, Wordsworth and Southey, but provoked Jeffrey. The great Edinburgh reviewer, who thought in 1807 that the diligent readers of poetry consisted chiefly of "young half-educated women, sickly tradesmen and enamoured apprentices," added as a rider to this raillery: "The scanty stream of Montgomery's genius is never allowed to steal quietly along its channel, but is poured out in melancholy tears, or thrown up to heaven in all the frothy magnificence of tiny jets and artificial commotions." Which is good Jeffrey; but despite him the *ninth* edition of the *Wanderer in Switzerland* was being advertised in this country in 1822, a score of editions had been printed in America, and Montgomery had earned from it £800.

Collins thus had practical support for his own views of the poet when one summer evening he arrived without warning on Montgomery's doorstep. Of this meeting it need only be said that as with Wilberforce there was an immediate affinity between the two men, perhaps because they shared the same consciousness of life, death and judgment, and the earthly transience which Montgomery himself crystallised: *Man, like a shadow, flees.*

But William Collins was also a publisher. He offered Montgomery the sum of one hundred guineas to compile an anthology of sacred verse with a preface, and to write—also for the *Select Library*—an Introductory Essay to Cowper's Poems. By October (1824) Montgomery—a punctual craftsman—had finished the Cowper preface and when the book came out by the end of the year, the new publishing house had printed its first volume of poetry. Work on the sacred anthology, known for generations as *The Christian Psalmist*, also went rapidly forward. It appeared in 1825, reached its fourth edition within twelve months, was then extensively used by American publishers of hymn books, and is now lauded in Chambers' *Cyclopædia of English Literature* as "having laid the foundation of scientific hymnology."[1]

But this phase of apparent progress is nearing its end. By extraordinary exertions William Collins both at home and in England had made his name known, especially in Evangelical circles where Wilberforce and his friends had continuously proclaimed the merit of his work. The outlook, in fact, seemed so set to fair that prosperous spring of 1825, that neither William Collins nor Charles Chalmers seem to have sensed the stealthy approach of disunion and disaster.

[1]This book is frequently mentioned in Julian's Dictionary of Hymnology. There are also many flattering references to it in *The English Hymn* by Dr. Louis F. Benson of Pennsylvania University (Hodder & Stoughton, 1915). Montgomery's *The Christian Psalmist* reached its ninth edition in 1846; his Cowper its ninth edition in 1868.

CHAPTER V

Escape from Jeopardy

1825-1829

I

SINCE THEIR first meeting the instinctive affinity between William Collins and Dr. Chalmers had become, in the public eye, a close unbreakable union. Not only did they read and ride together at St. Andrews several times a year, but in the intervening months their correspondence reflected no cloud on either their personal or financial relations. It could only have been with utter sincerity that Dr. Chalmers made this remarkable entry in his *Journal:*

> "Heavy till Mr. Collins came. Much interested in his visit and desire to be humbled that I find not an ever-present God enough for me. Let me at the same time thank Him for all his creatures. Mr. Collins has enlivened my prospects as to my future condition. But why should I lose faith? O my God guide me through my approaching difficulties as to college matters. Let me not suffer this visit of Mr. Collins to pass away without spiritual benefit."

From Glasgow, on the other hand, came such messages as: "Give my affectionate regards to Mrs. Chalmers whose kind and welcome smile so often cheered me."

At the beginning of 1825 this harmony was still undimmed. So far as Dr. Chalmers knew, his friend's affairs were prosperous though Mrs. Collins' ill-health was a perpetual anxiety. He himself had received substantial fees for his literary work in the form of bills which were dutifully met—seven hundred pounds in 1822, one hundred and fifty in 1824, four hundred in 1825.[1] The interest on his loans to the partners was always paid. And he must have been further encouraged in March when Collins, along with a parcel of quill pens and a present of books, not only returned a £600 bond for which Chalmers had been security, but promised repayment of the £800 loan to the printing company within a week.

This was a blunder. A new and sudden depression was already chasing out the boom of the past two years. A number of book-sellers delayed payment of their accounts. Scott, the trusted shopman who had always tried to keep a wary eye on the un-businesslike Charles, left the firm to join Longmans in London. Revenue had also been lost as the result of the too-optimistic arrangements with John Foster, and with Edward Irving who was now responsible for another discomfiture.

In the summer of 1823 he had promised an immediate Essay for *Horne on the Psalms*. Collins over-trustfully printed the rest of the book in advance and waited in patience for Irving's MS. But all through 1824 it remained unwritten, until in March 1825 the publisher in desperation wrote to Dr. Chalmers:

> "As it is a serious loss to us to have £250 so long locked up and useless, what I have to beg of you is that you would allow me to take your Two Discourses on Jeremiah I, V, and appropriate them to Horne. . . . After the experience of Doddridge (*Foster's failure*) and Horne I never will print a book till I have the Essay in my possession. No promises will betray me into this again."

Within a few days of ascertaining Dr. Chalmers' compliance with the proposal, the London visionary, stirred at last to action, sent the graphic promise: "In a fortnight it will be finished, dead or alive." This pledge he kept; the book was published by

---

[1]At this time publishers usually paid their authors by post-dated "bills." This delayed form of payment gave publishers time to collect their booksellers' dues.

June; and Collins with great relief boarded the Irish steam packet for a bookselling expedition to Ireland. Of this trip he wrote on 14th June: "The great increase of Bookselling in Dublin is a very favourable sympton of the increasing education of Ireland, and I am told Bookselling has increased tenfold within these ten years."[1]

By the time he returned to the Candleriggs the plight of the firm had, however, worsened, and willynilly he had to borrow from friends to keep it from foundering. The *Select Library*, it is true, was still pouring from his press, but too copiously, since on some of its volumes he incurred a loss despite heavy expenditure on advertising. For each first edition he normally printed 1,000 copies. If published at 3s. 6d. he allowed 1s. 9d. on each copy for paper, print and boarding, and thus by his own reckoning made about £87 if the edition were sold out. But on some of the earlier volumes he made no more than £40 or £50 and on some nothing at all: some were a dead loss.

His plight may best be appreciated by an anticipation. By 1828 he had published thirty-six books in the *Select Library*, of which sixteen went into more than one edition. Many of his essayists, apart from such celebrated names as Chalmers, Wilberforce, and Irving, were men of high intellectual attainments—Charles Simeon who wrote the essay for *Walker's Christian*, Dr. John Brown, Isaac Taylor and Thomas Erskine of Linlathen, a devout and wealthy advocate who gave up his practice at the Bar to study theology. The work of men such as these undoubtedly stimulated the sales of the series. But in the summer of 1825 the best-sellers were still to come; and meanwhile, the financial structure of the business, being under-capitalised and carrying heavy and irreducible overheads, was therefore doubly vulnerable to any recession of trade. It was at this time that a rather frightened Charles revealed to his brother that the annual expenditure for shop and warehouse on rent, wages, taxes and other shop expenses came to about £1,300 a year—a figure which

[1] Collins' chief bookselling associates in Dublin were R. M. Tims and Wm. Curry, Jun., & Co.

seems to have excluded the maintenance of the printing works in Candleriggs Court.[1]

By late summer, the partners were forced into fresh borrowing, and in order to grapple more effectively with this and various other dilemmas Collins postponed his annual journey to England until 30th September. He had hardly arrived in London when Charles, trying at last to make a decisive contribution of his own towards the firm's salvation, sent his brother the following appeal:

MY DEAR THOMAS,

I should like to see you and have some conversations respecting the Bank Bond that was cancelled last January. (*Charles must have meant March.*) The truth is that £600 was too much to draw out of our business at one time. We could have managed it very well to have paid up £100 every four months but more than this we have not done with safety. At the time the Bond was cancelled we had plenty of money as our accounts are all collected at the beginning of the year, but at the end of the season a Bookseller is generally ill off as he lives out of his money for nine or ten months while his own accounts must be paid when they fall due which is at no particular season. I must therefore in consequence of our Cash Account having been cancelled candidly confess that I feel myself in difficulties.

I am, My dear Thomas, Yours, faithfully,

CHARLES CHALMERS

Within two days the Doctor had lent another sum of £400, repayable within a year, which gave the firm a breathing-space. But this proved to be a very brief respite. On Christmas Eve the Doctor received from Glasgow a new intimation of misfortune: "These are bad times. The Whittakers, our agents, have failed, but it is said they will go on again." Though this message should have heightened his anxiety, he still did not appreciate the gravity of the crisis. He certainly had no idea that William Collins—with a timid and shrinking partner who disliked the routine of

---

[1] In 1825, the printers got 23s. a week. Apprentices began at 3s. per week, rising 6d. each year. The hours in the warehouse were sixty-one a week and the only rest-day was Sunday. Sixty-six hours a week were worked in the printing office.

the book business—was now in immediate danger of following Whittaker into bankruptcy.

II

During the first week of January 1826 William Collins and his partner grimly faced each other in the Wilson Street bookshop. Their situation was desperate. Together Collins and his wife's family had £6,000 invested in the business. The bookshop debt to Dr. Chalmers was £1,200. And although the partners had secured a new credit of £1,000 from the Royal Bank, its guarantors, suddenly alarmed by Whittaker's bankruptcy and the rumours of more sensational failures to come, had asked to be released from their bond. As this demand was peremptory and the firm had other pressing obligations, the worried partners faced each other in ominous circumstances.

Their conversation was not ill-tempered though relations between the partners had been chilly for some time. Charles considered the firm's plight was chiefly due to what he called Collins' "venturesomeness." To this Collins, who thought his partner "did not have his mind fully in the business," replied that the publishing and printing side of the business had always made a profit, but the retail side under Charles' supervision—this included the sale not only of literary works but of school and commercial stationery—had for some years been running at a loss. Neither partner, it is strange to discover, had any idea of the value of their stock; but both agreed that one way and another they had extended the business far beyond the limit of their capital, and they certainly had a clear vision of the stream of creditors' demands for payment which had poured into Wilson Street at the New Year.

On the 9th, when they met again, Charles was so alarmed at the prospect of the Chalmers' monies in the business being swept away in a grand insolvency, that without consulting his brother, he proposed an immediate dissolution of the partnership.

It was one of those moments where a man who has been long perplexed suddenly becomes clear-sighted. Without demur William Collins accepted the proposal. He would have to raise fresh funds not only to pay off Charles but to discharge the firm's debts—that he knew; but being the father of three children —William Junior aged eight, a five-year-old daughter Elizabeth, and a three-year-old boy John—he also perceived that the business during a prolonged period of trade insecurity could not provide ample income for two family men, of whom one entirely lacked business aptitude.

With the issue thus decided he began to act more resolutely. As a first step he called in his lawyer to draft a "Dissolution of Co-partnership." He persuaded one of his brothers-in-law to lend him £1,000 to meet the bank's immediate demand. Next, he cajoled a promise of £2,800—a very large sum in terms of contemporary purchasing power—to be lent when required by his three brothers-in-law jointly so that both Dr. Chalmers and his brother could be paid out in full. Lastly, he strove to collect debts due to the firm by tardy booksellers.

At this point, while Collins was showing superabundant vitality, Charles—nervous and ill-adjusted to commerce—again took fright. "Your brother mentions that the agreement was no sooner fixed than he felt distressed particularly for not having consulted you," wrote Mr. Montgomerie, a Glasgow man of business who had been implored by Dr. Chalmers to discover the "real" reasons for the break-up. "This he pointedly admits it was his duty to have done, a position too plain to admit of doubt. Accordingly, he so far wished to retrace his steps, but found that Mr. Collins had made his arrangements to fulfil and follow out the agreement and therefore was not inclined to give it up."

After this imbroglio both partners felt it their bounden duty to explain matters to the Doctor at St. Andrews. Collins went first, Charles a few days later. The effect of their visits on the worried divine may be judged from his *Private Journal:*

23rd Jan. Disturbed by Mr. Collins with matters of business.

30th Jan.   Charles arrived from Glasgow. Variously agitated with
his affairs and those of the College.

31st Jan.   Had more talking with Charles. I'm greatly disappointed
in Mr. Collins, but let me be calm and fearless.

By this time, it must be remembered, not merely the House
of Chalmers and Collins but the whole publishing world was
tottering. Towards the end of the month the bubble of bills,
counter-bills and mutual credits built up by Archibald Constable,
James Ballantyne, Hurst and Robinson (Constable's London
agents), and Sir Walter Scott had suddenly burst; and in consequence publishers everywhere came under anxious scrutiny. It
was a doleful setting which more than ever persuaded William
Collins that his future lay in cautious independence. For this
independence, however, he was to pay a heavy price in personal
anxiety. Unknown to Collins and perhaps only half-realised by
himself, Charles was sowing seeds of mischief which were to
produce later a bitter crop of suspicion between Collins and his
brother. The first seed, it is clear from the *Journal*, was planted
in Dr. Chalmers' mind on 31st January. The second, with lustier
roots, was sown on the 15th of March when Charles sent his
brother the following letter:

"When I returned from St. Andrews I made the proposal of
taking stock to Mr. Collins. He was at the time in great perturbation of mind in consequence of a demand upon us for £1,200 and
therefore would not listen to the proposal. He said he did not
value the friendship of any man at that time when I told him that
I thought the continuance of your friendship towards him depended
upon his doing exactly what you requested. He has since got his
Brother-in-law to come forward with £1,000 to relieve us, which
certainly would not have been forthcoming had not Mr. Collins
got greatly the advantage of me in the bargain which we had
made. It will, however, save us from Bankruptcy for we are not in
circumstances at present to pay away £1,200 out of the concern. . . .
The only information which I received from Mr. Collins respecting
your interview with him in Edinburgh was that you had acquiesced
in our arrangement, that you had given Mr. Collins instructions
to lodge your £1,200 in the Royal Bank, and that you have some
idea of selling the copyright of one of your Works for which Mr.

Collins is disposed to give you £300. This I think is too small a sum. I am certain you would get more for it in London from some of the booksellers there."

This was hardly a helpful epistle. None the less, by the end of March, winding-up arrangements were satisfactorily completed. Collins persuaded his wife's relatives to advance him the promised £2,800 at once; and on 1st April 1826 the two erstwhile partners signed an agreement which Charles, to his credit, thought generous. Its chief effect was to make the whole of the firm's stock, including the copyright of books already published, William Collins' property. Collins for his part paid Charles £800 as his share of capital stocks, £300 as his share of profits on 9th January, £200 as salary from 9th January until 1st September, and £100 worth of books published by the firm. He also gave Charles a bond of indemnity against all other liabilities, signed by himself and his three brothers-in-law: John Barclay, superintendent of the cotton factory at Catrine, James Barclay, superintendent of the bleaching works at Catrine, and George Barclay, a Paisley manufacturer.

Thus ended the uneasy partnership of six and a half years. The ex-partners immediately discharged their respective obligations and Dr. Chalmers was completely reimbursed for every penny he had invested in the business.

Only one further commentary on the break is needed. At no point in the dismal tangle of events was the rectitude of William Collins called in question. This is made clear beyond controversy by the following extracts from Montgomerie's cool and balanced letters on the subject to Dr. Chalmers:

> *15th April.* Mr. Collins mentions that from his own monies and those of his friends he had in the concern £6,000 besides the Bank credit of £1,000 which he has been obliged to provide and pay up, making £7,000 as the amount of his advances. This certainly is a large sum of money entitling Mr. Collins to consideration in the views he must have of managing the business.
> *19th April.* I have not a particle of doubt that it is the fixed and

Dr. Chalmers

determined purpose of Mr. Collins to pay these debts as they fall due. He has stated this so explicitly, and his correctness in these matters may be so much depended on that your mind may be at rest on that score. . . . At my last meeting with Mr. Collins to-day he mentioned that a friend had obliged him with the loan of £400 which he thought he could not better appropriate than by remitting it to you as the amount of your debt against the Company.[1] . . . The whole of these money transactions evidently sit heavy on his mind. I am convinced he has every wish to act justly. . . . With regard to my observation of regret as to the necessity of a dissolution, his admission is that he did say once but only once to your Brother that since the retail branch could not pay but was going back, it was too much to expect that he should continue to feed it from the publishing branch which had been doing well. . . .

By the beginning of May, when these unhappy shadows had begun to subside, William Collins notified his ex-partner in friendly fashion that his services in the bookshop would no longer be required; and Charles, not loth to leave, rented a small house in Edinburgh. Out of that house was to come distinction; for Charles, though his future was to be jeopardised by one final misfortune, was now on the brink of a career more suitable to his talents.

On arriving in Edinburgh he angered his brother at first by using his share of the Glasgow settlement to start *Chalmers' Journal of Useful Knowledge*, a widely-ranging periodical in which he explained some of his own scientific inventions. His late partner promised to assist in its distribution, and it eventually appeared in March (1827) with a fossil elephant as frontispiece and the name of Collins among its joint publishers. Charles, unhappily, proved to be as ineffective a journalist as he had been a bookseller. The *Journal* came out only six times, by which time, his funds having melted away, he was imploring an advance from his late father's settlement to pay his papermaker,

[1]Despite this reassurance, Dr. Chalmers noted in his *Private Journal* on the 22nd: "Felt degrading anxieties about a bill that I had sent off to Glasgow by post." On the 23rd he added: "Found a letter from Mr. Collins with a Note in payment of the Bill that I sent off yesterday. Saddened myself about Charles."

his printer and his engraver. Then suddenly his fortune turned. Eagerly and in much-improved health he turned again to school-mastering, and in this sphere at last found ambition worthily fulfilled. By November 1827 he had started a boarding-school with three boarders—two sharing a room at a cost of seventy guineas each per annum, and one with a room to himself at eighty guineas. And that, with the help of a £100 loan from the much-tried and still-doubting Thomas and his own subsequent leasing of Lord Napier's house in Edinburgh, was the start of the famous public school—Merchiston Castle.[1]

III

For at least three years William Collins, now thirty-six, was to swim slowly upstream with a chain of debt round his shoulders. But in the manner of Sir Walter Scott in Edinburgh who had started with not a moment's delay to level his own mountainous obligations, so, in a less epic setting, William Collins in Glasgow could also say: "My own right hand shall pay my debt." He set to work with the utmost energy. Less trustful and wishful-thinking than before, he set his face against "rash and speculative" ventures. His business arrangements became prompter and more efficient. Extravagant hopes were still to permeate the printing office from time to time; but the optimist had learned a sufficiently bitter lesson to make him study his orders, his manuscripts and the promises of his authors with a more dis-cerning eye. Now and then there were natural lapses. Crusades and commerce are seldom happy yoke-fellows, and William Collins at the height of his crusading could be absorbed enough to forget more mundane interests. Cunningham, the Harrow clergyman, complained occasionally, for example, that books he had ordered were not forthcoming. So did Chalmers. But perhaps the best proof of his forgetfulness—a very delightful one—is

[1]Charles Chalmers became a popular and accomplished teacher. After 1848 when he retired from schoolmastering, he published several valuable papers on scientific matters. He died in 1864.

James Montgomery's letter to his Quaker friend, Miss Rowntree. He had ordered for her a copy of the Collins edition of the *Olney Hymns* with his own preface. As it did not arrive, he wrote as follows:

> "MY DEAR FRIEND,
>   If you will just put on your bonnet and cloak, and step into the Glasgow mail, after travelling, I know not how many hours, day and night, you may, perhaps, reach that great city; then inquire for a certain street, the name of which I cannot give you, but, when you have found it, look at the shop-boards for ' William Collins, Booksellers, Printer, &c.' Enter boldly, as if you were going to stock a library from his shelves,—when peradventure the good man himself, half as thin as I am, but twice as brisk, bowing behind the compter, will say,—as well as ten pinches of snuff within the last five minutes will let him,—' Madam, what is your pleasure?' Then, without making a curtsey (because I know you won't even to oblige me) you may say, ' How comes it, William, that thou hast not sent to James Montgomery, of Sheffield, the package of books which thou promised him six weeks ago?' *His* answer, whatever it will be, will contain the secret of my long silence towards you."

IV

One of William Collins' first arrangements after achieving independence was to become co-publisher with Smith Elder of *Donnegan's Greek and English Lexicon*, a volume which ran into many editions and was still popular a quarter of a century later. In his own right he published, in two volumes, Edward Irving's *Babylon and Infidelity Foredoomed*, a characteristic book on prophecy foretelling an early " glorious and overwhelming revolution " which would bring Christ back to earth.[1] That summer he also went on his usual tour of the English booksellers. But his

[1] The first volume had 17 errata, the second 19. This was not altogether Collins' fault. In his Preface, Irving wrote: " The desire that the momentous matters herein set forth, might be first offered to the Church of Scotland, moved me to publish it at a distance from my residence, which hindered that complete revisal of the press which I desired to give."

prospects, owing to a general malaise in the book trade, were not bright; and in Glasgow, where most of the city's power-loom factories were on half-time, the state of business was so depressed that he dismantled one of his three printing presses before setting off on his journey by chaise. An old and faded Order Book used on this tour shows that he travelled to London, Nottingham, Birmingham, Worcester, Gloucester, Bath, Bristol, Taunton, Exeter, Plymouth, Devonport, Portsea, Colchester and Cambridge —no mean journey, and one which was indifferently rewarded. In Birmingham he sold only twenty-three books. In one town, unnamed, he took orders for a mere handful of the *Select Library* works, two algebra books, two copies of *Walton's Compleat Angler*, and only one set, in three volumes, of Chalmers' *Christian and Civic Economy* (which had originally come out in shilling numbers). A Devon bookseller ordered but two atlases. And though Bath and Bristol were more congenial hunting grounds, Mr. Longman and Mr. Seeley of London ordered only about a hundred volumes between them. It was with acute disappointment that he returned to Glasgow by July to wrestle for many months there with an acute trade slump which was only relieved slightly when he secured a contract to print a large law book.

In the New Year of 1827 a slow improvement began. Economy and improving sales enabled him to repay several hundred pounds of his debt to his brothers-in-law, though this unfortunately got him into difficulties with Dr. Chalmers.

"I paid your two Bills which were presented by the Bank of Scotland," he wrote on 28th March 1827, "and I write at present to solicit a particular favour and that is to beg you would allow your Bill for £212 (£200 of this was author's fees for Vol. III of the *Christian and Civic Economy* on which he had spent £30 in advertisements), which becomes due in May to stand over till I come to St. Andrews in July when I shall pay you with interest. I shall be rather scarce of money till July but this would allow me to get my Irish and English half-yearly accounts collected. I have been printing chiefly for other people lately, which occasioned me little outlay, and I have been purchasing little, so that my engage-

ments are few, and I shall be quite in circumstances by that time
to pay you with convenience."

He met with less sympathy than he had expected. A cloud
about the size of a Divinity professor's hand was now forming
among the spires of St. Andrews, and Collins' letter, which also
offered £100 for a new edition of 1,000 copies of the *Tron Church
Sermons*—"the utmost number I should wish to print"—merely
provoked a sombre entry in the *Journal*. "A letter from Mr.
Collins which now is always disturbing, and it will require
management and Christian wisdom to shape my future conduct
to him." The cloud soon grew threatening. Within a few days
the Doctor upbraided his publisher for "not paying attention"
to an order for schoolbooks sent him by Charles Chalmers, and
got in reply the mild explanation that owing to bad weather no
carriers' wagons had been able to make the journey between
Edinburgh and Glasgow for at least a fortnight. Having accepted
the offer of £100 for the new edition of the *Tron Church Sermons*,
Chalmers then offered to sell the copyright—a proposal on which
Collins stalled for the time being. "That could be better
negotiated when I see you at St. Andrews," he replied. "In the
meantime that the volume may not be suspended in its sale I
shall proceed immediately with the printing of the new Edition."
It was to be a year before the new edition of that luckless book
could be published.

Meanwhile, he printed a recent Chalmers' sermon for which
he paid the Doctor £37 10s., and set off for London. His southern
journeys were speedier now. Mr. Telford's new road from
Glasgow to Carlisle allowed the mail coach to cover that part
of the journey, ninety-five miles, in nine hours; and the whole
journey took only some forty-seven hours. But he had many
other places to visit; and the little red Order Book shows that
he roved far and wide with considerable success. Hatchard ordered
250 books this time, Seeley more than a hundred; Bath and
Bristol stood as firm as ever. (They were supplied, his Order Book
shows, "by the Stage Coach Company's van to Bristol, from

White Bear, Basinghall Street, London.") Nevertheless, his tireless journeying about the cities and towns of England on top of
his long struggle to stave off bankruptcy, his incessant proof-
reading, and his church activities had taken severe toll of his
strength. In October he was forced to bed with severe inflammation in his breast and side, returned to work prematurely, and
had a relapse. Despite much bleeding and blistering he recovered,
and in January 1828 went to St. Andrews to relax for three days
under the Doctor's roof.

Most unfortunately, for both men, the lowering cloud of
suspicion which had darkened the old-time relationship ever since
Charles Chalmers' retirement from the business was not to be
dispersed easily. While William Collins was under his roof, Dr.
Chalmers noted in his *Journal*: "Mr. Collins from Glasgow
arrived. He brought good large accounts of publication in my
favour. I am not altogether satisfied with his shop account
against me." There is then silence between the two friends until
All Fool's Day when the ill-starred Tron Church chickens again
came home to roost. "Enclosed," wrote the troubled Collins to
his friend, who had just been nominated for a professorship in
Edinburgh, "I send you my Bill for £100 which is for the *Tron
Church Sermons* which were published on Saturday last. I subscribed them yesterday in Glasgow, but did not sell a single copy
and I sent the volume to Edinburgh to Wm. Whyte & Co. to
subscribe and he only disposed of six copies. I hope it will do
better in London where I believe it is scarcer."

It must be noted here that Collins had wrought manfully for
this book. At loss to himself, he had even put out a remunerative
printing contract to an outside printer to ensure publication of
the *Tron Church Sermons* by the appointed time. But he got no
sympathy from his friend at St. Andrews. The failure of the
book merely added another boulder to the cairn of suspicion and
resentment which Dr. Chalmers had been raising. It needed
now only a touch to bring it rumbling down on William's head.
The touch was duly applied.

Captivated by the American *Memoirs of Mrs. Huntington,*

Collins had asked the Doctor for a few pages of preface. Unluckily, Chalmers received the request along with a letter from Waugh the Edinburgh publisher, who claimed that as he was already printing the Huntington book the house of Collins was jeopardising his "rights and interests." Chalmers, imagining also that his publisher was infringing an American copyright, impetuously charged him with double-dealing.[1]

"I am very much surprised," Collins replied stoutly. "The Work is an American publication and is not copyright in Britain, and several Booksellers have already published the Work as well as he. Every Bookseller in the Kingdom has an *equal right* with him to publish it. . . ."

He was, however, already printing the book—a piece of news which brought so enraged a declamation from the Doctor that the worshipper at last turned swiftly on the hero.

"I am very much grieved," he wrote on the 22nd April 1828, "at the spirit in which your last letter was written. Though you deemed it necessary to tell me, that as circumstances stood, you could not consent to give a Preface to *Mrs. Huntington*, yet it certainly was not necessary to do it in such a tone to a man who, for twelve years past, would, if it had been possible, have plucked out his own eyes to serve you. I am far, very far from being insensible of the many sincere returns of kindness and friendship and devotion to my interests which I have received from you, but even this reciprocity might have modified at least any expression which might wound my feelings."

He then disclaimed once more that there was anything illegal in his actions, and ended with typical pertinacity:

"If you finally make up your mind to have your Article cancelled *it shall be done* and I can easily find some other friend who will Preface it for me."

But the Doctor by this time was conscience-stricken. He sent an appeasing reply, and the storm blew over.

The tide of Collins' fortunes had now turned—for two reasons.

[1]The lack of copyright laws between the U.S.A. and Britain, in the first half of the nineteenth century, created many controversies, notably those roused by Charles Dickens' complaints of American pirating of his novels.

He himself had become more cautious in his business affairs. Equally important, most of his friends had rewarded his loyalty to *them* with fidelity and support for *him*. Thus James Montgomery was the "friend" who helped him out with the Huntington preface so quickly that within a few weeks of the Chalmers eruption the book, which rushed into four editions, was in the bookshops.

Montgomery was now a powerful buttress. Thrice he had helped Collins to produce a popular volume; for in addition to *The Christian Psalmist* and the Huntington Essay, he had edited—for a fee of one hundred guineas—a famous anthology, *The Christian Poet* (1827). Both publisher and essayist-editor deserved their success with this book. Montgomery, after combing hundreds of volumes of poetry for *The Christian Poet*, thought that the hundred volumes finally represented contained "millions of lines—wagon loads of chaff and straw, with here and there a grain of gospel truth in genuine poetry." "The winnowing," he declared, "has been no small nor brief toil." And indeed it is impossible not to admire the conscientiousness with which Montgomery cast his net. He even solicited John Clare.

Clare—a poet of luminous simplicity—had sent the *Sheffield Iris* a number of poems of his own under the names of several Elizabethan and Caroline poets. When, however, the suspicious Montgomery asked for a loan of the old and rare book which Clare mentioned as the source of the poems, on the ground that it might aid his own compilation of *The Christian Poet*, he received not only a confession of the forgery but a promise:

> "I shall be very glad of the opportunity in proving myself ready to serve you in your present undertakings; and could I light on an old poem that would be worth your attention, 300 or even 1,000 lines would be no objection against my writing it out; but I do assure you I would not make a forgery for such a thing, though I suppose now you would suspect me; for I consider in such company it would be a crime, where blossoms are collected to decorate the 'Fountain of Truth.'"

The promised poem was not forthcoming. But success shone

on *The Christian Poet*. Within two months, two thousand copies were sold. It then went into several editions in different formats, at prices ranging between 4s. and 10s. 6d. And although published about the same time as Keble's *The Christian Year*, it successfully survived even this formidable competition.

For such a gratifying result the weighty influence of *Blackwood's Magazine* was partly responsible. In the issue for December 1828, Professor John Wilson (Christopher North) wrote an elaborate twenty-two-page joint review of *The Christian Psalmist*, *The Christian Poet* and *The Christian Year*.[1] His references to Keble's volume were as cursory as his references to Montgomery's were extensive and glowing.

> "As we meet with Montgomery seldom," he declared, "and as the two little works which have chiefly suggested our article, and from which some of its pages have been framed, may not have fallen—may never fall—in the way of many thousands of *our* readers—we conceive that we have been doing some service to the cause of piety—and poetry—by thus attempting to widen the sphere of their circulation. They seem to be fast going through editions—*The Christian Psalmist* having reached a fifth. . . ."

Professor Wilson, who did William Collins this good turn with his generous review, was a lion-hearted giant of a man whose enthusiasm often unbalanced his criticism. However that may be, he gave William Collins a helping hand when he most needed it, despite the gentle barb in his review that William Collins of Glasgow was likely to publish small works which the great public of William Blackwood of Edinburgh might overlook. Or, had he remembered how, during the previous year, William Collins had rejected—in the best tradition of all publishers—a poem which might have brought him a small fortune? This poem, *The Course of Time*, on no less a subject than the history of the world, was the work of Robert Pollok, the young author of the *Tales of the Covenanters*, who in 1823 had "so esteemed Mr. Collins." Four years later Pollok, in a state of rapid decline and

---

[1] Montgomery always believed that this review was written by Thomas Carlyle. Messrs. Blackwood's records show that Wilson was the author for a fee of one guinea a page.

about to follow the Keatsian path to Italy, offered *The Course of Time* outright to William Collins for £50. But Collins refused the offer. His refusal may have sprung from his latter-day caution. Or he may have seen, what most critics failed to see for a long time, that Pollok's disjointed and unbalanced poem was too much a hollow echo of Milton's sonorous cadences without the master's organ-note. Certainly the poem was not rejected lightly. There were passages in it which must have appealed to his Calvinistic sense—for example Pollok's stricture on Byron who:

> " *Drank every cup of joy, heard every trump*
> *Of fame, drank early, deeply drank, drank draughts*
> *That common millions might have quenched: then died*
> *Of thirst, because there was no more to drink.*"

Despite this, he refused the poem. And Pollok, wisely from his point of view, took it to Professor Wilson who enthusiastically passed it on to William Blackwood with an earnest request for publication on the half-profits system. Blackwood agreed, and *The Course of Time* was duly published in the New Year of 1828 with phenomenal success. Within a year 12,000 copies had been sold; in the early 'forties it reached its sixteenth edition; and by 1870 its total sale exceeded eighty thousand copies. To-day, it is remembered only perhaps by two epitaphs—Frere's inscription on his own copy of the work: "Robert Pollok, A.M., this work of yours is meant, I do not doubt, extremely well;" and Professor Oliver Elton's: "Robert Pollok's *Course of Time*, a blank verse, and otherwise blank, history of the world between the creation and the doomsday, is an impossible work."

The resilient Collins was not likely to brood long on his oversight, if oversight it was. The tide, though not yet at the flood, was flowing strongly. His own prestige as a publisher was mounting. And his *Select Library* in particular was by this time being widely sold and discussed.

But here we must take a last look at this series. It was destined for a long life, but 1829 was its peak period, with almost fifty

volumes in circulation, including two recent additions of note—
Wilberforce's *The Practical View of Christianity*, with a preface
by Daniel Wilson (a future Bishop of Calcutta) which Simeon
considered to be "one of the finest compositions in our language;"
and an edition of Cowper's *Olney Hymns* which as late as 1915
won a scholar's tribute from Dr. Louis F. Benson of Pennsylvania
University: "The best study of the *Olney Hymns* is Montgomery's
introductory Essay written for Collins' Glasgow edition, and
often reprinted." These volumes added greatly to the fame of
the series, though the publisher was bitterly disappointed that
Wilberforce's failing eyesight had precluded him from writing
his own preface to his own book. They also added considerably
to the series' English circulation which, thanks to its own merit
and William Collins' travels, had been steadily growing.

In Scotland the success of the *Select Library* was no less notable.
One particularly warm supporter was the Duchess of Gordon, a
lady of renowned piety. Book by book, the series had been sent
to her castle where she lived devoutly behind mullioned windows,
a vast iron gate, a "canonically fat porter in white stockings and
gay livery," lawns of velvet green, and an ancient inscription on
the grey castle stones:

TO THAES THAT LOVE GOD AL THINGIS
VIRKIS TO THE BEST

So enthusiastic indeed did the Duchess become that she invited
William Collins to reprint sacred works of her own liking such
as Boston's *A View of the Covenant of Grace*. But even ducal
blandishments failed to persuade him that yet another edition of
Boston's *Fourfold State* was not a better proposition.

So we come to the end of a striking phase. Collins, now in
very bad health, was exhausted with his three years' struggle.
But he had secured his position in the spirit of Sir Walter: "I
was born a Scotchman and a bare one and was therefore born
to fight my way with my left hand when my right failed me,
and with my teeth, if they were both cut off." He had repaid
much of his debt. His twelve-year-old son William had left

Glasgow Grammar School[1] and, as an apprentice in the business, was working ten hours a day for six days a week. His books were selling satisfactorily. And only continued ill-health seemed to darken the future. William Collins' approach to this spectre was characteristic. In the third week of June 1829 he undertook his annual English journey as usual, and on his return threw his weary frame into a startling new crusade for the moral uplift of his fellowmen.

[1]Now Glasgow High School, which boasts among its former pupils Sir John Moore (of Corunna), Thomas Campbell, James Gibson Lockhart, and two Prime Ministers—Bonar Law and Campbell-Bannerman.

CHAPTER VI

Greatheart of Glasgow

1829-1837

I

DURING HIS first ten years as a publisher, William Collins
had seen calamitous changes in Glasgow's social life.
The city was still flinging itself outward into the quiet
partridge fields: inwardly, in those less temperate days, its heart
was being corroded by whisky which, after the spirit duty was
reduced in 1823, flooded into Glasgow as a cheap and easy anodyne
for the misery of the wynds.

The hard toping of an earlier day was still widespread among
all classes in Scotland, though the upper and middle strata of
society were now more leisurely in their cups than they had been
in the late eighteenth century and the start of the nineteenth. In
those roaring years, a man of sensitive stomach often found that
his host's hospitality verged on violence; a laird could declare—
with pride and a touch of the old mordant humour of his race—
that he had never known anyone who had been "actually killed"
by drinking, but he had known some who had "died in the
training;" while according to the whimsical Scottish novelist
Thomas Hamilton: "The office of mingling the discordant
elements of punch into one sweet and harmonious whole, is
perhaps the only one which calls into full play the sympathies
and energies of a Glasgow gentleman."

However, by the eighteen-twenties Glasgow's unquenchable thirst—in the city's higher reaches—had diminished, although, as in every Scottish town, an ample stock of liquor was still considered an essential amenity in all but the poorest houses. It is not without interest as a reflection of contemporary social custom —few Scottish ministers of to-day could or would emulate it—that in September 1824 Dr. Chalmers' cellar contained 71 bottles of Madeira, 41 bottles of port, 14 bottles of sherry, 22 bottles of Teneriffe, 10 bottles of claret and 44 bottles of whisky. And Chalmers, though hospitable, was a temperate minister. In contrast, the poorest classes in the city had given the latest fiery cross from the Highlands such a welcome that even noisy babies were given whisky; at New Year celebrations small children were often seen drunk; and the city faced not only the danger of open revolution caused by the long delay over Reform, but far-reaching social degeneration.

There were two men in the West of Scotland whose conscience rose in challenge to these excesses. One was John Dunlop, a Greenock lawyer; the other was William Collins. Collins, sensitive to the point of heart-break, had brooded on the problem for many years. But it was not until 1829 that he felt free to hurl himself into a passionate crusade for temperance reform. During that autumn Dunlop visited Glasgow to found a temperance society. Round a table the project was discussed with twenty leading citizens, including one minister. After much abortive talk, the minister drew from his pocket a motion condemning the project root and branch. The long, uneasy silence which followed was dramatically broken by William Collins who rose to his feet and said in vibrant tones that for years his heart had been so burdened with the problem, that very often he could not sleep at night; his mind was haunted by the dreadful conditions of the poor and working classes, in consequence of their dissipation; he had pondered and planned without effect; and now for the first time he saw a ray of hope. From that utterance sprang Britain's first Temperance Society with William Collins, who subscribed £75 to it in two years, as its first member. A public meeting was fixed in its support, though all but one of the Glasgow ministers were hostile. There were other difficulties. It was arranged that notes should be sent to all the clergy, asking them to announce the meeting from their pulpits. But the messenger selected arrived for his duties extremely drunk. Fortunately, Robert Kettle, William Collins' suitably named coadjutor, procured another equally suitable herald—"a clean, sleek, Methodistic-looking character, his hair combed straight down his forehead, and as sober as a judge. A bright brass plate gleamed from his breast, and seemed to reflect the purity of his intentions, and afford a guarantee for the faithful fulfilment of whatever commissions might be entrusted to him." Neither the brass plate nor the purity of the new herald's intentions were to sway the clergy, but despite this, the meeting—enlivened by two noisy drunks—was duly held, and William Collins, of whose speech 15,000 copies were printed, had begun a new career as a powerful and original temperance orator. He was now forty.

Requests that he should make speeches on this startling new topic soon poured in from all parts of Scotland; he rejected none; and his speeches when delivered were described in contemporary reports as "thrilling," "enthralling," "powerful," and "lengthy." It was certainly a very remarkable essay in endurance. In the winter of 1829 he spoke all over Glasgow. In March 1830 —a year in which almost nine thousand Glaswegians were committed for being drunk and disorderly—he thundered in Edinburgh:

"Temperance Societies have arisen on our darkness, like the cheering star of hope. . . . And could we but persuade temperate men to join these Societies—could we but persuade the friends of Christianity, and the lovers of our country, to confederate themselves under their banners, and go forth in their might against the destroyer we would soon turn back that mighty tide of evil that now rolls over us; we would soon arrest the progress of that plague which is withering her beauty and her strength; and Scotland would again rise, in the might of her moral grandeur, a glory among the nations! "

Thirty thousand copies of this homily—with its many Chalmersian echoes—were printed on the Collins printing presses. Then he went into the highways and byways. At Kilsyth he delivered an "astonishing" speech which, according to the Press, persuaded three hundred people to join the local Society. At Hamilton, where he was "lucid, instructive, thrilling," the audience was at first mystified by the appearance of the church beadle ahead of him, carrying a large white pillow. "In the lecturer's zeal to direct public attention to the fearful ravages of strong drink he was then addressing meetings, in different parts of the country, almost every night, and had somewhat inflamed his hand; hence a considerate friend had suggested the use of the pillow," said an eye-witness. "Mr. Collins placed it on the desk before him, in order to protect his hand, which, in the great earnestness and enthusiasm of his advocacy, he brought so frequently, and with such force, upon the desk that but for the pillow between him and the hard board it would probably have been lacerated. Very soon the feathers in the pillow were driven to each end, whereupon, he took it up in both hands, shook the feathers hastily together, and proceeded with his address. This he did several times, until ultimately, as if impatient of such repeated adjustment of the pillow, he doubled it up, and keeping hold of it by the two ends with one hand, knocked away with the other; and before he had reached the last half of the lecture he became so animated that the pillow was abandoned altogether. It was apparent to all that the good man's soul was on fire, and he set and kept others on fire too. He was intensely earnest—he believed what he said—and hence he prevailed upon vast numbers to follow his praiseworthy example."

Soon the news of these pyrotechnics spread to England. After addressing meetings without a pause right through the spring, he spoke at a meeting of almost two thousand people at Bradford in June 1830. In October he travelled south again by steam packet from the Clyde to address the first meetings of the Liverpool and Manchester Temperance Societies. At Manchester, said the now-defunct *Manchester Times*—"The address of Mr. Collins occupied

nearly two hours in delivery, when he requested leave, in con-
sequence of exhaustion . . . to rest himself for a short time. Mr.
Collins again addressed the meeting for upwards of an hour. . . .
His discourse was blended both with instruction and amusement."
At the end of this meeting, several of the reporters at the Press
table joined the Manchester Society, which had just elected Sir
Oswald Mosley, Baronet, as its chief office-bearer. Thirteen
thousand copies of this speech were printed.

The Candleriggs presses were now running without cease. In
1830 alone, over and above the house's normal publications, they
turned out half a million temperance tracts and the *Temperance
Society Record*, a magazine of which for five years Collins was not
only publisher and printer but editor as well. But the pace was
becoming too fast. For not only was this wholehearted campaign
absorbing too much of his physical energy, but he was as deeply
involved as ever with business cares and with the Glasgow
Educational Society (a body which provided model schools for
the training of professional schoolmasters); and he still suffered
from persistent ill-health. Yet enfeebled as he was, and despite
the urgent representations of his friends and family, he went in
June 1831 to a London meeting attended by dignitaries of the
Church and the War Office, where he claimed the honour of
having founded London's first Temperance Society.

"I stand on this platform," he said, "with deep emotion to
witness the first public meeting of the Temperance Society in the
Metropolis, which I claim to have the high honour of being
founder. I had come to London, and after trying for several
weeks, I could not get a single person to join me. I left for home,
and when about 50 miles on the way God put it into my heart to
turn back and make another attempt. This second effort was not
more successful than the first. I went to Bristol, and succeeded
in forming a Temperance Society there. This induced me to
return to London, and make a third attempt in which I rejoice
to say that, under Providence, I was successful." Like his others,
this speech when printed seems to have had a wide circulation
in view of a South African clergyman's testimony that it

persuaded a hard-tippling trader who was exchanging beads and buttons for native hides and horns to sign the pledge, and throw his 22-gallon cask of brandy into an African river. In August, still unresting, Collins helped to found a Temperance Society in Dumfries.

II

The business had not been neglected meanwhile. In 1829 he issued ten new volumes of the *Select Library* and a new translation of *Herodotus* by Isaac Taylor (published jointly with Houldsworth & Ball of London); he was also elected President of the Glasgow Company of Stationers. His son, too, was showing promise though as yet he was such an inexperienced apprentice that Collins' own business energy had to be unabated. Proofs he conscientiously read himself, and not a day passed without consultations with Rore his foreman printer on questions of type and format. He was also planning new projects, the most important of which took shape in September 1831 when he lent himself unreservedly to the fulfilment of Dr. Chalmers' "chief earthly ambition"—the preparation of a treatise on Political Economy.

This work was the dream of a decade, but not until the spring of this year had Chalmers been able to undertake it in earnest. Unquestionably it was the only Chalmers work of which his publisher disapproved, but fidelity over-rode prejudice. The publisher only made one demand on his author—that he should be constantly supplied with copy so that the work might appear as arranged in the New Year of 1832. This required a flail on the author's back. "I beg you will send part of the MS. by the Mail to-morrow evening," is a typical September appeal; and in November: "I will thank you to send me more MS. by the Mail on Monday evening. . . . I beg you will not disappoint me."

Despite the whirling flail and much advertisement, the New Year of 1832 brought sad tidings. Collins had advertised the book widely both in Scotland and in London. He had printed prospectuses with lists for subscribers' names, pasted them on boards, and sent them off to the leading booksellers. He had even written long personal letters to the chief booksellers in London stressing the book's importance. Yet all these efforts brought him, within a fortnight, orders for only 175 copies. In Glasgow especially, his overtures met with such a stony reception that he felt bound to give the ecclesiastic-economist the un-varnished reasons:

"Your friends here," he wrote in January, "are indignant that occupying as you do the Theological Chair in the first University in Scotland you should busy your head with Political Economy. Some of your best friends who frequent my shop seem grieved at this circumstance. I have occasion to know that this feeling is not confined to Glasgow. . . . I do not intend to come to Edinburgh for the settlement of my half-year's accounts with the Booksellers till the volume is finished that I may subscribe the work myself in Edinburgh. I shall leave no measure neglected which may make the work known and secure its circulation, and shall be careful to inform you of its progress."

Twelve days later, he reported that the London booksellers had now ordered 300 copies and the prospects were brighter. By the first week of February, the book was in the bookshops at 12s. od. under the ponderous title: *Political Economy in Connection with the Moral State and Moral Prospects of Society*. But the reviews were hostile, the *Quarterly Review* in particular describing Chalmers as "incompetent to reason on this subject."

It was an unfortunate reception, for the Doctor had expected better results. His pride was hurt; and he began to brood—as he had done over John Smith's handling of the *Tron Church Sermons* —on the deficiencies of his publisher. The inevitable result was continued sniping during the rest of the year. All the Chalmers accusations need not be described in detail. They included tempestuous charges that his publisher lacked "sufficient sym-pathy" with his *Political Economy*; that he had not been told of or paid for a third edition of his Edinburgh Sermon (Collins on this point referred him by date to the appropriate bill); and that his recent works were inadequately distributed in London (a charge which Collins met by dispatching to his author a long list of Metropolitan booksellers to whom the works had been sent). But it was all so wearisome, that the publisher turned aside, almost with relief, to support a petition to the Lord Provost and Magistrates that no new licences should be granted in view of the 2,198 public houses already established in the city and its suburbs. A month or two later, when he set out on his annual journey to London he left behind him the most tragic community in Britain.

III

Glasgow in 1832 was so ravaged by cholera and by political unrest over the Scottish Reform Bill that the flow of business virtually stopped. In Glasgow alone his book sales should have been greater than ever since the city's population had risen by sixty thousand in ten years and was now more than two hundred thousand. The advantage of this expanding market at his door was, however, suddenly vitiated. Glasgow was naturally inured to political upheavals. But cholera—the most frightening visitation in the history of the city—developed with such virulence that Lady Holland in London asked, in a frenzy, why a cordon of troops had not been thrown round Glasgow to stop all communications between that city and the outside world; and William Collins, like most leading citizens, contributed three guineas to a fund for a special Board of Health to "guard against the visitation of that awful calamity, the CHOLERA MORBUS."

By May, when the Clydeside death roll was 600, panic tore through the streets, and doctors were even assaulted for their failure to provide a remedy. Many ships flew a warning yellow flag from the mast-head; the quaysides at Glasgow and Greenock grew green with grass; and the ravage was still spreading. At the end of July, while William Collins was on his summer visit to England, the deaths were nearing 1,000. By the first week of November, when the death roll was nearly 3,000, he must almost have dreaded returning from business in the evening lest he should find the "grisly foe" at work in his own household.

But cholera was not the only shadow on Glasgow in 1832. It was the prime preoccupation, certainly; but the citizens, who had once noisily demonstrated against the Act of Union, were even more united and vociferous for the Reform Bill. Although a moderate Tory, the shrewd eyes of William Collins had already perceived the dangers inherent in failure to concede the popular demand. On his return from his late summer journey to England in 1830, he had seen ricks burning beside Mr. Telford's new roads, and angry impoverished people with faces as chalky-white as the pages of his own books. His discussions with booksellers in Manchester, Liverpool and Sheffield, and even in the ancient University cities had disclosed, too, that most of them were pledged to Reform as the only salvation from civil war.

There was another compelling reason for the unrest, and one to which William Collins himself had contributed. Still striding forward under the protracted, powerful eighteenth-century impulse, education's broadening of the national mind had fostered hopes to which Reform seemed to promise satisfaction.

It is therefore not surprising that by 1832, political passion—compounded of knowledge, desire for natural rights, and despair engendered by depression—had soared in Scotland to fever point; so that William Cobbett, who in October drove past the Collins bookshop in a carriage and pair, received wild acclamation for his many and varied tilts against the anti-Reform party.

The fiery Cobbett also remarked during this trip that there was too much drinking in Scotland. This was hardly an original viewpoint to William Collins, who disapproved even the moderate potations of Dr. Chalmers. He now sent his friend a copy of one of his own widely circulated Edinburgh speeches, *The Harmony between the Gospel and Temperance Societies*, with the aside: "I am glad you are persevering in your cold water experiment. Every week will still more confirm your convictions of its advantages."

But the Doctor was more engrossed with a pamphlet which he thought had been tardily printed and sparsely distributed.

To the first charge Collins replied that the recent political excitement, so "grievously adverse to bookselling," would have made
earlier publication quite useless—a plea which had as much
effect as an iceberg has on the Equator. As regards the second
charge the headstrong Doctor, chafing as usual at delays, made a
strange sortie of his own into the bookselling business towards
the end of the year. Without consulting his publisher he arranged
privately with the London firm of Ridgway for his pamphlets'
English advertisement and distribution.

This was the last straw. On the 29th December 1832 Collins
wrote Chalmers a letter worth reproducing in a few extracts for
the light it sheds on the resolution which now marked his
maturity, and on the curious fact that whereas most pam-
phleteers had usually published their pamphlets gratuitously as
propaganda, Dr. Chalmers received substantial sums for his as
literary works.

> "I regret exceedingly," Collins began, "that you should have
> embarrassed me with your arrangements with Mr. Ridgway. It
> has quite paralized me and made me heartless in the matter. I am
> quite sure had you understood matters rightly you would not have
> done it. Mr. Ridgway is but a subordinate retail Bookseller, and
> has no better means of getting a pamphlet disposed of than I or
> any other Bookseller has. He advertises the pamphlet, and by
> making it known, produces a demand for it throughout the
> Kingdom, but the Booksellers must write for it, *not to Mr. Ridgway*,
> but to Longman, Hamilton, Simpkin and Marshall and the other
> large Houses who supply country orders. This is the *alone* medium
> through which a pamphlet can obtain circulation. Now I com-
> pletely occupy all these channels myself, and therefore they can be
> of no use to Mr. Ridgway."

His reply then became more personal and illustrative, as he
pointed out that one of the Doctor's recent pamphlets had
involved him in a publishing loss of £90, explained why in great
detail, and ended:

> "I am always glad to receive any suggestions from you but you
> ought to leave it to my greater Professional Knowledge to adopt
> the means best fitted to accomplish your wishes. From my long

devotedness to your interests you might have trusted to my fidelity, and you are quite aware no wish of yours is regarded with indifference by me."

If Collins thought he had pacified his friend, he erred sadly. True, the Doctor, realising the unwisdom of intruding on his publisher's preserve, countermanded his arrangement with the London bookseller. But his New Year gift for 1833 was a criticism of the distribution of his pamphlets in Edinburgh. Again he got the stout reply that even after the booksellers had returned unsold copies at each half-yearly settlement, every Chalmers book and pamphlet could still be got from Oliver and Boyd, Collins' Edinburgh agents, within ten minutes. "There is a lingering feeling in your mind as if your Pamphlets were not easily accessible," he added. "I can assure you, my Dear Sir, it is as much my interest, and not less my wish than yours to make them as accessible as possible. But I do not know how to make them more so."

In the middle of March, shortly after presiding over the annual meeting of the Scottish Temperance Society, he began a long-awaited move to new premises at 155 Ingram Street (a street which in the eighteenth century had been dignified by the name of Back Cow Loan). At the same time he gently complained in his correspondence of "a return of the giddiness in my head which so oppresses and paralizes me as to render me unfit for any exertion while it continues." Despite this he threw himself into a flurry of work for his favourite causes, published a small book on infant training, and wound up the year by advertising as "suitable" Christmas presents for children—Defoe's *Robinson Crusoe* (published elsewhere) and Dick's *Christian Philosopher* (published by himself).

At this stage of the story our admiration for the resource and the vitality of spirit which spurred his frail physique to such labours cannot be stinted. For he needed repose. He was about to throw himself into the most imposing of his many crusades. And all through 1833 and 1834 he walked in dark and distressing shadows of family bereavement and the loss of old friends. Thus in 1833 the idolised Wilberforce, amid scenes of high memorial pomp, went to his saintly rest in Westminster Abbey. In the following year a melancholy fate overtook the once-flashing northern light of Edward Irving. In the late 'twenties, Irving's swaying intellect had been obsessed with Biblical prophecy and the supposed gift of miraculous tongues, until even his oldest friends—much to his surprise—became alarmed at his irresponsible utterances. Thomas Carlyle who loved him to the end was horrified but sympathetic. William Collins, too, for a time, out of sheer generosity of spirit, tried to defend him, or at least to put the best face on his peculiar declamations. But even *his* sympathy was so alienated that Irving once noted with pain: " Collins spoke to me as a heretic." Sir Walter Scott, on the other hand, who had studied him with keen and friendly interest at a dinner party, noted in his *Journal* that there was "talent on his brow " but "madness in his eye."

The tragedy of Irving had then still a year or two to run before the last, slow-falling curtain. But by 1831 his Church had become a scene of tumult which Carlyle described characteristically as "puddling and muddling in the midst of certain insane jargonings of hysterical women, and crack-brained enthusiasts, mostly ' Ohs ' and ' Ahs '. . . ."

Although Collins deplored this strange turn in his friend's life as much as Carlyle, he had nevertheless published a second edition of Irving's *Babylon and Infidelity Foredoomed of God* by 1832—the year in which Irving's followers founded the Holy Catholic and Apostolic Church which still survives. But in spite of this monument to his labours Irving's day was over. During a March twilight the following year, in a church half-lit by a single candle, he was deposed by the Presbytery of Annan and went out to face darkness and doom. For a time he wandered about the Midlands and Wales. Two years later, at the age of forty-two, he was back in Glasgow, broken-hearted and ill, with strange shadows flickering over his tired, illusioned mind. "For a few weeks," wrote Mrs. Oliphant, "he is visible about Glasgow —now appearing against the sunshine in a lonely street, his horse's hoofs echoing slowly along the causeway, his gaunt, gigantic figure rising feeble against the light." But before Christmas he was dead, and William Collins was standing with tangled memories before his grave in the crypt of Glasgow Cathedral.

Before then he had also been standing beside the grave of his fourteen-year-old daughter, Elizabeth, who had died after a prolonged illness during the summer. Here, indeed, was heart-break. For although the little girl had long been an invalid like Mrs. Collins, her gentle beauty of face and disposition had scattered light about the household; and most fittingly she left a legacy worthy of her spirit. It was a chance death-bed remark of little Elizabeth's which launched William Collins on a new and utterly selfless endeavour.

IV

On a wintry day early in 1834, he was sitting as he did every day for a while beside his daughter's bed. At these affectionate daily vigils, his topics by custom roved over all his activities— the Church, the printing works and bookshop, his visits to England and Ireland, his early life in Eastwood, and the busier life of the city. On this particular day he spoke with unusual emotion of his visitations in the dark and stricken wynds, and especially of distressed and churchless families he had just seen. "Can nothing be done for them?" asked the little girl. It was a simple question which pierced the father's heart; he left her; but already the question had become a restless, all-absorbing litany: "Can nothing be done?"

In William Collins' copious vocabulary negatives never had much currency. But for once the word "nothing" kept ringing in his ears. He pondered for many days, till suddenly there came the vision splendid: he would build churches for the poor, churches with ministers and towers and spires that would bring the radiance of Heaven to the halt, the blind and the poor. So he got to work, talked to his friends, and drafted so many schemes that finally his vision was transmuted into a colossal plan—at which any ordinary man would have blenched—for the erection in Glasgow alone of twenty new churches complete with ministers, funds, congregations. To accomplish his dream, he formed the Glasgow Church Building Society with himself as Honorary Secretary, put his printing presses at the disposal of the new Society, prepared subscription lists, and set out cap in hand to beg subscriptions from Glasgow's wealthy citizens. His own contribution was £200—a very generous donation, for in the same year his old Temperance Society wound up in favour of an absolute "long pledge" body which he felt he could not support, and left him to discharge a debt of a like sum. By July he had collected almost £12,000, and by October £22,000—a sum then equivalent to a resplendent fortune. Meanwhile, in June, his little daughter died.

Endless repining would have been regarded by William Collins as a selfish betrayal of that faith, transcending human loss, in which he lived and in which his daughter had died. So he hid his sorrow among the many cares of his church building drive and the collection of evidence on "Drunkenness" which he had been ordered to give before a Select Committee of the House of Commons. Then he hastened to London.

On 27th June 1834 he unloosed a deluge of facts and figures on the Select Committee—the result, he said, of two or three hours' daily study of the problem during the previous five years. This is not the place to recapitulate his evidence, which in the official report covers about twenty closely printed foolscap pages. But one of his assertions was striking and apparently true—that the Royalty of Glasgow had one spirit dealer for every fourteen of its 19,500 families. (The figure for Glasgow with suburbs added was one for every eighteen of 40,000.) These formidable statistics were embellished with a familiar rhetorical ring. For example:

'So much has spirit-drinking become associated with all our

customs and practices in Scotland, that there is scarcely an event in life, scarcely a circumstance that occurs, not a transaction can be done or a change can be effected, with which spirit-drinking is not associated; it is associated with our births, and with our deaths, with our marriages and baptisms; it is associated with a man's entry on any employment, with his apprenticeship, with his change of employment in the same work; it is the symbol of hospitality where friends meet, and forms the complimentary usage of life among the middling and lower orders; it is employed in making bargains, at the payment of accounts, at fairs and roups, and every possible circumstance of life. And that is the greatest difficulty we have had to contend with: it struck its fibrous roots into everything so deeply, that to tear up the spirit-drinking practices is like tearing up the whole social system."

He then urged the complete suppression of distilling, made a passionate appeal to the Government to "destroy this withering angel," and returned weak and ill to Glasgow to inspect the progress of his church extension plan, now so widely recognised as a great personal triumph that the Presbytery of Glasgow accorded him a vote of thanks for his "voluntary exertions," and the General Assembly of the Church of Scotland singled him out for special acclaim.

Not every visionary sees the consummation of his dreams during his lifetime. William Collins' terrestrial reward for his high endeavour was a series of invitations to lay the foundation stones of most of the twenty churches; until by 1841 the last of them had pierced the city's smoky skies, and all stood in their allotted space.

V

Two chequered years were now to pass quickly. In 1835 the house of Collins stood well above tide-mark. Its old debts had been repaid. Its books were selling well not only at home but in the United States, where William Collins had secured the services of Messrs. Leavitt, Lord and Company as his New York agents. Even more encouraging to the father was the success of William

Junior, a tenacious, painstaking youth of eighteen who was never in any danger of forgetting orders, as his father had sometimes done, nor of delaying their dispatch. Together, father and son looked hopefully forward to a period of expansion.

That this would affect Dr. Chalmers was inevitable. In the preceding years that divine's reputation had remained in the ascendant. Since the start of the decade he had become one of King William IV's Chaplains for Scotland (1830), Moderator of the General Assembly (1832), author of a famous *Bridgwater Treatise* (1833), Fellow of the Royal Society of Edinburgh and Corresponding Member of the Royal Institute of France (1834), and Doctor of Laws of the University of Oxford (1835). He was also by this time fairly prosperous—with realisable assets of about £9,000—although the Town Council of Edinburgh, which by time-honoured arrangement paid his professorial salary, was insolvent, and the salary in arrears.

In view of his spreading renown, the time seemed ripe for a uniform edition of his works. This ambitious project, canvassed in 1834, was reopened by William Collins on 5th March 1835. "My mind has been much turned to the subject," he wrote, "and as your Classes will close in a few weeks, I would like that we lost no time in addressing ourselves vigorously to the enterprise, and give our best thought and strength to it." This overture was followed by long discussions in May during the General Assembly. At the end of August, Collins, whose health, in his own words, was "in a very prostrate condition," discussed the great design further at Burntisland.

A month later we get a charming sidelight on him in a letter written by Ann Chalmers to her father (19th September). Addressed to "My Dearest Papa," the letter recounts how she had met Mr. Collins in the Edinburgh-Glasgow coach. "No accident happened but they put in a restive horse at one of the stages and after sundry ineffectual attempts to make it proceed had to take it out, the passengers declaring they would not stir with such a dangerous animal. Mr. Collins was very kind."

By this time, Mr. Collins was deeply engrossed in his preparations for the *Collected Works*. He bought a new fount of type, and
printed 80,000 prospectuses which, he told his author, "I intend
to distribute profusely in all the Towns and Villages of the
kingdom where there are any Booksellers. I am anxious that not
an hour should now be lost in commencing the Work, and will
esteem it very kind if you can forward me copy without delay.
. . . It will require the utmost exertion to get the first volume out
in time." This plea had immediate effect. Chalmers, who was
revising and expanding all his printed works, at once dispatched
seventy-five pages of MS., and two or three days later Collins
wrote again: "I am happy you are so far advanced in your
preparation, but I shall soon overtake you."

By November the printing presses were working under severe
pressure; and their owner was complaining that a proof sheet
had been delayed: "I should like very much if no omission took
place from neglect, as it makes me lose nearly a day, and I have
not an hour to lose."

This race against time was hardly prospered by a legal
entanglement. Twelve years earlier, it will be remembered, he
had taken additional premises in Wilson Street. In March 1832,
with three months of his lease still to run, he closed the Wilson
Street warehouse and pasted up large yellow placards on its
frontage announcing his move to 155 Ingram Street, near the
Royal Exchange. His landlord, an Edinburgh man who felt that
his property was being unduly depreciated, took umbrage:
Collins' closure of the warehouse—without warning and three
months before the expiry of the lease—he described as "illegal
and unwarrantable"; he had not been given time to find a new
tenant; the shop had been made to assume a "most deserted and
abandoned look"; and lastly, his "valuable" shelving and most
of his mahogany counters had been removed. This indictment,
which Collins and his lawyers considered a "most nimious,
oppressive, and uncalled for action, for the institution of which
nothing but a morbid spirit of litigation can account," the
landlord persisted in taking to court, with a claim for £500

damages and £100 costs. The case drifted on through the year, and after various hearings was decided against William Collins by a jury. But the eventual result seems almost like a moral victory, for the Court of Session in assessing the damages (26th November 1835) mulcted Collins for only £25 and the pursuer paid more in costs.

This lawsuit was not his only distraction. The year 1835 crackled with religious controversy over Church patronage and the merits of State establishment. The Evangelicals, so far Erastian as not in the main to oppose the broad principle of patronage, were however most bitterly opposed to the intrusion of a minister by a patron *against the wishes of a congregation*. The Moderates, although many of them disliked patronage and the traffic it entailed,[1] were anxious to avoid controversy on the issue—in the interests of general tranquillity. But over against this trumpeted the strident counterpoint of extreme Dissent or Voluntaryism, eloquently repudiating patronage, Establishment, State Endowment of church extension, and, indeed, anything about which clung the faintest Erastian aroma. To the Voluntary clamour, the Evangelicals especially, being passionate for church extension with State aid, opposed a stout front. Thus, throughout 1835, in order to stem the Voluntary tide, leading Glasgow churchmen delivered lectures on Church Establishment, of which a contemporary theologian wrote, "The lectures themselves were remarkably able; they were listened to by immense and excited crowds, and they told, there can be no doubt, very materially on the issue of the conflict. Mr. Collins published them in a cheap form immediately after their delivery, and they were scattered broadcast all over Scotland." As we should expect, Mr. Collins not only devoted his printing presses to this cause but, despite his delicate health, took to the platform as well. He also published

---

[1] The *Glasgow Herald* on 23rd November, 1835, reported under a heading—"Value of Church Patronage ": "The Church patronage of the parish of Ochiltree, in the County of Ayr, was exposed to public sale on Wednesday in Edinburgh, and bought by the Most Noble the Marquis of Bute at the price of £240. The upset price was Fifty Pounds." The extensiveness of patronage may be seen from its incidence in June, 1833, when, of 944 livings, 582 were under the patronage of individuals, 274 under that of the Crown, and 62 of Town Councils.

during the year an edition of Thomas Dick's *On the Mental Illumination and Moral Improvement of Mankind*—a book which he thought "suitable" as a gift for children, and the future Lord Macaulay, when he heard of this in India, "quite absurd."

By December, zero hour for the first 6s. volume of the *Collected Works* was nigh and relations between Dr. Chalmers and his publisher became tense. A week before Christmas the publisher hastened off the first complete copy of Volume I, bound in embossed cloth with a gold-lettered title, which he accompanied by the remark: "I am making the most convulsive exertions to get the volume out, and I think I will succeed to have it out in time." Although in the saddle, so to speak, he could be a galloper himself, Chalmers disliked being pulled along at the tail of some-one else's horse, and wearying also perhaps of his publisher's sustained entreaties to send MS. for the next volume, his temper was already a little frayed when he scanned Volume I in its published form and lit upon errors clearly attributable to excessive haste. The rumblings of weeks broke in a minor typhoon. He fastened on a cluster of errors on one unlucky page, though the answer he got must have caused him acute surprise. It certainly seems conclusive:

> "I am much grieved at the errors in Page 146 which have given you so much uneasiness,"

wrote the publisher, who had meanwhile corrected the plate, on 20th January 1836,

> "but on referring to them I find that the Proof was corrected by yourself, and there are corrections of your own on that very page, and yet you have not noticed one of them. Though I regret the errors yet I am glad we are not responsible for them, as I never take the responsibility of any Proofs that are sent to you, and indeed never read them with the view of corrections."

He also assured the Doctor that every sheet left to the printing office to read was scrutinised four times. But the stubborn Fifer was difficult to convince. He renewed his criticisms by return of post. And also by return he got the following picturesque

answer coupled with the usual urgent appeal for more copy for
the next volume:

> "I hope to have the pleasure of seeing you next week when I
> shall hear all the complaints you refer to respecting the volume.
> I shall be sincerely happy to have any suggestion which may im-
> prove its appearance or promote its sale. I am too deeply interested
> in its success, as well as yourself, not to avail myself of every hint
> which may conduce to its advantage. But I am sometimes annoyed
> with men, who, because they have the temerity and folly to find
> fault with everything, think themselves sufficiently wise to instruct
> men in their own peculiar profession although absolutely ignorant
> of that profession in all its details. Of this I had a most signal
> instance this very day, in the case of Mr. McKenzie, who, though in
> the most consummate ignorance of printing and papermaking and
> all that relates to the business of a Publisher found fault with every-
> thing about the volume. What led a man so utterly ignorant of
> the whole matter, to offer his opinion so confidently I cannot tell,
> but it is sufficiently annoying to me, after having given so much
> thought and labour to it, and after producing a volume which has
> given *such satisfaction to the London Trade*."

The trouble over these early volumes must be a classic example
of too-hasty preparation for a large-scale undertaking, for Collins
had many other publications in hand. Early in 1836, finding the
task beyond his own printing resources, he was forced to enlist
the aid of Edward Khull Junior, a printer of German extraction
who later exchanged printing in Glasgow for bullion broking in
Australia. Khull was thrown into a frenzy by Chalmers' hand-
writing to which the Collins printers had long been inured.
Here is an example—from one of his manuscripts:

Khull had been given the task of printing Volume III. "I wish to state," wrote Collins (10th March), "that it would be desirable if your copy could be transcribed before you sent it. Mr. Khull's men found great difficulty in making it out and complain of the hindrance in deciphering it."

By the beginning of April, notwithstanding these difficulties, Volume II was on the market; and William Collins, with a slight sense of freedom was using his surplus energy to promote two minor campaigns—one to establish a Savings Bank in Glasgow, the other to get subscriptions for a fund to relieve the "suffering Protestant clergy of Ireland." He was also beseeching more copy for Volume III. But Dr. Chalmers was still anxious about the fate of his *Works*. After studying Volume II, his wife sent renewed reproaches to Glasgow—which Collins answered forthrightly:

"Your good lady is at her complaints again about the boarding of the work. To the charge as respects the first volume I plead guilty, but I demur a little to the charge against the second. There may be incidental copies in which the stitch is missed and consequently there may be a loose leaf or two, but as a whole I have got credit for the manner in which the volume is finished, especially from the London Trade. I have spared neither labour nor expense in having them well done and I am satisfied they will stand a comparison with any of the London publications."

Laggard sales also caused anxiety. To stimulate them, Chalmers reminded the Rev. J. W. Cunningham of Harrow that although much new matter was being included in his *Works*, the public might think it was merely a matter of "re-publication"; that many London periodicals had meted out to him "harsh and injurious treatment"; and would Cunningham draw the attention of London reviewers to any new matter, particularly the *Christian Observer* and *British Review*. Collins, on his own initiative as a publisher, secured the powerful backing of *The Times*, whose review began:

"We have much pleasure in calling the attention of our readers to a new cheap and uniform edition of the entire writings of this eminent individual, now in the course of publication."

H.O.C.   H

For a month or two the Chalmers household became less carping and the great task went steadily on. Despite the difficulties of getting out the *Works* with regularity, along with the *Select Library*, pamphlets and other books, William Collins still found time to further his favourite causes with unfailing zest, and even wrote a sixty-page booklet himself to prove the need for church endowment.

His greatest achievement of the year was, however, his publication of *Leitch's Practical and Economical Readers*—a striking portent of a new competitive age. Before 1836, several Scottish publishers had been advertising schoolbooks. But William Collins in that year widened and intensified their competition in a realm which, as an ex-teacher, he understood. With modernistic eyes he had brought his business through the stresses of industrial unrest in an ancient if factory-laden city; and being himself a virile product of the eighteenth century urge for learning, he foresaw the coming era of widespread popular education. Few publishers in fact can have been more suited to move in step with a great popular transition. His publication of *Leitch's Readers* (in full brown sheepskin with rather crude wood-cuts)— of which more than one and a half million were sold within fifteen years—was therefore as significant a step in Collins' personal and publishing history as the contemporary trial of the first electric telegraph and the crossing of the Atlantic by the first iron sailing ship were to the life of the country as a whole.

But this was a vintage year, and such a season in any sphere of creation—grapes, roses or poetry—is always rich and satisfying. In addition to *Leitch's Readers* and the *Collected Works* William Collins published a permanent best-seller, Nathaniel Paterson's *The Manse Garden*—"a book," said a Scottish churchman, "that would be read for the sake of its poetry, and wisdom, and kindness where there are no gardens, and for the sake of other days when there are no manses." Long recognised as a minor Scottish classic, *The Manse Garden* was written by the grandson of Scott's character Old Mortality, and Paterson himself had been a frequent visitor to Abbotsford in Sir Walter's lifetime. At first he wished his MS. to be published anonymously but could not find a publisher; and after several rejections he was almost in despair of ever seeing it in print when fortunately, as he told his brother in June 1836: "Collins undertook for a 1,000 copies at his own cost. It has spunked out, not by his fault. . . . Mr. Collins tells me it is succeeding beyond his expectations." Eighteen months later the book had reached its fourth thousand, and henceforward William Collins—the wheel of time's revenges having come full circle—was to get an ample and ever-increasing recompense for his financial oversight of Pollok's *Course of Time*.

The year 1836 was a vintage season in another familiar field. Hearing that Greenock suffered from what the church extensionists called "religious destitution," he visited the town and personally collected £1,000 for his cause. In September, he went for relaxation to Largs on the Ayrshire coast and perceiving that this holiday resort also stood in need of spiritual renovation, amassed by a personal house-to-house collection the extraordinary sum for such a small place, as it then was, of £632. It was most unlucky that Dr. Chalmers, who praised this achievement in the General Assembly the following year, did not know about these pious errands when he wrote, contemporaneously with Collins' Largs activity, a letter probably only censorious because it misunderstood the nature of a printer's problems. At any rate, Volume IV was printed by this time, Volume V was on its way, and the New Year (1837) should thus have brought with it a warming sense of achievement. Catastrophe came instead on the 3rd January when Collins' fourteen-year-old boy John was taken seriously ill. On the 5th, while racked with anxiety and in the middle of printing a Chalmers' pamphlet, he received severe reproaches from Mrs. Chalmers—on the Doctor's behalf—for an apparent failure to forward proof sheets of Volume V. This was another poniard in his heart, but again he sent a reply which seems unanswerable:

"I am deeply distressed at the contents of Mrs. Chalmers' letter which I received this morning and I am too much engrossed with *urging forward* the printing of your Pamphlet just now to reply to the various subjects it notices, which I shall do when the Pamphlet is fairly out. The delay in sending Proof Sheets arose from circumstances which I could not control, namely my men not being generally at work since Monday. I regret you should insinuate any want of cordiality and friendship on my part. I most cordially concurred with you in the necessity of publishing, and since I saw you I have consulted *with no man* as to the propriety of it. You know I am not the man to shrink from your determination, or compromise in any way your feelings and reputation."

Three days later, his son—after much suffering—died of erysipelas. On the 9th, Collins, shaken with sorrow but still blade-bright in his faith, sent this " deeply afflicting intelligence " to Dr. Chalmers. "It is a solemn warning to us all," he wrote, " that the boy whom you saw in blooming buoyant health last Monday is now no more. It is a sore bereavement to me, but I trust that He who does not chasten for His pleasure but for our profit, will enable us by His grace so to be exercised with it, that we may richly share in the blessing he intends to communicate by affliction—to make us more partakers of His holiness. Pray for your afflicted friend." Two much-loved children had now died, his wife was a chronic invalid, and he himself was frail. Unbroken by these misfortunes, he plunged anew into his work, and within a few days was pleading the cause of church extension in the illustrious presence of Sir Robert Peel.

VI

Sir Robert Peel, who became Prime Minister for the first time in 1834, was one of those statesmen—like Burke and Wilberforce —whose integrity adorns his politics. Lacking the luminous eloquence of Pitt or Canning, he left his mark on the country not only by the repeal of the Corn Laws and the creation of a Police Force, but because like Stanley Baldwin in our own times, he materially softened by conciliation and example some of the political asperities carried over from previous periods of inflammation—in Peel's instance the Reform Bill, in Baldwin's the 1926 General Strike. Having been elected Rector of Glasgow University, Peel travelled to Scotland in the New Year of 1837 to deliver his Rectorial Address and attend a public banquet in his honour at the very time poor William Collins was treading his more dolorous road.

Collins, while politically conservative, was of course far from obdurate. Unquestionably he was more progressive than Dr. Chalmers, whose refusal to illuminate his Edinburgh house at the passing of the Reform Bill cost him broken windows; and in common with most of Glasgow's business men, he had a particular respect for the forward-looking views of Sir Robert Peel. Above all, he was ambitious to enlist Peel's sympathies behind State endowment of church building. Accordingly, as arrangements were in progress for addresses to be presented to the Conservative Leader by many public bodies, including the Glasgow Church Building Society, Collins, at the beginning of his son's illness, consulted Peel by letter about the necessary arrangements. The consequence was that on the 15th, he duly presented an address, in company with a deputation from the " operatives of Glasgow," who made a quaint presentation of their own " Freedom of the City in a Silver Box " and a complimentary address for which the subscription paper had lain in the Collins bookshop. He also attended the public banquet. This mammoth affair—attended by more than 3,000 people in a specially erected pavilion—began at 5.30 p.m. Eight hours later, only one half of the thirty-seven toasts on the list had been drunk, and the exhausted Collins, despite his respect for the guest of honour, had slipped quietly away, to renew his acquaintance with Peel at a later date.

Meanwhile he had resumed his business duties, which meant a flood of entreaties to Dr. Chalmers to send him more copy for Volume VI and VII of the *Works*. In March during a printers' strike his pleas became insistent. " The Master Printers," he wrote on the 8th, " have agreed to assist each other in forwarding these works which are indispensable to be got out, and I have suspended everything else but your works. Let me have some copy without delay that I may be getting on as fast as I can in the meantime."

He was also now receiving recognition in Church affairs. In the same month two Presbyteries—Glasgow and Hamilton —competed for the honour of having him as one of their lay representatives at the General Assembly. A still greater honour befell him a few months later when he was chosen as a member of the Church of Scotland deputation to go to Court and present the young Queen Victoria with an address of congratulation on her accession to the Throne—a singular mark of appreciation which must have wakened many memories of the long eventful journey from the Eastwood schoolroom.

CHAPTER VII

In High Places

1837-1843

I

ON THE morning of 20th June 1837, when King William's
death brought the Princess Victoria to the Throne, Dr.
Chalmers, who had planned to go to London in company
with both William Collinses—on a further attempt to force
Government aid for church extension—postponed his visit.
Collins, anxious to introduce his twenty-year-old son to the
London booksellers, adhered to the original plan, leaving Dr.
Chalmers to join him later with other ecclesiastics for the
presentation of the Church of Scotland's address to the new Queen.
The younger William fortunately kept a diary of his first London
trip from which the following extracts are taken (the comments
in square brackets being the present author's):

> On Tuesday, the 27th day of June 1837, having made every
> necessary arrangement for a visit to London, I started from
> Glasgow at 4 o'clock p.m., and after a very pleasant drive reached
> Edinburgh at nine in the evening, where I joined my father, who
> had proceeded thither the day previous.
> Having secured our berths in a steam vessel—*The Leith*—we
> then took a ramble through part of the city, after which we were
> conveyed in an Omnibus to Newhaven, where we embarked for
> London.
> At length, we reached Blackwall, where we landed, after a

pleasant passage of 41 hours, which—the distance being nearly 500 miles—is at the rate of about 11½ miles per hour. On landing we found Omnibuses waiting to convey passengers into the city, so, getting into one of them, we drove away, through street after street, for nearly an hour, when we reached Cheapside—in a small street off which we took up our abode.

[The Collinses' lodgings were Mrs. Andrews' at 22 Ironmonger Lane.]

Going along Cheapside, I was surprised at the immense number of vehicles running along:—Omnibuses, contracted to ' Buses ' by the Cocknies: cabs of a great variety of shapes; flys, sedans, vans, waggons, stage and hackney coaches; together with little carts drawn by dogs (a good preventive against their mischief and madness) of which latter there are not a few: so that what are generally a nuisance in our Scottish Towns, are there put to a useful service.

Thursday, 29th June.

We made our way to Paternoster Row, the great mart of literature, it being the last day of the month, on which parcels of magazines are sent away to every bookseller of note in the kingdom, estimated at 1500. All was bustle.

Returning to St. Paul's, which was now open for divine service, we entered it, when, though prepared from what I had heard, for something great, I was lost in astonishment. The walls are adorned with rich monuments to celebrated warriors and statesmen, of which the one to Sir John Moore pleased me most.

[Sir John Moore was a citizen of Glasgow.]

Friday, 30th June.

From this we proceeded until we came to Southwark Bridge. It is of cast-iron, and has only three arches. The centre one is about 240 feet in span. There are tolls of a penny levied on foot passengers, so that, while London Bridge on the one side and Blackfriars on the other, which are free, are crowded with passengers, it is almost deserted. It is remarkable that every alternate bridge over the Thames has a toll while the others are free. They have a contrivance at them that have tolls, as at most of the public places, for counting the number who pass, which serves as a check on the collectors.

Saturday, 1st July.

Opposite to the House of Lords stands Westminster Abbey. It is interesting to know that the first printing press erected in England stood near this spot. [William Caxton's.]

Monday, 3rd July.

Visited Paternoster Row, took a Bus to Piccadilly, and then walked to Berkeley Square. Here I left my father to make a few calls and went to Hyde Park. Visited Westminster Abbey and House of Lords, where Lord Belhaven presented a memorial from the General Assembly regarding Endowments, which he accompanied with a few remarks.

[Collins Senior sent Dr. Chalmers a long account of a conversation with Lord Belhaven which ended with the following hint of the great improvement in his financial stability since the dark days of 1826: "You need not bring any money with you to London as I shall give you plenty when you are here, and shall give you money to remit home to your account in the Commercial Bank ".]

Thursday, 13th July.

This forenoon we visited Messrs. Clowes' printing office, which is the largest in London—indeed I should suppose the largest in the world. We were first conducted through the machine-rooms, in which were about 20 machines, throwing off at the rate of 750 sheets, printed on both sides, per hour. These machines were driven by a steam engine.

Saturday, 15th July

I went to visit the most stupendous undertaking, the Channel Tunnel.

[This is not, as might be supposed, a reference to the proposal for a tunnel under the English Channel. William Jr. inspected Sir Isambard Brunel's tunnel between Rotherhithe and Wapping. Begun in 1825 and finished in 1843, it was the first Thames tunnel and cost £433 per linear foot.]

Monday, 17th July

This being the day the Queen was to dissolve Parliament, the Queen was most enthusiastically greeted with cheers and waving handkerchiefs as she passed along, which loyal expression she returned by bowing most graciously. She was most magnificently attired, with a beautiful crown upon her head. On Her Majesty's landing at the House of Lords a salute was fired. After waiting for about half an hour, during which time Her Majesty had delivered her maiden speech, the procession returned to the palace by the same route. So soon as I had seen the procession leave the House of Lords, I made my way to the front of the palace, which I saw Her Majesty enter.

Visited the Zoological Gardens and saw a balloon ascent.

Returned to our lodgings and here I found Dr. Chalmers who had arrived from Edinburgh, to present an address to the Queen from the University.

Wednesday, 19th July.

I proceeded to the end of Pall Mall opposite to St. James's Palace. After waiting there about an hour, to see the arrivals and departures, I returned to our lodgings, and in the evening got a description of the levee from Dr. Chalmers, who presented the address I formerly alluded to.

[One wonders if Dr. Chalmers told the Collinses that having kissed the Queen's hand he forgot to give her the address, but did so after a reminder from one of the Lords-in-Waiting.]

Friday, 21st July.

This forenoon I accompanied my father to the West End of the Town where he joined a number of gentlemen who composed a deputation from the General Assembly of the Church of Scotland to present an address to Her Majesty. After seeing him dressed out in court suit and away with the rest of the deputation to St. James's Palace, I went out to the Queen's Palace where, after waiting a little, I saw the Queen proceed in a two-horse carriage to St. James's Palace to receive the address.

On returning to where I left my father, I found he had returned from court, and with the rest of the deputation had had the honour of kissing Her Majesty's hand. Her Majesty read her answer to the address in a very neat manner.

[Matthew Leishman of Govan, who was one of the deputation, left the following account of it:

' Retiring from the Royal Presence, the Moderator's remark made in my ear was amusing and characteristic. "Only think, Leishman, that growing lassie to be the Sovereign of these realms. Why! she is just like a modest manse bairn." This in the broadest Scottish accent. Court gossip said that Her Majesty, who at that time knew little of her northern kingdom outside the pages of her school history books, observed as the deputation withdrew:— "Well, I think I have snubbed these Knoxists!" ']

Monday, 31st July.

Set sail in steamship *Monarch* from Blackwall to Leith.

[The *Monarch* sailed on one occasion from London (1836), with the Lord Provost of Glasgow on board, at 1 a.m., on Thursday morning and arrived at Newhaven on Friday afternoon at 2 p.m. As the Edinburgh coach left for Glasgow two hours later and arrived at 8.30 p.m., the journey according to the newspapers, was completed ' in the remarkably short space of 44 hours.']

Wednesday, 2nd August.
  Arrived Edinburgh, but could not secure a seat in any of the coaches for Glasgow.

Thursday, 4th August.
  Started from Edinburgh this forenoon crammed in the inside of a coach with five other passengers.

Thus began the journey to the high places. But father and son had little time to dwell on present glories. Within a week of his return, William Junior was writing out in a fair hand for the printers three of the Doctor's sermons for Volume IX of the *Collected Works*. And within a month, William Senior with unabated energy was pleading the cause of church extension at Wishaw, Cambuslang and Barrhead.

II

It is perhaps time, as William Senior approaches his fiftieth year, to glance again at his character in maturity. He had suffered much. But though he was still very thin, his dark hair was untouched by grey and he had a strangely youthful appearance. Always impulsive, he abounded still with the old enthusiasm which would have driven him to attempt a citadel singlehanded without a scaling-ladder, and his faith was as unshakable as ever. He still believed of course in temperance and in the abolition of strong spirits. But he was still unprepared to advocate a total abstinence which would have forbidden light wines and was consequently assailed by many of his old temperance friends. As a result of this schism, which had divided the temperance movement by 1838 so thoroughly that a lath splitter in Glasgow and a rope spinner in Gourock are reported to have taught themselves Hebrew to study the wine question in the Scriptures as thoroughly as possible, we get a slant on our publisher written by his old comrade John Dunlop. Dunlop, in 1837, "strove with

William Collins to go into the new total abstinence plans, in vain."[1] Early in 1838, he recorded a similar fruitless attempt which criticises Collins on some counts which we know to be warranted, and on others where superior contrary evidence and Dunlop's very zeal for his cause reduces the value of his estimate. Some of his remarks are noteworthy:

"Mr. Collins has many good points, and great energy of character. He was prodigiously useful in the Temperance Cause originally. He does not speak, however, very well, and is prolix. I don't know that he excels much in writing: but he is acute in argument.

Mr. Collins has rather a sharp, unconciliatory manner, but he does not fear to declare the whole counsel. He is accused of being Diotrephes-ly inclined.[2] I am not sure that he is calculated to lead large masses along with him: and his Temperance career must be considered defective, if he proceed no farther than he has done. I asked him to give me a memoir of his personal operations; this he declined."

Dunlop's note was made in March. Earlier in the year, Collins had renewed his acquaintance with Sir Robert Peel. "A short time ago," he told Dr. Chalmers on 1st February, "I addressed a letter to Sir Robert Peel on the subject of the religious destitution of Scotland, the necessity of more churches, and other matters which it might be of use for him to know when the subject came to be discussed in Parliament. I received in reply a very long, kind and intelligent letter thanking me for my information, putting a number of queries to which he wished a reply, and inviting further correspondence and information of which he would gladly avail himself."

Soon after this interchange, although it was evident that Lord Melbourne's Government was averse to any but meagre help for the Church of Scotland, Collins was chosen as one of a deputation to go to London for a final attempt to get funds. To prepare the ground, an advance guard went to London,

[1]Autobiography of John Dunlop, privately printed by Spottiswoode, Ballantyne and Co., Ltd., 1932.

[2]See the Third Epistle of St. John v. 9: "I wrote unto the church: but Diotrephes, who loveth to have the pre-eminence among them, receiveth us not."

composed of himself and two Glasgow ministers—the Rev. Robert Buchanan, future historian of the Disruption, and the Rev. Dr. McLeod.

No longer, we find, was the journey made by stage-coach alone; for the railway age was in full swing and Collins' trip involved travel by steam train, ship and stage-coach. From a full and fascinating diary of the trip kept by Buchanan,[1] it appears that the trio left the Broomielaw at 9.30 a.m. on the 8th March 1838 and sailed down the Clyde in the steamer *Commodore*. By four o'clock in the afternoon, Ailsa Craig lay on the *Commodore's* beam. At five the following morning they were in the Mersey, anchored in a dense fog 200 yards off the Liverpool landing-stage and calculating their chances of catching the six-thirty train to Birmingham. Unfortunately, as the boatmen who took them off the ship lost themselves in the fog and rowed about for an hour before finding the landing-place, they missed this train and had to wait five hours for the next.

"We drove to the rendezvous of the steam-carriages," wrote Buchanan who was making his first train journey, "got three places in the third carriage of the train, and at half-past eleven started from Liverpool. The carriages are large and handsome; each passenger has his own compartment, like an arm-chair, three on each side. The motion at first seems tremendous, giving one the sensation rather of flying than moving on the face of the earth. But nothing surprised me so much as the quickness with which one gets used to it, so that it seems nothing out of the way; and we got impatient if we were not skimming along at twenty or thirty miles an hour." The ninety-seven-mile journey to Birmingham took four hours and forty minutes, and Buchanan added with the charming naïveté of inexperience: "Railway travelling is delightful for its ease and expeditiousness, but will never be resorted to by anyone who wishes to see the country. The motion is too rapid to allow the eye to survey any one scene with accuracy or minuteness; and, moreover, to

[1] *Robert Buchanan, D.D., an ecclesiastical biography* by N. L. Walker, 1877.

secure a level, much of the railroad runs in lanes or cuts where the banks hide everything from the view."

At Birmingham Collins got an inside place in the Mail Coach, the ministers two places in the Emerald Coach where they met "two sulky, unsocial fellow travellers"; so began a bitterly cold night journey to London. By noon on the 10th they had reached the Union Hotel in Cockspur Street, where alarming intelligence awaited them that the Government was about to reject their proposals for church endowment without further ado. This was a situation admirably suited to William Collins' quick impulses. In rapid succession the trio saw Lord Aberdeen, Lord Tweeddale and Sir Robert Peel, all of whom urged them to see Lord Melbourne as speedily as possible. The following letter was accordingly sent to Downing Street:

"The Rev. Dr. McLeod, Rev. Mr. Buchanan, and Mr. Collins of Glasgow beg leave respectfully to inform Lord Melbourne that they have arrived in town as a deputation from the General Assembly's Committee on Church Extension in Scotland; and to solicit the favour of his naming a day when they may be allowed the honour of an interview with his lordship in reference to that subject, as they are anxious to have an opportunity of submitting certain important facts and considerations which they venture to hope may not be disregarded in any decision to which Her Majesty's Government may come regarding it."

This missive was at once acknowledged, and soon after three o'clock in the afternoon of 15th March, William Collins and his two friends were ushered into the presence of Lord Melbourne at the Treasury. "We were shown into an ante-room," said Buchanan, "and after waiting about fifteen minutes were told his lordship was ready to receive us. On being introduced, we found his lordship standing with his hat in one hand and his stick in the other. He bowed, invited us to sit down (rather stiffly, I thought), and remained silent." The deputation then put its case, ending with a parting shot that if the Government did nothing to relieve Christian destitution in the big Scottish towns the Church would be forced into a state of permanent hostility. "During the interview," noted Buchanan, "his lordship kept very much on the reserve; preserved his usual air of *insouciance.* . . ." It was, however, agreed that he should meet the full deputation when it arrived.

In the meantime the advance guard went on with its lobbying. It pressed its claims on the Duke of Richmond; the Lord Advocate who "interrupted insolently "; Lord Haddington; the Bishop of London ("He is a good-looking, gentleman-like man—bald, a round prominent forehead—clear, intelligent countenance—and but for that absurd-looking piece of Episcopal dress, the black apron, he would be a fine-looking man "); and, most transcendant figure of all, the victor of Waterloo. Again, Buchanan's diary tells admirably the story of their reception by the Duke of Wellington:

" *Wednesday 21st March.*
    A few minutes before 12 we were at the gate of Apsley House. The servants seemed to have received intimation of our visit as we were admitted without a question being asked. We were shown into a sort of ante-room looking into the park. . . . After we had waited about ten minutes, a door at the upper corner of the room was opened and the Duke appeared, and requested us to walk into the inner room, which was the library—a very large and elegant apartment, the floor of which was occupied to a great extent with writing and other tables, on which lay a multitude of books, papers, &c. His appearance everyone knows. The large acquiline nose, the high-arched eyebrow, the clear penetrating blue eye, small mouth, rounded and prominent chin, would be recognised at once by everybody who has seen any one of the ten thousand engravings scattered through the bookshops of all the towns and villages of the Kingdom. Nothing could be more simple and unostentatious—nay, more kind and familiar—than his manner of receiving us. Instead of calling his servant to set our chairs, or leaving us to do so ourselves, he busied himself lifting a package from one chair and a picture from another and drawing them forward until he had accommodated us all; and then, advancing his own chair close to the little circle we formed, he sat down almost in the midst of us."

The Duke of Wellington was sympathetic, especially when the

dangers of Church animosity to the State were explained. He said:
"If religion be overturned in Scotland it will not stand here. To
set up in Glasgow and Edinburgh, and the great towns in general,
what they call the System of Voluntaryism (and as he uttered
this word in a tone of peculiar emphasis, his eyebrows shot up
into its highest curve, while his eye sparkled, and his mouth
curled with a most comical expression), is the most monstrous
thing that was ever heard of—totally inconsistent with the peace
and good order of society. Why, I think Old Popery was bad—
very bad; but this Voluntaryism would be forty times worse.
Independent of the religious interests of the people, which would
be sacrificed, it would be impossible to govern society with such
a system prevailing." This must have heartened Collins and his
friends. Equally, they must have scented their coming defeat
when the Duke ended: "Gentlemen, you will get nothing. That
is my opinion. I am sorry for it; but so you will find it."

Nevertheless the deputation, now entire, continued to press
its claims. After leaving the Duke, they had another interview
with Lord Melbourne who again received them with "his
customary nonchalance of manner." On the following day they
stood on the crimson carpets of Lambeth Palace to plead their
cause to the Archbishop of Canterbury. In the Home Office they
strove to persuade Lord John Russell. And in the evening William
Collins sat round Sir Robert Peel's dinner-table with a brave
array of notables, including the Earl of Aberdeen who wore the
star and blue ribbon of the Garter; Sir David Wilkie, the Scottish
painter; and young Mr. Gladstone, "grave and thoughtful,"
who though not yet twenty-seven was already considered the
rising hope of the *Conservative* Party. According to Morley, Mr.
Gladstone long remembered this occasion though in recalling it,
he seems to have got the date wrong.[1] The relevant passage is as
follows:

"In 1837 Mr. Gladstone says in one of the many fragments written
when in his later years he mused over the past, ' we had a movement

---

[1] *Life of Gladstone*, Book II, Chapter V, Macmillan, 1903 edition. The year, since
Collins is mentioned by name, must surely be 1838.

for fresh parliamentary grants to build churches in Scotland. The leaders did not seem much to like it, but had to follow. I remember dining at Sir R. Peel's with the Scottish deputation. It included Collins, a church bookseller of note, who told me that no sermon ought ever to fall short of an hour, for in less time than that it was not possible to explain any text of the Holy Scripture."

Other dinners followed—at Lord Aberdeen's and the Bishop of London's—but Collins soon chafed at the contrast between the opulence of his successive entertainments and the Government's reluctance to endow religion in the Candleriggs and the Gallowgate. In the end his impatience found a characteristic vent. The deputation was being shown the Duke of Sutherland's art collection by an "upholster and groom of the chambers," pending the Duke's own arrival. William Collins was certainly not overawed by the gorgeousness of his surroundings. He had wandered round rooms decorated with scagliola, fluted Corinthian columns richly moulded in gilt, silk and satin damasks in green, crimson and yellow. He had sat on chairs covered with purple satin embroidered with gold-coloured leaf and admired the Duke's tables, each with blue velvet let into a frame of gold with gilt carvings. Last of all, he had inspected the Duke's proposed new picture gallery, magnificent with its ceiling of rich stucco gilded fretwork. It was in this room that William Collins, to whom a righteous cause was always more glorious than worldly splendour, exclaimed at last with sudden passion: "Here are we fighting to get a paltry fifteen or twenty thousand pounds, and now we are under the roof of a man who spends as much on a single room." Within a day or two, he was appealing for voluntary funds for his Church at a public breakfast of well-known London Scots.

III

As if public cares were not enough, poor William Collins had now to suffer another Chalmers thunderstorm. "That damned fellow," as Melbourne always called him, was about to deliver a series of lectures on Church Establishments in London where his vogue was as great as ever. Still pining a little for London print, he suggested that the lectures could be printed more speedily in the south. Collins naturally held a different view. While still in London, he replied that it would be cheaper and more efficient to print and bind in Glasgow, and added shrewdly that in any event London printers could not print from the Doctor's MS.

The Doctor, meanwhile, was preparing his Lectures on Establishments in a state of considerable perturbation, which his publisher innocently aggravated with a demand that he should write a public appeal for church extension funds. Chalmers, evidently objecting to Collins' assumption, and indeed advance publicity, of the appeal's arrival, wrote two vehement letters to which the publisher, now back in Glasgow replied on 12th April 1838:

"After receiving your last two letters in London I felt myself foreclosed from writing you again. You seemed to be labouring under some grievous and unusual state of excitement which, whatever might be its cause, gave me very great pain. I can assuredly say for myself, what you well know, that I would subject myself to inconvenience, and encounter any labour to promote your ease, and peace, and comfort, but no inconvenience or labour could be so grievous to me as to observe the unusual state of excitement, and consequent suffering under which you seemed to be labouring. I know you have suffered many and grievous wrongs, but in these your friends have deeply sympathised, and you cannot forget how often they have stood by you, and carried you triumphantly through."

Though it must have been difficult for any other tree to grow very tall under the vast beechen shadow of Dr. Chalmers, the increasingly spirited replies of William Collins to the Doctor's distempered effusions are significant of the enhanced maturity of his own judgment and his determination to spread his own branches. The very spirit indeed with which he rebutted Chalmers' more impetuous rebukes frequently evoked from the Doctor a note of sincere contrition. On this occasion the Doctor's penitence was expressed on a proof sheet, and Collins wrote again: "I received your communication on the proof sheet yesterday, and I cannot tell how much it has relieved me, and I rejoiced the more that it gave indications of your own mind being relieved from the excitement under which you seemed to be labouring and which was distressing me. I thank you for it, and I can assure you it has proved oblivious of all my former feelings."

In the second half of April Dr. Chalmers arrived in London, where he delivered his first lecture on the 25th, and where once again triumphal scenes took place before picked audiences studded with Royalty (the Duke of Cambridge who thought Chalmers "a monstrous clever man "), and, in Hanna's words, with "dukes, marquises, earls, viscounts, barons, baronets, bishops and members of Parliament." "The concluding lecture," said Hanna, "was graced by nine prelates of the Church of England. The tide that had been rising and swelling each successive day now burst all bounds. Carried away by the impassioned utterance of the speaker, long ere the close of some of his finest passages was reached, the voice of the lecturer was drowned in the applause, the audience rising from their seats, waving their hats above their heads, and breaking out into tumultuous approbation."

Emblazoned with eloquent passages, the Lectures were almost bound to enjoy a wide sale. But before they reached the bookshops William Junior, who in Glasgow was setting up the Lectures contemporaneously with their delivery in London, accomplished a quick-fire printing feat. Printed, bound, and published in the Candleriggs, the Lectures were widely advertised and rushed south. Within a fortnight the first edition had gone and the firm was being urged by the London booksellers to send at least another 1,000 copies. To cope with the demand a new edition of 2,000 was printed within eight days, though the Coronation, said William Senior, "has produced a great stillness and cessation of all literary matters." But not of the Lectures. Within a year 8,000 copies of the book—now included in Volume XVII of the *Collected Works*—had been sold (including a London printing), and the *Works* got a new impetus. Thus October saw the XIIth Volume. By November he had finished printing Volume XIII.

In December he wound up this year of intense personal activity
by a single-handed endeavour to collect funds for his favourite
scheme, embarrassed now by a deepening schism in the Church
over patronage. "Everywhere there is a sickening apathy," he
warned Chalmers. "I intend to try subscriptions in Glasgow
single-handed and wait for nobody." But for the first time even
this prince of beggars failed. For three days he tramped or drove
from one address to another, secured only two subscribers, and
turned again to business so utterly exhausted that in the New
Year (1839), from spacious new premises at 111 and 113 Montrose
Street where he lived above his office with his wife and son, he
wrote the unaccustomed, despairing words: "All seems darkening
and closing in around us from every quarter." However, to his
everlasting honour, Glasgow's Greatheart had never been a
capitulard. He turned to one of Glasgow's wealthiest citizens,
William Campbell of Tullichewan, found him willing to give a
subscription of £25 for each £1,000 raised to build one hundred
new churches, and from his own more slender resources offered
a similar donation of £5. He had already contributed £500.

IV

The year 1840—year in which the house of Collins published the
first of its series of *Illustrated Dictionaries* edited by the Rev.
James Boag—started with yet another ecclesiastical explosion.
In the previous year, the Dean of the Faculty of Advocates in
Edinburgh had written a pamphlet on the patronage issue,
strongly attacking Chalmers and his fellow non-intrusionists.
As the issue was now ripening fast to a State quarrel of the first
magnitude, Chalmers composed a trenchant reply entitled
*Remarks &c., occasioned by the Publication of a Letter from the Dean
of Faculty*, and urged for it the widest possible circulation both
in Scotland and in London. Collins pushed his presses hard
therefore, the pamphlet was quickly distributed, and by the first
week of February had reached a fourth edition. Yet for some

reason the turbulent Doctor was again dissatisfied. He complained to Collins' old friend Buchanan that his publisher was neglecting his interests—a complaint as unfounded as it was bitter. For of Dr. Chalmers' injustice on this score—springing as usual from natural impatience and the urge not of antipathy to anyone but apparently of sheer zeal—there can be no shadow of doubt. On the very day the publication issued from the press it was sent off in large parcels to Whittaker, Hatchard, Simpkin and Marshall, Hamilton Adams & Co., Nisbet, and Seeley—in fact, to all the leading London booksellers. It was advertised in *The Times*, *Standard*, *Record*, *Morning Herald* and *Watchman*. Review copies were sent to the *Globe*, *Courier*, *Patriot*, *Christian Observer*, *Christian Guardian*, *British Critic*, *Church of England Quarterly*, the *Quarterly*, and to thirty newspapers in Scotland. Within a week two thousand copies had been disposed of. The Doctor surely should have been soothed not only by Collins' explanation of these steps, but by his transmission of £380 outstanding in author's fees, and an assurance that the first consignment of yet another volume of his *Works* was on its way to London (where the house had just opened its first London office—at 10 Stationers' Hall Court).

How complex this relationship had become! By 1841 every Scotsman with an interest in either books or the Kirk knew, or supposed, that Dr. Chalmers and Mr. Collins were inseparable. Mrs. Oliphant was later to call the publisher the Doctor's " chosen and beloved friend." And somehow, despite temperamental differences, this was true. The sky under which Collins lived had occasionally been riven by the thunder and lightning of the Doctor's choler; and in the earlier days, as we know, there had sometimes been valid grounds for complaint. But, as time passed, embroilment in Church controversies so sharpened Chalmers' natural impatience as to render him, it seemed, unable to brook with any ease even the smallest delays in his friend's presentations of his views. Perhaps, also, his very intimacy with his publisher encouraged a candour and a freedom of utterance which he would scarcely have used to anyone else. Certainly he found it difficult to realise that William Collins, if the life-blood of his business was to be kept flowing, had interests in many other publications. Nor in his haste did he always appreciate how often his publisher-friend even risked his own business prospects by giving precedence to Chalmers publications. None the less, pained as he not infrequently was by his friend's vehemence, Collins considered it to be a natural heat of the blood, a distemper to be mastered by Chalmers if possible, but, if not, to be transcended by understanding. So the breaches were quickly healed.

Here we must break the chronological sequence of the story and leap across the stormy months of 1841 to the following year when the Doctor sent illuminating views to a lady who had consulted him about the publication of a book:

> "People do not read large works as they were wont," he wrote.[1] "My last work on Pauperism has only had about 300 purchasers— and this though the gross price of all that has been sold will not defray the expense of the advertisements alone. It is true that Mr. Collins of Glasgow is a Provincial Bookseller, nor have I yet found my way to a London Publisher whom I might make the principal in the concern, and at the same time have the command of one or more of the best London Reviews. I would earnestly advise your securing this object first, before adventuring on the publication of one or more volumes. . . .
>
> "In conclusion, let me beg that you will not make transpire what I have said to you of Mr. Collins, whom I have not ventured privately to name as your *chief* publisher—only because of his position—for he is a man of great personal worth, beside being my particular friend."

The old hankering for London is still reflected in that letter. But perhaps no comment on its other remarks is needed. Let us return to 1841.

This was a year of considerable expansion during which William Collins advertised in Scotland that his traveller Mr. Ruthven, first of a long and honoured line of salesmen, would "call and await the esteemed commands of his customers" in a

---

[1] It is noteworthy that in the same year Thomas Campbell wrote to a friend: "For several years past, the sale of all Books—and that of mine among the rest—has been going down lower and lower."

horse and trap. It was also a year of constant stress during which
the Doctor not only kept up his frequent complaints about the
printing, binding, and distribution of his works, but seems
to have nourished the suspicion that his literary revenue was
less than it ought to have been. It is also noteworthy that
Chalmers' pre-occupation with the patronage controversy brought
others besides William Collins within the ambit of his fretfulness,
judging by the following entries in his *Private Journal:*

> *4th June.* Rode with Mr. Collins to Kinghorn Loch. Tendency to
> impatience with others which I must watch and labour to
> overcome.
>
> *12th June.* Unfortunate collision with Mrs. C.
>
> *16th June.* Unfortunate parley with Mrs. C. who is still confined
> to bed. Quite unable for my evening devotions. O that religion
> were uppermost at all times.
>
> *11th Sept.* This want of self-restraint is deplorable.

The *Journal* must be interrupted here. Sometimes, as we have
seen, Dr. Chalmers in his very zeal unwarrantably infringed his
publisher's province. On 22nd September he did so once again
by tendering, in a letter, rather gratuitous advice on how to
advertise his new work on pauperism. He then resumed his
Journal:

> *23rd Sept.* Brooded hurtfully on Mr. Collins' negligence in reference
> to my new publication.
>
> *25th Sept.* A quieting letter from Mr. Collins.
>
> *2nd Oct.* O that I could control all anger and fretfulness.
>
> *14th Oct.* Have sad exercise anent Mr. Collins and his inertness
> respecting my publication. Let all be kept in its proper place
> by a right sense of God and eternity.
>
> *15th Oct.* The devil is taking a great advantage of me through the
> medium of Mr. Collins by whose neglect and inattention I have
> been sadly discomforted all this day.
>
> *16th Oct.* I have written Mr. Hanna (Chalmers' son-in-law) to
> undertake the looking after of the business part of my author-
> ship. It is a melancholy view of my spiritual weakness.
>
> *23rd Oct.* Mr. Hanna on Tuesday. Have seen Mr. Boyd (*of Oliver
> and Boyd*) and heard from Mr. Collins and things now in a

better train. Devolved on others my correspondence on the
business of my authorship.

13th Nov. Wrote Mr. Collins anent the pecuniaries.

Here the *Journal* must again be interrupted. By the 18th
November there had been a new turn in the Collins-Chalmers
business relationship. It was evidently decided that for the time
being Mrs. Chalmers should take over the business side of her
husband's literary affairs, in view of a letter which Collins sent
her on the 18th, enclosing a bill for £44 10s. 6d. (outstanding
from the sale of the *Collected Works*) and acknowledging that she
was "now to be the custodian of the documents." He added that
the book trade was slow, and that the latter volumes of the
series had not interested the public mind.

"Hitherto," he explained, "I have realised nothing from the
New Series, for the outlay on it up to this time, has exceeded
by several hundred pounds all that I have realised from the sales.
. . . You have had plenty of English newspapers of late containing
advertisements of the new work. It is very affecting to see the
advertisements of the work standing alone, unassociated with
books of any kind, save perhaps Annuals, as booksellers are wisely
not expending money in advertising at present. . . . You cannot
fail also to observe that the advertisements of the new work,
by standing alone, have been smothered among soap, oil, hygean
medicines, rheumatic pills, liquorice drops and endless quackeries.
Perhaps the Englishers may think that the new work has its
befitting place among the other quackeries of the day, though
I am quite satisfied that were they to make trial of the grand
specific which the work contains they would find it would help
to renovate the *constitution* of English society."

The *Journal* then continues:

22nd Nov. More encouraging accounts of my late volume.

26th Nov. Read an American review of my works which has greatly
interested me, and also a letter from an American bookseller
(*Mr. Carter*), which exercises me somewhat anent the secularities
of my authorship. Guide and influence me aright, O Lord.

15th Dec. Sat up very late, till after one in the morning with a

conversation on the subject of the affairs of my authorship between Mr. Collins, Mr. Hanna, Mrs. Chalmers and myself.
17th Dec. Prayed with Mr. Collins, Mr. Hanna and Margaret in the drawing-room after all the others had retired.

It is difficult to understand the Doctor's anxieties on some of these matters. He seems to have desired a wide circulation of his new work on pauperism, but the publisher's difficulties were overlooked. For between the 17th and 20th October 1841 (although he was going to devolve on others his literary correspondence), Chalmers called on Mr. Boyd, Collins' agent in Edinburgh, and asked how best the book could be widely circulated. On the 20th certainly, Collins was writing to Boyd: "Dr. Chalmers is intensely anxious about the circulation of this work. . . . I completely sympathise with him, and enter fully into his anxieties. . . . I would therefore take it kind if you would instruct your travellers to keep their eye on it for some time, and dispose of as many of the work as they can in their wanderings. I mean to advertise it very largely, even though the sales may not compensate for the expense, but just to force the work to the utmost on public attention."

Under a less glittering spotlight than his famous author William Collins, too, was securing public attention. In September he had laid the foundation stones of three churches in Glasgow. In November he took the chair at a large city demonstration against Sunday trains—a matter of some moment, for the Edinburgh-Glasgow railway was to be opened the following year. He was also printing and selling his first editions of the Scriptures, a development of the highest importance to the firm, as we shall see later, and one of engrossing interest to himself.

From that pleasing task he turned aside to greet James Montgomery, now almost seventy and visiting his native land for the first time in sixty years. Montgomery's visit—on behalf of Moravian missions—attracted great interest. The newspapers devoted columns to his speeches. The *Glasgow Herald* even printed a phrenological study of his old and saintly head. And

at his main meeting in Glasgow, where the ageing poet appeared
in an out-moded suit of black with breast ruffles, William Collins
introduced him to the audience in language peculiarly his own:

> "If I were to give expression to the fulness of my heart, I could
> say much; but his presence must repress my praises. And even were
> I able to overcome the delicacy of my own feelings I should find
> a still more insuperable obstacle in the delicacy of his: and I shall
> only say that Mr. Montgomery, the distinguished Christian poet
> of Great Britain, stands before you—a man whose genius has been
> sanctified and inspired with fire from the altar of Heaven, and
> which he has always consecrated to the honour of God, the service
> of his Redeemer, and the good of man."

After this devoir, so gracefully performed, Collins commissioned Montgomery to write an introduction to a new
edition of *Paradise Lost*. It was also in 1842 that he completed
the twenty-five volumes of the Chalmers' *Collected Works*, and
thus left a permanent memorial not only of the famous divine's
intellectual energy but of his own incessant toil and devotion.

CHAPTER VIII

The Final Crusade
1843-1853

I

DAWN IN Edinburgh on Thursday the 18th May 1843
was cold and leaden, untinged by the stormy crimson
which so often gives the high ridge of the Old Town
its unique morning beauty. By the dawn-token, the streets
should have been grey and silent. Instead, excited crowds were
thronging into George Street to witness one of the historic
occasions—like the signing of the Covenant, or the Bonnie Prince's
ride to Holyroodhouse—which seem to illuminate Scotland
towards the middle of each century.

On this day, at the General Assembly of the Church of
Scotland, men awaited such an event with tense expectancy.
The General Assembly, about to be confronted by an issue of
conscience, was an institution deeply interwoven with the
country's social life, as it still is. In the Chalmers era and earlier,
its high level of debate encouraged earnest and promising young
advocates to cut their forensic teeth. The leading nobles of
Scotland were its senators equally with the merchants of Glasgow
or the sheep farmers of the Borders. So illustrious, indeed, was
the Assembly's tradition that to take but one example—when it
met in Glasgow Cathedral in November 1638, to reject the
episcopacy proposed by Charles I and Archbishop Laud—its

members included not only Argyll but the great Montrose, sitting as an elder from the presbytery of Auchterarder. In 1843, the heads of many great Scottish families—lacking only the slashed doublets, the pistols and swords, and the armed retainers of their forebears—were still among the Assembly's laity, and again facing an issue of conscience which went to the very roots of the country's life.

For ten years Scotland had been convulsed by the conflict over Church patronage. An ever-increasing number of congregations during that troubled time had asserted their Presbyterian right to veto undesirable incumbents. On the other hand, the patrons whose power of presentation had sometimes a financial as well as a prestige value, regarded the congregations' resolutions as an infringement of their legal rights; and in this they were supported by the courts and the Government. The General Assembly by solemn Act was on the side of the congregations, and many of its officers endeavoured to persuade Sir Robert Peel's government to alter the law in their favour. These efforts were in vain. Peel refused to take action in the hope that the storm would blow over and in doing so revealed, for such a far-sighted statesman, a strange misunderstanding of the Presbyterian temper. Thus by 1843, when the combustible elements had reached flash-point, the dominant Evangelical party, fully prepared to sacrifice the material and spiritual benefits of Establishment for their principle, had already resolved to disrupt the Kirk and set up a free denomination of their own.

At this fateful Assembly William Collins was an early arrival —ardent as ever, but, since he was no easy violator of traditions, probably breathing more sensitively than some that almost ponderable air of impending fate, when institutions vested with the mystique of ancient and cherished splendours are about to be broken or abruptly remoulded. He was soon to hear, as at former Assemblies, the crisp rhythms of marching and the brazen din of pageantry modulating into the National Anthem as the Queen's Commissioner, the Marquis of Bute, made his entrance and assumed his place on the Throne. From his own place in the

Assembly he watched the Moderator, "very pale, but full of dignity, as one about to do a great deed," first as he read a protest against encroachments on the Church's spiritual powers which Collins himself had signed, then, after bowing to the Queen's representative, as he made for the door with Dr. Chalmers beside him—the old impetuous Chalmers who had already grasped his hat impatient to be gone. It is pretty certain that by this time he had his own hat in hand and was hastening to join the stream of seceding ministers and elders.

Soon the long, historic procession with Chalmers in its van was marching four abreast amidst cheering multitudes through Dundas Street and Pitt Street to Canonmills, where a vast hall was awaiting the First General Assembly of the Free Church of Scotland. And, still close behind his old friend, marched William Collins. It is not difficult to guess his emotion during the fantastic, stirring scene when Chalmers was proposed as the first Free Church Moderator and "the whole assemblage rose, waving hats and handkerchiefs and loudly cheering for some minutes "; or when the Doctor gave out a psalm in the ever-moving Scottish metre:

> O send Thy Light forth and Thy Truth;
>   Let them be guides to me,
> And bring me to Thine holy hill,
>   Ev'n where Thy dwellings be.

The final act, quick and inevitable, drew on in grim splendour. Four hundred and seventy-four ministers signed the Act of Separation—a sublime sacrifice which stirred Mr. Gladstone to describe it as "a noble and heart-stirring spectacle ", and Francis Jeffrey, now Lord Jeffrey and a judge, to hurl his book on one side when he heard the news and exclaim: "I am proud of my country. There is not another country upon Earth where such a deed could have been done." For the sacrifice was very great. Seventy-year-old ministers turned the key for the last time in doors of manses which had been both home and sanctuary for perhaps thirty or forty years, and passed with their families through crowds of weeping parishioners. Dr. Duncan, the inventor of Savings Banks, left his parish manse at Ruthwell after forty-three years' unbroken happiness there. The eighty-five-year-old minister of Collins' own birthplace was too old to have taken much part in the skirmishings and pitched battles which preceded the Disruption. Nevertheless he proclaimed himself on the side of the Disruptionists with the exclamation: "Nil timendum Christo duce," and died two months later.

Some of the quitting ministers moved into huts and miserable inns pending the erection of new churches and manses for the Free Church. But even this was fraught with difficulty. In the north, where the Duke of Sutherland declined to give an inch of his vast territories for Free Church buildings, many church services were held in the open air. On at least one Highland sea loch the minister preached from a boat anchored offshore to large congregations assembled on the beach. Some, until their new churches were built, preached at cross-roads on the public highway. University professors who favoured the Disruption had to resign their Chairs, as Chalmers did.

To assist in the relief of these manifold difficulties, William Collins, who had made his twenty-six-year-old son a partner during the year, spurred his flagging body to a further supreme effort. He was elected to eleven of the new Church's Committees, contributed not only £200 to its general funds, but £100 to a fund to build manses for homeless ministers, and though suffering from recurring attacks of bronchitis, spent the rest of the year campaigning for the Free Church with the same flame-like enthusiasm with which he had supported the old Church and all his other causes—temperance, education, savings banks, the abolition of slavery and "No trains on Sunday." Within a few weeks he was addressing a great Free Church demonstration in Glasgow's City Hall. He became an elder in the Free Tron Church and laid the foundation stone both of this edifice and Free St. John's. He attended the many Committees to which he had been appointed by the Free Church Assembly. But by Christmas, worn out with these exertions, he was ill in bed, though not for

long. In 1844 he undertook extensive printing commitments
for the Free Church, notably the re-publication of the writing of
the "Scottish Reformers and the Divines of former days" and
rejoiced that at least forty thousand subscribers saw the printer's
name on the first volume, the *Select Practical Writings of John
Knox*. He still went often to Edinburgh. He spoke in several
provincial Scottish towns. And despite his increasing lassitude
he was, in 1844, contented in his very ardour for this new and,
for him, final cause. The one thing he could not possibly know
was that the next act in the personal drama of his life was already
being played out not in Scotland but among the dissolving snows
of Switzerland where the news of the Disruption had fallen on
the ears of a famous historian like the sound of a resurrection.

II

The historian was Merle D'Aubigné. For several years, the early
volumes of his *History of the Reformation* had been world-famous;
and by the spring of 1844 his work and fame had stirred Chalmers
and the Disruption leaders as profoundly as the immensity of their
own sacrifice had moved D'Aubigné. William Collins naturally
shared the Free Kirkers' admiration. He was in constant contact
with their leaders, being one himself, and despite the ordeal of
many fiery furnaces he and Dr. Chalmers were still fast friends.
Neither could have discerned in the dark, inscrutable face of the
future, certainly not in the brilliant aspect of the Swiss scene,
the seed of bitter, irrevocable collision.

Knowing D'Aubigné's enthusiasm for their cause, Dr.
Chalmers and Dr. Candlish—a noted leader of the Free Church
with a flair for ecclesiastical management—devised a scheme for
a comprehensive distribution of the *History of the Reformation*
among Free Church adherents. One hundred thousand subscribers in advance, they suggested, was a desirable circulation.
The work was to be published by a Church committee, and
printed by either an Edinburgh or a Glasgow printer. How far

William Collins figured in the early conversations is uncertain, and Dr. Chalmers' *Private Journal* throws little light on the proposal. Possible references are:

> *30th April.* Mr. Collins and a startling proposal.
> *6th May.* With Dr. Candlish and Mr. Collins.

It may be that the "startling proposal" concerned D'Aubigné. Whether or not, a committee with Dr. Chalmers and Dr. Candlish as its leading members was formed under the formidable title, *Association for the Wider Circulation of D'Aubigné's History of the Reformation;* and D'Aubigné himself decided not only to visit Scotland for a meeting with the Free Church representatives, but to arrange exclusive British publication of a new volume (Vol. IV) of his *History.* To further this project he kept in close touch with Dr. Chalmers who "earnestly recommended" him in April 1845 to "take no offer from a London, or from any other bookseller, and settle on no plan of publication till you have come to Edinburgh."

D'Aubigné, travelling from London to Newcastle and then by stage coach to Edinburgh, was met on the Queen's birthday by Chalmers—"that man," he noted, "who for these thirty years has been all over Europe the representative of Scotland."

But Volume IV of the *History* was his main pre-occupation, and fortunately for his financial expectations publishers both in London and Scotland were competing for the rights. This battle was eventually won by Messrs. Oliver and Boyd, a long-established Edinburgh firm who were reluctantly persuaded by the Free Churchmen to let 20,000 cheap copies of the volume be distributed through Free Church machinery—D'Aubigné getting £3,000, and a wealthy backer of the Church, Archibald Bonar, guaranteeing the firm against loss up to £1,000.

A tangled situation soon arose. Several publishers were already issuing the first three volumes, among them Blackie of Glasgow, Longman of London, and William Collins. Most of the Collins edition, admirably translated from the French by Henry Beveridge, advocate grandfather of the present Lord

The Trongate, Glasgow, 1837
Coloured lithograph by S.D. Swarbreck

Beveridge, had won favourable notices. But William Collins, full of restless energy, had also decided to issue the *History* in phenomenally cheap editions and go all out for gigantic sales. Strange events followed.

The first inkling Oliver and Boyd had of the Collins scheme was a letter, dated 13th August 1845 from a Glasgow friend who reported that William Collins, in addition to the volumes already published, intended to issue them in twenty-two 4d. weekly numbers, starting at the end of the month. Collins, said Boyd's Glasgow informant, had also suggested that church beadles should become canvassers for the weekly numbers and get an allowance of 1s. for every subscriber they obtained. "This," he added, "is going the whole hog."

Boyd, sitting at the centre of his own sales web, received advices on the same day from a Perth bookseller that Collins, who requested an answer by return of post, had asked one *bookseller* in each town to become agent for a *People's Edition* of the earlier D'Aubigné volumes.

On receiving this intelligence Oliver and Boyd wasted no more time. In the last week of August they announced their exclusive purchase and early publication of Volume IV, promised a new edition of *all four volumes*, and protested to the Glasgow publishers that their recent activities were improper—a censure which evoked a protest from Blackie to Boyd that certain of his charges were "not in the best taste seeing that you are well aware of Mr. Collins' high character for integrity." Blackie added that his own house had no intention of suppressing their own two volumes already published so long as they could be sold. So the war went on, until in the summer of 1846, when the ears of the Scottish people were almost deafened by the sound of D'Aubigné's name, the general confusion became still worse confounded.[1]

In June, unknown to the Free Church leaders, both Blackie and Collins agreed with Oliver and Boyd on an impressive cash offer of £1,750 for the joint right to publish Volume IV. The only

[1]Collins also published D'Aubigné's *Discourses and Essays*.

condition was that Collins and Blackie should not announce their editions until 6th August so that the Oliver and Boyd edition might have a few days' precedence.

The imbroglio now took its last strange twist. A Free Church circular calling on "all Protestant clergymen" to get 100,000 subscribers for the Oliver and Boyd edition, suddenly drew from the storm clouds their hoarded lightning. In Edinburgh the incensed booksellers urged the Free Church to disentangle itself at once from the bookselling business. In Glasgow Collins and Blackie struck shrewdly and hard. On 10th August 1846 they jointly advertised a protest in the *Glasgow Herald* and other leading newspapers that although Volume IV (for the right of printing which they had paid £1,750) was already on sale at 14s., yet the Free Church D'Aubigné Association was to sell it to its subscribers at 8s.; nor had they been informed of Oliver and Boyd's arrangement with the Free Church.

Seven days later Oliver and Boyd—now thoroughly entangled in disputes with the Scottish book trade, with a New York publisher who claimed that D'Aubigné had promised the copyright of Vol. IV to him, and with the London booksellers[1]—issued a considered reply. They explained that the Collins-Blackie agreement gave them the right to issue the book at any price to anyone they thought fit: which was perfectly true. But the storm in the book world had become too widespread for peace and comfort, and the scheme was wisely abandoned.

III

A thunderous cloud meanwhile had loomed up from another horizon. At the beginning of 1846 the D'Aubigné affray had not reached its height, and relations between the Doctor and his publisher were still so friendly that on the 15th January Collins promised Chalmers £5 for his new church in the Westport of

[1] Oliver and Boyd had made an arrangement for the book's London distribution through the Religious Tract Society.

Edinburgh, adding a warm assurance that his last address had given him "serene and unmingled delight." The delight was soon to die in astonished grief.

At the end of March or the beginning of April, the Doctor—in a sudden tempest of annoyance, and only four years after he had claimed Collins in his correspondence as a man of "special worth and my particular friend "—suddenly transferred his literary interests and goodwill to Oliver and Boyd.

The affair is reminiscent, though the circumstances are by no means comparable, of the final breach between the ruined Archibald Constable and Sir Walter Scott in 1826. Scott was a great Scotsman—as Chalmers was—but in one of the very few ungenerous acts of his career, as John Buchan has said, he let his broken publisher hobble down the Castle Street stairs without a word of kindness. William Collins was not ruined like Constable —far from it: he had become prosperous and his long devotion to Chalmers bore no comparison with the more formal relations 'twixt Edinburgh and Abbotsford. Thus, if the two men—the great divine and the publisher—faced each other at all in an open rupture, as Scott and Constable did, the stormy reproaches of the one would waken more grief than anger in the heart of the other as he left his old friend for the last time. But perhaps they did not meet at all; perhaps, even, they were reconciled later as friends if not as publisher and author.

Careful research has so far yielded no certain reason for this lesser disruption, though Chalmers' increasing irritation over the prolonged D'Aubigné haggle must have been a contributory cause. The only available clue at present seems to be a letter from Chalmers to Boyd (dated 11th April):

"I beg that you will proceed immediately with the printing and publication of that pamphlet, and should Mr. Collins venture on a prosecution I am willing to defend it. I put a work into his hands which he undertook to do and failed in what he promised. It will be very strange if he step forth as an injured man on the ground of a very grievous injury done to me by himself."

There was no reprisal. Another "auld sang" had ended, and

William Collins evidently realised that any immediate *rapproche-ment* was out of the question. In the absence of complete informa-tion as to the rights and wrongs of the cleavage, it is vain to imagine his emotions as the last clap of Chalmers' thunder broke over his head. But certainly on the financial grounds which had formed a bone of contention in 1841 he could hardly have reproached himself for neglecting the Doctor's interests.

By this time, Dr. Chalmers must have made at least £14,000 by his pen. It is difficult to estimate his literary earnings precisely, owing to lacunæ in those personal accounts of his which have been preserved and the destruction of many of his publisher's records. But his income for certain years is known, and a reliable estimate can be made for the others. We know, for example, that he received more than £3,000 from Smith and Whyte, and that for miscellaneous work in his earlier days he got substantial fees from William Blackwood, from Jeffrey (who paid him £50 for a single article in the *Edinburgh Review*) and other publishers. For writing his *Bridgewater Treatise* in 1833 he got £500. Thus from extra-Collins sources he derived about £4,000.

By William Collins he seems always to have been well paid, even in the dark days. For a score of essays in the *Select Library* he got, on the average, £35 each. For his legion of Sermons, pamphlets, and General Assembly speeches his receipts per manuscript varied between £28 and £75 for a first edition alone. Large volumes such as the *Commercial Sermons* which went into a number of editions must have brought him in sums exceeding £1,000. He certainly made several thousand pounds out of the twenty-five volumes of his *Collected Works;* for although the exact figure is not known, it is significant that his ascertainable assets rose from £9,000 in 1836, when the *Works* began to appear, to £13,000 in 1842 when they were completed.[1] The sum of £14,000—much larger in value then than now—seems therefore to be a reasonable estimate of his literary earnings.

However that may be, William Junior, when the break came,

---

[1] Charles Simeon received £5,000 for a large collection of his sermons published in serial volumes.

acted quickly and efficiently on the assumption that it would
not be repaired. He began to negotiate the final settlement of
Dr. Chalmers' literary affairs with Mr. Boyd—in itself a heavy
task, for all the works outstanding had to be brought back from
the booksellers: intricate copyright difficulties had to be ironed
out, and bills computed for Oliver and Boyd's purchase of
Chalmers publications in the Collins warehouse. Thus many
weeks went by, till the Doctor's natural impatience sharpened
into petulance on 1st June, when he wrote to Boyd: "Should
not the settlement with Messrs. Collins be completed now that
all might be ready for the proposed operations in July (*a reprint
of the Works*). There seems a tardiness on their part which it
were well should be terminated."

On the following day William Collins Senior also wrote to
Boyd:

> "It was my intention to have called again to see you, but I was
> unexpectedly required to return home last week, to see an old
> friend who is unwell, and who had expressed an anxious wish to
> see me. I now send you my concurrence with the agreement."

This hastened the transfer arrangements. By the beginning
of July—while the city bells of Glasgow, by order of the Lord
Provost and Magistrates, were ringing a "merry peal" in honour
of Sir Robert Peel's passage of the Corn Bill—most of the outstanding Chalmers volumes had been dispatched to Edinburgh,
and Oliver and Boyd were meeting a series of accounts for them.
One of these—for "262 Chalmers Vol. 17—£17 3s. od."—has been
preserved on notepaper headed: "William Collins, Printer,
Publisher, Bookseller, and Wholesale Stationer, South Frederick
Street, Glasgow and Paternoster-Row, London."

The house had, it will be noticed, changed its London address
from Stationer's Hall Court to Paternoster Row (No. 34), a
famous literary highway since the days of Queen Anne.

IV

Boyd had kept Dr. Chalmers in the dark about the sale to Collins and Blackie of the right to publish D'Aubigné's fourth volume. Thus when the Free Church scheme collapsed, when, too, Oliver and Boyd called on Archibald Bonar for his £1,000 guarantee, and the Collins-Blackie arrangement became known, the suspicious Chalmers protested and then retreated into an angry silence, despite Oliver and Boyd's repeated assertion that the scheme had ended because of booksellers' resistance and for no other reason.

However, on the last day of the year (1846), in a lengthy letter, Chalmers made peace with his new publisher. There is no need to reproduce it all here. But the purport of two passages must certainly be recorded. They show that Chalmers had himself offered Bonar £100 as a contribution to his guarantee. This offer was refused, a provisional agreement being reached instead that a hundred "friends" should contribute £10 each. Then followed a revealing postscript:

> "There is one piece of information which I meant to have given you when we last met, but from forgetfulness omitted it. The Glasgow booksellers with whom you made the bargain have proffered their subscriptions and I think given Mr. Bonar reason to hope, that they would head the list with very handsome sums."

Glasgow's Greatheart was evidently still generous. He certainly remained so in the eyes of Dr. Chalmers' son-in-law Hanna, who, with all the relevant documents in his possession, must have understood his father-in-law's affairs better than anyone living when he wrote the standard *Memoirs of Dr. Chalmers*. In that extremely able work he omitted all references to publishers' quarrels, the D'Aubigné tangle, and many other issues here brought to light for the first time. As many of the chief actors in these controversies were then still living, he could do little else. Yet knowing all the facts, he could still describe William Collins in the first volume of the *Memoirs* (1849) as a

man "who, after such a life of honourable service in the cause of
Christ as few laymen among us have ever lived, in that retirement
into which feeble health has forced him still cherishes with
unabated zeal those interests, which in bygone years he toiled
so much to further."

But the lights are dimming on this chequered stage. Within
a few months of his reconciliation with Boyd, Dr. Chalmers was
dead. Quietly, in a strangely tranquil contrast to the tumults of
his temperament and the storms of his career, he died in his sleep
during the night of the 30th May 1847—"half erect, his head
reclining gently on the pillow; the expression of his countenance
that of fixed and majestic repose."

The tributes to him were many, for despite certain temperamental defects he was a resplendent figure. "The greatest of
living Scotsmen," said Lord Cockburn at the time. "One of the
greatest of our race: a commanding character, a superb orator,
the most illustrious Scottish churchman since John Knox," said
Lord Rosebery in 1915. Or, in the words of John Buchan later
still—"one of the noblest figures in any Church, as far above
Knox in vision and wisdom as he surpassed him in charity."

These tributes still reflect the great divine's untarnished
lustre. Across the world at least a dozen bays, capes or mountains
bear his name; Scotland is studded with Chalmers churches,
streets and statues; and at least a score of books and a hundred
commentaries have been written about him. Such resonant
echoes from the shades could only be evoked by a man of trans-
cendent genius. But this has never been in doubt. Except for his
contemporary Sir Walter Scott, Chalmers—as orator, moral
teacher, leader of a great ecclesiastical army, and with an intellect
of high quality—was surely the greatest Scotsman of his time.
Though his temperament had a more asprous tinge than Sir
Walter's, and he suffered fools less gladly, there could hardly be
better proof of William Collins' own high qualities than that he
retained the intimate friendship of such a man for more than
thirty years. But here we must leave him. In Edinburgh, church
bells tolled all over the city during his burial and massive crowds

lined the streets for the funeral procession. Queen Victoria, although he had left adequate resources, immediately conferred a Civil List pension of £200 a year on his wife and daughters. Newspapers and periodicals all over the world devoted many columns to his achievements, not only as an unsurpassed preacher but, despite his literary orotundity, as an author. "He is the only Scotch clergyman whose professional writings have commanded general and distant admiration," said Cockburn, himself the author of a classic work, *Memorials of His Time*. "There is scarcely a place where English books are read that does not delight in the rich and lofty animation of his works."[1]

William Collins had done his work well.

V

William Collins (I) the father, in this year of breaking links, was almost fifty-eight years of age; William Collins (II) the son, who had married Annabella Proudfoot Glen in 1845, was thirty; William Collins (III), the grandson, was born on 6th September 1846 in a world that was changing fast. When William II travelled to London, he no longer endured the romantic ordeal of coach-travel as his father had done: the railway line from London to Carlisle extended now to Glasgow and the clip-clop of the horses across the moors had yielded to the roar and shriek of the railway engine. Even correspondence in business affairs had been speeded up by the penny post and the electric telegraph; while the house of Collins, making its own small contribution to the age of speed, had published the first of its famous Ready Reckoners.

But again—as in the firm's foundation year—unrest threatened from many sides. In 1846 the price of bread soared after the destruction of the crops by a bad season. A year later, the railway

[1] 4,000 copies of Chalmers' *Lectures on The Epistle to The Romans* were sold by one bookseller in New York between 1843 and 1845.

speculation bubble suddenly collapsed in a spatter of bank-
ruptcies. By 1848, the long depression—after frightful harvests,
the failure of Ireland's potato crop, and the sweep of violence
across Europe—suddenly became menacing. In Glasgow, where
scores of factories closed down, an angry mob even raised
barricades in Argyle Street and the Saltmarket where William I
had laboured. The military were called out. The Riot Act was
read by the Lord Provost, and seven of the rioters were killed
when the troops opened fire. As a final personal catastrophe, both
William I's wife, a shadowy invalid figure of whom little is
now known save that she was described once in a newspaper as
"a lady of great amiability," and his sister Jessie (born in 1783),
died during the year. He had thus lost all his family except his
son William. Quiet as a saint in these last crushing sorrows, the
man of many words and enthusiasms went down the Clyde to
Rothesay, took comfortable lodgings in 11 Argyle Place and
started a mission in the town for poor people. Here also he
found relief from the tensions of the times in the reading of his
favourite devotional books, in voluminous correspondence, and
frequent visits from old friends. His son's visits were specially
acceptable as he brought reports of the firm's continued expansion, and once (1848), the exciting news that the base of the
family pyramid had broadened with the arrival of a second
grandson, Alexander, grandfather of the company's present
chairman.

In August 1852, he also heard a full account of fresh negotiations with the irrepressible D'Aubigné, whose fifth volume was
now due. Though William Collins and his son had lost three or
four hundred pounds on Volume IV—Blackie's lost £700—and
the country was saturated with D'Aubigné editions, publishers
were still competing keenly for the next volume.[1] This time
D'Aubigné asked for £2,000. But Collins, Blackie and Oliver and
Boyd made him a joint offer (on 4th August 1852) of £1,350 for

[1]When Queen Victoria asked Lord Macaulay's opinion about his *History*, she received
the answer that it was not to be implicitly trusted; that the writer was a strong partisan,
and too much of a colourist; but that his work well deserved a perusal and would
greatly interest and amuse her.

the new volume. For a while the negotiations lagged, till the parties eventually compromised on a figure less than D'Aubigné's demand and more than the publishers' offer. Of the sum as finally fixed, Collins and Blackie jointly paid £450, and the volume was duly published the following year.

But William Collins during this winter was failing fast. The storms were over. Happy in his faith and therefore serene in the gloaming of his life, he daily scanned from his window the sailing ships steering towards the Cumbrae Islands. He still sent large donations to his favourite causes—£100, for instance, to a fund for evangelising Glasgow—but he seems to have lived simply. His effects at Rothesay after his death were valued at only £71 16s. 6d.: and these included fifty-four books and a gazetteer, the sofa on which he lay before the fire, a tea-urn and a coffee-pot, a set of fire-irons, and a carpet described as "very old" which was valued at five shillings.

At the close of 1852 he had only a few more days to live. His friend, the Rev. J. A. Wylie, who wrote a number of books for the house, including a most popular work *Modern Judea*, recorded of a visit shortly before his death that he could never forget the "sweet serenity of spirit which breathed forth in every word and look." It was in that spirit that he died of chronic bronchitis on the 2nd January 1853, in his sixty-fourth year.

Several newspapers paid him tribute. "The memory of such a man," declared the *Scottish Guardian*, "cannot fail to be blessed. The recollection of his burning zeal is at this moment 'provoking' some at least to devote themselves to the same noble cause of making their city flourish by the preaching of the Word.[1] The lesson, too, of liberality which he taught, of liberality upon a scale so immensely beyond the stinted and narrow limits of all previous giving to the cause of Christ, has already been so learnt as to have effected an entire revolution upon that subject in the minds of most Christian men. Above all, the strength and the simplicity of his faith in facing difficulties

---

[1]Glasgow's original motto was: "Let Glasgow Flourish By The Preaching of the Word." Now it is: "Let Glasgow Flourish."

that seemed insurmountable, a faith of that kind to which all things are possible, will not be lost in the way of an example to others.

"In addition to the honour in which his name must ever be held for such achievements as these, his memory will in this city, at least, be long and gratefully cherished for all those personal excellencies by which his character was so richly adorned. His unobtrusive humility, his unselfish spirit, his warm affections, his generosity of heart, his ardent and impulsive mind, his extensive knowledge, his catholic charity, his readiness for every good work—above all, and as the spring of all, his deep and devoted piety, combined to constitute a character that was a preserving salt in society while he lived, and that will leave a sweet and wholesome savour behind him for generations to come."

William Collins had left other permanent memorials. Over thirty-four years of ceaseless toil he had created a prosperous publishing firm with vital ancillaries—printing, binding, and stationery. He had founded a family destined to play a distinguished part in national and local government, on the battlefield and in the world of literature. Even his death became the man. For he died on a Sunday morning at the very moment when the church bells of Rothesay began to sound across the waters of the Clyde, and only a few miles away from the village of Innellan where, a few years later, the blind hymnist George Matheson was to write lines which William Collins and James Montgomery would have included with pride in their *Christian Psalmist*:

> *O Cross that liftest up my head,*
> *I dare not ask to fly from Thee;*
> *I lay in dust life's glory dead,*
> *And from the ground there blossoms red*
> *Life that shall endless be.*

CHAPTER IX

A New Order

1853-1865

I

GLASGOW'S SPIRIT of Energy had so triumphed by 1853 that the city offered even stranger contrasts than during the sharply-tinted days of the Regency. For refined industrial science had, as elsewhere, mated with a coarser greed to produce an ill-matched progeny; and Glasgow thus presented the spectacle of fine new roads and prosperous mansions fleeing like opulent refugees ever farther and farther from the Gehenna of gaunt tenements to which the ancient academic quarter had been reduced.

During the Regency an inquisitive professor had once excavated in that quarter twenty-three Irishmen huddled together in two rooms—one measuring thirteen feet by eleven, the other fifteen by eight. By the mid-Victorian age, fifty thousand Glaswegians swarmed within ninety acres of caverns and tenements in the Gallowgate and Saltmarket, a literal and metaphorical dung-heap so fever-laden and depraved that the minister of the Tron Kirk, evidently a worthy occupant of Chalmers' pulpit, described the area as "the wretchedest, foulest, immoralest corner of Scotland, nay of Great Britain—one mass of moral and physical filth, the worst under the canopy of heaven, a seething sea of sin and devilry and bestiality rolling eternally around it, the very steeple pointing its finger as if by protest to that heaven which the breathing multitude around it so fearfully forget."

This grimy backcloth behind the spreading silhouette of William Collins' printing works deserves a closer glance, since it largely conditioned his career.

By the New Year of 1853 intemperance was so rife in the city that while the printers in Montrose Street were working on the long-awaited fifth volume of D'Aubigné's *History of the Reformation*, the *Glasgow Herald* was saying: "There has rarely been exhibited so much open intemperance as on New Year's Day; and the scores of degraded wretches who staggered along the streets or were trundled to the various Police Offices in a state of drunken insensibility, contrasted most disgustingly with the crowds of well-dressed and respectably conducted artisans, who looked on and lamented." That was in January. By March, Edinburgh's *Scotsman* and Glasgow's *Herald* were embroiled in a quarrel over the drinking powers of their respective communities. This ended, after much angry talk of "lies" and "calumnies," in a Glasgow victory, since Edinburgh committals for drunkenness and disorderly conduct proved to be one for every seventeen of the population—the Glasgow ratio was one for every twenty-two—and the *Glasgow Herald* was also able to report with gentle malice: "On Saturday a special train, with 1,200 tee-totallers from Edinburgh visited this city, and after spending a few hours in the western capital, returned to Auld Reekie, very many of them in a state of intoxication; in fact, it was one of the most drunken trains that ever left the Queen Street terminus." Though incidents like this were splendid ammunition for the old inter-city slanging match and may have been exaggerated, the social perils of unbridled drinking were exceedingly grave. Not only were the city's Bacchanalians even drugging their whisky with snuff—so desperate their search for a nepenthe—but most public houses were reeking dens where the dregs of humanity sat, or more often stood, in constant session. Nor was this the only threat to civic order. In the first three months of 1848 alone, more than forty thousand destitute Irish immigrants had poured into the already overcrowded city—a torrent which aggravated the housing shortage and brought with it endless religious squabbling and even hand-to-hand fighting.

But all this composed the darker side of the city's scutcheon. Its other aspect revealed a Glasgow which by this time had become one of the world's busiest workshops. More than one quarter of Britain's pig-iron came from the West of Scotland. Lanarkshire on the southern fringes of the city was rapidly becoming the greatest coal-producing county in the British Isles. And the night sky of Glasgow flared so luridly with the blaze of furnaces that Alexander Smith the Ayrshire poet was soon to write in mingled love and horror of his adopted city:

> *Draw thy fierce streams of blinding ore,*
> *Smite on a thousand anvils, roar*
> *Down to the harbour bars:*
> *Smoulder in smoky sunsets, flare,*
> *On rainy nights, with street and square*
> *Lie empty to the stars.*
> *From terrace proud to alley base*
> *I know thee as my mother's face.*
>
> *When sunset bathes thee in his gold*
> *In wreaths of bronze thy sides are rolled,*
> *Thy smoke is dusky fire;*
> *And, from the glory round thee poured,*
> *A sunbeam, like an angel's sword,*
> *Shivers upon a spire.*
> *Thus have I watched thee, Terror! Dream!*
> *While the blue night crept up the stream.*

In the light of his upbringing and environment, it seemed natural for William Collins II to put on his father's mantle. In one respect he went further. He was one of those conscientious people whom a modern Collins author, Dr. Arthur Bryant, has saluted thus in *English Saga:*

"All over England and Scotland isolated individuals began to tackle self-imposed tasks, each striving to cleanse his or her own small corner of the Augean stable. Such were provincial doctors who faced fever and vested interest in a tireless campaign against insanitary conditions, devoted clergymen and non-conformist ministers, city missionaries and temperance workers, and young men and women of comfortable circumstances—often evangelicals or quakers—who gave up their leisure hours to teach in ragged schools or to organise clubs, sports, and benefit societies for their poorer neighbours."

As one of this devoted band, William Collins chose temperance reform as his chief social interest and soon became the most ferocious total abstainer in Glasgow's history.

This puritanism of his accorded well with his politics. Being a manufacturer from the dominant middle-class which had risen to power after the Reform Act he looked over distant horizons through an exporter's eyes, saw his publications travelling across the oceans to the book marts of the world along with tweed, cotton goods and Clyde-built ships, and inevitably fastened his faith to Free Trade. He was therefore a Liberal. But William Collins had inherited too much of his father's Christian humanity to accept, as did many Liberal manufacturers of his time, the cruel laws of the "dismal science." While Cobden and Bright could with a clear conscience oppose Factory Acts as impious interference with the divine operation of the universe, William Collins, less consistent but warmer-hearted, could not so blind himself to the contradiction of pelf and poverty around him. Hence his fervour for good causes.[1]

In 1853 he was in his thirty-sixth year—the age at which his father, too, had faced an independent future without a business partner. In few other respects were their positions comparable. William I had looked out from the Candleriggs in 1826 on a future which would have been misty indeed but for his own moral strength and optimism. William II, on the other hand, was the owner of a publishing house which if not grandiose was a waxing concern; and he had two healthy sons to sustain its tradition

---

[1] An early sign of this appears in the *Glasgow Herald* for 29th December, 1854—a record of a subscription of £10 to Glasgow's Patriotic Fund; and towards maintaining the wives and children of soldiers, sailors and marines presently serving in the East." Henceforward, his benefactions to charity were to be many and generous.

some day, though William III was still only six years of age and Alexander four. He also had the advantage of a more settled environment. True, Glasgow in his first winter of independence was ravaged by cholera virulent enough to cause almost 4,000 deaths; there was also a strike of cotton spinners; and the outbreak of the Crimean War was disturbing. But the Chartist movement—last substantial social eruption in the first half of the century—was quiet in the early "fifties," and the next quarter of a century was to be a period of unbroken economic advance.

We can see this second William, then, as a well-found apostle for the vigorous new age which stretched ahead. He had inherited from the first William a sticking quality, a Calvinistic rectitude in business, and a marked determination to surmount obstacles. Except on the temperance question and Gladstonian concepts of economy, William II's blood was never fired with quite the same passion that had driven his father on one mission after another. A more ambitious business brain, unfailing shrewdness, a natural love of the counting-house and an inherited zest to see commercial plants grow under his hand, marked a difference, not so much in the man, as in the area on which the second William chose to concentrate.

By good fortune his robust physique enabled him to work long hours at a stretch without undue strain. "You may talk as you like, but the greatest part of all genius is hard work," he told the children at a school prize-giving. It was a precept characteristic of the preceptor, and one which he carried into such relentless practice that men in the printing works used to recall how, during his first fifteen years in the business—from 1829 onwards—he was often in his office at six o'clock in the morning and was known to have taken only three holidays. He took more relaxation later on, but in general his deep-rooted adherence to the gospel of work, as we shall see, was to govern his business life for another forty years—and he was already nearing forty! Such a long span itself symbolises the strength of the age. But like Queen Victoria herself, William Collins

Sir William Collins, 1817-1895

was to grow—by every known connotation of that regal adjective—more "Victorian" as the years passed. He believed not only in expansion, but in consolidating his position as he went. Though very radical in outlook, he put his trust in the good order of society; in the divine mission of Great Britain to reproduce that good order in all parts of the globe; and in solidity—the solidity of Victorian newspapers, the Scottish baronial style of architecture which got fresh impetus from Prince Albert's reconstruction of Balmoral and Holyrood, and the painted draperies of Winterhalter. One suspects that his house was gravid with heavy upholstery, bookcases of stern carved oak, and huge vases. Soon he had an imposing carriage. Later came a steam yacht and a summer residence at Oban—in the authentic tradition of the Victorian magnate—with croquet, crinolines, and country house parties. Even his Bibles had massive brass corners and double clasps in supreme token of Victorian respectability and his position as an elder of the Free Kirk. It was natural of course that such a man—he was twice married and had eleven children in all—should be endowed with a strong patriarchal sense.[1] Though he was far from being a Barrett of Wimpole Street his sense of duty dictated a benevolent despotism over his family and especially over his roguish sons, William and Alexander, by whose peccadilloes he was, in the manner of his venerated Queen, not always amused.

How then shall we sum him up? He sounds like a typical merchant prince in the callous confident age of *laissez faire*. But that he was not. Unlike many honest manufacturers of his time, he was a humanitarian with a keen social conscience and a genuine concern for the workers in his employ. By every other token he was a characteristic Victorian to the very roots of his Victorian beard.

It was lucky that the founder of the firm had left a son so admirably fitted to be a master of mass production. For the Romantic Age of literature, more suited to the father than the

---

[1] After the death of his first wife he married again—in 1863—a Glasgow lady called Helen Jamieson by whom he had two children.

son, was over, and much of the old picturesque intimacy had
departed from the Scottish bookselling trade. In 1819, when
William I threw down his modest gauntlet to the established
booksellers of Scotland, Lockhart, in his *Peter's Letters to his
Kinsfolk*, had written truly:

"Instead of Scotch authors sending their works to be published
by London booksellers, there is nothing more common nowadays,
than to hear of English authors sending down their books to
Edinburgh, than which Memphis or Palmyra could scarcely have
appeared a more absurd place of publication to any English author
thirty years ago."

But in those resplendent years the creative impulses of
eighteenth-century Scotland were still unexpended. Sir Walter
Scott, in the admiring gaze of the world, was limping up the
Mound from Castle Street to Edinburgh's Parliament House or
driving down to Abbotsford, revered chief of a goodly company—
Lockhart himself, Jeffrey, James Hogg the Ettrick Shepherd,
Lord Cockburn, and Christopher North. By 1853, that fellowship
had been broken by death or old age, and there were no successors
on Scotland's horizon. Robert Louis Stevenson was still only two
years old, Andrew Lang nine, James Matthew Barrie unborn.
And though the Scottish instinct and reputation for literary
creation were being kept alive, this was due not to any illustrious
figures at home but to the four Universities and to certain
London Scots: John Ruskin whose northern ancestry seemed
already remote and unreal; Thomas Carlyle, a Scot to the end
but withdrawn in flame and fury to Chelsea: and Lord Macaulay,
compiling history by this time with the magnificent colour
he had deprecated in D'Aubigné. The Northern Kingdom, after
a long period of creative energy, had reached what probably was
a necessary pause.

Though the Scottish literary scene showed "old December's
bareness" compared with England's "teeming autumn"—this
being the age of Tennyson, Browning, Matthew Arnold, Dickens,
Thackeray, Trollope, Charles Reade and the Brontës—the Scottish
publishers and printers were still fully capable of forcing a

living from unpromising soil. In particular, William Collins, with new and up-to-date steam presses, was meeting the old Scottish demand for educational books, a demand which the nation's new prosperity was creating in all parts of the British Isles. He was printing reference books and directories by Post Office contract. On the title-page of the Post Office Annual Glasgow Directory for 1848-49 appears the imprint: " Printed by William Collins & Co., 111 Montrose Street, for the Letter-Carriers of the Post-Office." He also planned a series of books on travel and science.

Already, in the 'forties and early 'fifties, the house had published a number of travel books about the Pacific, North Africa, Turkey, Greece and Palestine, which were no doubt inspired by the wanderings of the Victorian rovers who had succeeded the travelling milords of the previous century. Its scientific output had included works on geology and astronomy —Thomas Dick's *Celestial Scenery* for example—and several scientific cyclopædias. Since the steam presses made it possible to print the classics and books of reference in bulk, there had also been an ever-increasing stream of dictionaries, household works like *The Pilgrim's Progress* and the *Holy War* (in cheap numbers),[1] and reprints such as Thomas Campbell's edition of Shakespeare. This last volume strongly influenced the fortunes of the house. Campbell, describing it modestly as "the stuff I have to write about old Shakey," originally compiled the book in the late thirties, with a preface, for a well-known publisher, Edward Moxon of Dover Street. To procure it, since the copyright had many years to run, the house must therefore have purchased either the plates or the sheets of the original edition. Whatever the arrangement, it was a useful purchase and the herald of many similar reprints—Glassford Bell's edition of Shakespeare for example—during the rest of the century.

Schoolbooks, too, had been pouring out in an unending flow.

---

[1] It will be remembered that one Collins edition of D'Aubigné's *History* was published in cheap numbers. This became a popular feature of publishing in mid-century. In 1849, for example, Longman, William Whyte and William Collins co-published *The Chronicles of Edinburgh* by R. H. Stevenson in six 1s. monthly parts.

It is a remarkable tribute to their longevity that William Collins V, almost a century later, received a letter with the following tribute:

> "I have a book, *Complete System of Practical Arithmetic*, published by William Collins, 203 Buchanan Street, 1849.[1] This book has been of great assistance to me in my studies."

Of this long-lived text-book more than one million copies were eventually sold—a figure significant but not really surprising, for the standard and speed of printing had so improved in the 'forties that by the 'fifties William II was already dreaming of mass production. In 1856 he gave his dreams solid reality with his first atlas. But even more important, within six years he was appointed publisher to the Scottish School Book Association, a body formed to improve school texts in daily use; and again the tide of his fortune perceptibly rose. When about the same time he was also invited to act as publisher for the Irish National Schools, to which he sent 2,320,500 copies of thirty-one books in just over ten years, the tide of fortune was flowing irresistibly. It was to become mightier still when he launched out on large-scale production of the Bible.

II

Men's varying reactions to the teaching of the Bible have shaped the whole history of the western world. Even nowadays when the Bible is not so widely regarded as a source-book of divine revelations, it is still the greatest single influence on modern thought, and those least conscious of this fact readily admit its

[1] This address was one of many occupied by the firm during its great period of expansion between 1839 and 1861. The printing machines alone remained at Montrose Street. The rest of the business was carried on successively at 7 South Frederick Street; 7 South Hanover Street; 201 and 203, and later 198 Buchanan Street. In 1861 it was finally established at Herriot Hill in Stirling Road (now Cathedral Street).

supremacy as a work of English literature. For the Bible is the culmination of the greatest age of English writing: hence the permeation of prose and poetry on both sides of the Atlantic by its rhythms and images. Surely therefore it is appropriate that a publishing house whose founders based their lives on Bible teaching, and whose authors have made no negligible contribution to modern English literature, should have made its greatest advance by printing and publishing the greatest of all books.

Until the eighteenth-century Foulis brothers achieved European renown, Scottish typographers had lagged behind the English craftsmen. It was not, indeed, until 1508—thirty years after Caxton's first book—that King James IV of Scotland authorised Mr. Chepman and Mr. Myllar of "Our Burgh of Edinburgh" to bring a printing press from Flanders and set it up in the Cowgate. Even then, seventy-two years were to pass before Alexander Arbuthnot, "Printer to the King's Majesties, dwelling at Ye Kirke of Field," was licensed to print a full copy of the earlier *Geneva* or *Breeches Bible*—delightfully so-called because its rendering of Genesis III, 7, read: "They sewed fig leaves together and made themselves breeches."[1]

During the next two centuries, a score of Bible printers were licensed, the last being His Majesty's Printers for Scotland—Sir David Hunter Blair and John Bruce—who printed many editions of the Scriptures between 1798 and 1839 and stoutly resisted the least infringement of their monopoly. Such intransigeance naturally roused opposition. The Scottish Bible Societies in whose development William Collins I had played a leading part were importing English Bibles printed under the authority either of the King's Printers in England (Eyre, Strahan & Spottiswoode), or of the Oxford and Cambridge Universities, and were loud in their demands for general free trade in the sale of the Scriptures.[2]

[1] Through the centuries many other Bibles have received jovial nicknames. Those include the Whig Bible, so-called because the beatitude by a printer's error read: "Blessed are the place makers"; and the Bug Bible whose old English translation of a verse in Psalm 91 read: "So that thou shalt not need to be afraid for any bugs by night."

[2] Under the Lord Protector's Act of 1657, Glasgow University had the same privilege of printing Bibles as Oxford and Cambridge.

Thus a quarrel soon arose in which the interest seems to have been commercial rather than Christian. In the early twenties, Hunter Blair secured an interdict preventing Edinburgh and Glasgow booksellers from selling "English printed " Bibles at prices forty per cent less than his own, and then, over-triumphant, took corresponding action against another batch of booksellers and Bible Societies. This proved to be his ultimate undoing. The Evangelicals, especially, reprobated the idea of the King's Printer reaping a monopolistic harvest from sacred seed, while the booksellers were so resentful that another uproar and further lawsuits followed. In 1828, however, the Lord Chancellor pronounced judgment that the King's Printers in Scotland had the right to prevent importation of English versions, just as Eyre, Strathan & Spottiswoode had the right to prohibit importations from Scotland; and so a practice as old as the Reformation came to an end, to the intense annoyance of the Scottish commonalty who had no great love for the Hunter Blair Bibles. At once there was a new outcry of such violence that two successive Select Committees were given the problem to investigate. At the end of this prolonged examination the "Biblical " privileges of the King's (or Queen's) Printer in Scotland were abolished in 1839; English Bibles were allowed in Scotland at will; and all Scottish printers were given the right to print the Scriptures *under bond and caution.*

Most Scottish publishers of standing, including William Collins, Nelson, Oliver and Boyd, Blackie, and Constable immediately applied for licences; whereupon, to ensure accuracy, a Bible Board—consisting of the Moderator of the General Assembly, the Lord Advocate, and the Solicitor-General—was set up (1841) to collect from each potential printer a bond of security of £500 and to pass the proofs. This body worked with commendable zeal. When William Collins' first Testament— printed in 1841-42—was found to contain "three errors " he was required to alter them in the plates. Our old friend Edward Khull was cautioned for similar inaccuracies and requested to "wait on the Moderator as might suit his convenience." Another firm was told severely to look to the state of its plates of the Psalms and also to spell the Lord Advocate's name correctly. Clearly, then, the scrutiny, which continues to this day, was eagle-eyed. It is clear also that the abolition of the monopoly was equally justified, since it led to a reduction of prices on both sides of the Border, greater efficiency in printing, and wider circulation of the Scriptures.

As may be guessed, William I, who ever preferred crusades and commerce to run in double harness, had started to print the Scriptures with tremendous enthusiasm. It was no light task, for the Bible consists of 4,631,056 letters, all to be set up by hand. But he went ahead, and secured licences in 1841 for several New Testaments, including the Pearl Testament of which he printed 30,000 copies. In the winter of 1842 he was printing his first complete Bible. By the end of 1843 he had completed three Bibles —a Diamond 32mo Text, the Nonpareil 12mo Text School Bible, and a Pearl 24mo Text. The father had in fact laid down a granite-like paving. His son lost little time in fitting it with gold setts.

By the middle 'fifties—with ten single-cylinder steam printing machines, five old style printing presses and several litho presses in his works—he issued his first complete Family Bible in medium quarto and was about to embark on more elegant, and, in some instances, luxurious bindings. This was a notable advance. The firm's earliest Bibles—bound in plain dressed sheepskin with stained or sprinkled edges, or in cloth with blind blocking—could never have been classed as works of art. But William II persuaded the tanners to give him goat and calf skins, dressed and dyed; and these new leathers were often embellished by hand-chased brass rims and clasps, and blocked in gold design. By the end of 1860, his first Bible catalogue could boast eighteen editions of the Scriptures ranging from a majestic Imperial quarto size in Turkey morocco costing £4 10s. od. to a Pearl 24mo at one shilling. The sales of all these editions were satisfactory. Of a Royal quarto Bible in full morocco boards, costing one guinea, nine thousand copies were sold in twelve months. No fewer than

250,000 Collins Family Bibles with Henry & Scott's famous Commentaries were sold over the years (at prices ranging from £4 10s. od. for an elaborate production to a minimum of 28s.), until towards the end of the century these massive tomes began to go out of fashion. Equally popular were his illustrated Bibles, a characteristic feature of Bible printing in Victorian times on both sides of the Border. In Scotland William Collins employed David Roberts, R.A., a native of Edinburgh who had earned renown for his scene painting at Drury Lane, his painting of Scottish scenery on the wall of the Edinburgh Assembly Room for King George IV's entertainment by the peers of Scotland, and his cathedral pictures at the Royal Academy. Collins had thus a more than merely competent artist to supply drawings for his first illustrated Bible (1858). By this time, it is noteworthy, his output of Bibles of all sizes totalled about eighty thousand a year.

Not surprisingly, in view of such remarkable progress, he was summoned in 1860 to Westminster to give evidence before yet another Select Committee on Bible printing patents—an old, vexed question which had emerged again with the expiry of Eyre, Strahan & Spottiswoode's Patent as Queen's Printer. William Collins' views on the issue were bound to carry weight, since he was heading towards his ultimate monopoly of Scripture printing north of the Border, and his eyes were already on the teeming English markets.

In his evidence he made a strong plea that Scottish-printed Bibles should be sanctioned in England, although this was already happening unofficially. "English Bible printers," he said with candour, "have never interfered with the sale of Scottish printers' Bibles in England." He then gave the Select Committee the following information about his own progress:

"By 1860 I had printed 17 Bibles in different types and sizes with three more in preparation, besides editions of the New Testament. The number of editions of the English Bible in the catalogue of the Queen's printers for England in 1860 was 21.

"I am also a Binder, and issue the different editions I publish in about 300 various styles.

"I publish Family Bibles with commentary, text by Authority, at 21s. bound. My sale is 1,000 copies monthly.

"Before the abolition of the patent in 1839, the number of Bibles printed in Scotland was under 80,000. From 1831 to 1836 the largest number printed in one year was 105,600, the average falling short of 80,000. From 1854 to 1858 the average was 225,000, and I estimate that this year, 1860, the number may reach 300,000."

Question: "Is your edition similar to Oxford and Cambridge in respect of text and punctuation?"

Reply: "Yes, since I first commenced to publish."

These answers show how far the house had spread its tentacles and how swiftly the energetic publisher was approaching the golden future for which he had planned. In the following year when the House of Commons turned down the Select Committee's recommendation that the Royal Patent should be abolished— leaving Eyre & Spottiswoode as King's Printers to this day— Collins received the Highest Award of Merit at the Crystal Palace International Exhibition for an exhibit of two big Family Bibles. By 1862, when he was appointed Queen's Printer for Scotland,[1] he had also begun to publish many Bible Commentaries, of which the *Library* Commentary brought a spontaneous tribute from the famous Charles Haddon Spurgeon—"I think it is the best Commentary upon the whole Bible which has been issued within the last fifty years "—and an equally warm eulogy from Queen Victoria's favourite spiritual adviser, Dr. Norman MacLeod, a preacher of renown who—let us hope innocently—has since been described by Lytton Strachey as "an innocent Scotch minister."[2]

But Collins editions of the Scriptures were now well known. By 1865 sixteen thousand Bibles, Testaments and Prayer Books were flowing every month from the splendid new three-storey premises at Herriot Hill into which he had moved four years

[1]The 1862 edition of Thomas Campbell's Shakespeare had the imprint: " Glasgow: William Collins, Publisher and Queen's Printer." In the same year the house opened a branch at Cockburn Street, Edinburgh, to which for many years goods were shipped by the Forth and Clyde canal.

[2]*Queen Victoria*, Chapter IX. In the later Phœnix Library edition (Chatto & Windus) *innocent* has been altered to *strenuous* (which may be an *innocent* study in synonyms).

earlier, and where the house of Collins is still established on historic ground. Here, before the Reformation, John Herriot—a cleric in the service of the Cathedral—and other medieval dignitaries had walked among gardens and flowered sidewalks, gazing westward in the gloaming to the mountain sunsets of Argyll, and by day to the green smokeless lands of Eastwood in the south-west. It is unlikely that the go-ahead publisher lingered long among these phantoms of the past. He now had a first-class site, up-to-date printing machines and accomplished printers. Thus equipped, he launched himself into one of the most astounding expansions in the history of British publishing.

CHAPTER X

Across the Oceans
1865-1877

I

IT IS impossible to describe the next phase of this splendid advance in detail. We can only follow the hastening figure of William Collins through the Victorian heyday, see with what stubborn sagacity he widened the whole range of his business, and note the adventurous beginnings of the firm's imperial trade.

In 1865 he reorganised the direction of the business. During the 'fifties, despite his robust physique, he had found undivided control a tax on his powers. So he now invited three of his most able lieutenants to become co-partners in the business. The first subordinate was Robert Henderson, a traveller for the firm in the 'forties, who had spent his evenings in English and Scottish hostelries compiling a popular *Commercial Ready Reckoner*, forerunner of many similar handbooks issued by the house during the 'sixties and 'seventies. His other choices, John Morrison and John Walker, also justified his judgment; for although William Collins was still the all-highest, this cabal of four were able to agree on plans bold in their conception, especially in the field of science, and far-reaching in the result.

The middle decades of the nineteenth century were the seminal period of modern science. In the 'thirties came the

171

electric telegraph and Sir Charles Lyell's *Elements of Geology*; in the 'forties. Sir James Simpson's experiments with chloroform; in the 'fifties Charles Darwin's *Origin of Species*; in the 'sixties Tyndall's famous study on Heat, the founding of the periodical *Nature*, the work on submarine cables of Lord Kelvin (then William Thomson, Professor of Natural Philosophy at Glasgow University), and a multitude of experiments which were to end one day in a blaze of electric light, the clean whine of electric railways, and the telephone.

The partners of the house were intensely stimulated by these scientific revelations, though they had lived in a city of swift mechanical progress too long, and seen too many changes on their own threshold, to gape—like a mid-Victorian Highland chieftain or an English country squire—at the technical finesse of the matured Industrial Revolution. Instead, they planned a series of works encompassing electricity and many other branches of scientific inquiry—acoustics, for example, geology, chemistry, naval architecture, steam, and animal physiology. To this end no expense was spared. The whole series cost £30,000 to produce over the years, of which £10,000 went in authors' fees and royalties. And although part of this new spate naturally joined the steady flow of schoolbooks, many were advanced enough to meet the requirements of such clever students as Collins' own son, William III, whose University studies under Thomson had stimulated his natural mechanical genius. In all, of the seventy-two volumes in the series, thirty-two of them advanced texts, more than two and a half million copies were sold.

To look ahead, the *Science Series* was often to be accompanied by scientific publications of a more occasional kind. The house, for instance, issued in one volume a course of lectures delivered in Glasgow by such leading scientists as Kelvin, Tyndall, Geikie, and Siemens (1879). To look still further ahead, this tradition of deep interest in natural phenomena was to be sustained during the twentieth century by many admirable ventures which will be described in their place.

Reverting to the Victorian 'sixties, the firm's intense scientific activity did not distract them from older educational subjects. Laing's *English Literature* went into thirty-five editions. More than half a million copies were sold of Trotter's *English Grammar*. Dr. Bryce, Rector of Glasgow High School and father of the great jurist Viscount Bryce, wrote and edited a number of books on algebra, geography, astronomy and geology, until at the age of seventy his hammering of eruptive granite on the slopes above Loch Ness brought upon him instantaneous death under a falling mass of stone. Leonard Schmitz, a scholar of European fame, to whom as Rector of the Royal High School at Edinburgh Queen Victoria entrusted the education of King Edward VII and the Duke of Edinburgh, contributed among other works a *Manual of Ancient Geography*, and a *History of the Middle Ages*. John Bartholomew was recruited for the making of many maps. But the list of scholastic books and authors is too prodigious to catalogue. It need only be said that the men of vision at Herriot Hill recruited men of knowledge from the schools and universities to establish their educational reputation on a secure foundation.

It is interesting now to see how authors were rewarded for educational texts three-quarters of a century ago. Undoubtedly hard bargaining obtained between the firm and more than one contributor. When Canon Ridgway was offered £500 to prepare a set of six elementary readers, he stipulated instead for 10s. per printed page—a demand which seems to have produced silence till six months later a minute in the firm's contract book recorded acceptance of the Canon's offer. In the main and in accordance with tradition, educational works were bought outright. Morrison's *Composition* (154 pages) was purchased for £80, Laing's *Literature* for £60, Dr. Schmitz's *History of Rome* and *History of Greece* for £75 each, and Dr. Dick's *Outlines of Natural History* for £100. In the realm of higher education, Professor Young received £150 for his *Physical Geography*, and Professor Cleland £150 for a book on *Animal Physiology*. A few volumes were, however, published on a royalty, or, as it was then called, a lordship basis. Mr. Chardenal's three French books brought him, for every 1,000 copies sold, £12 2s. 6d. for the first book (published at 1s. 6d.),

£22 10s. 0d. for the second book (2s.), and £50 for the third (3s. 6d.).

But the demand for educational reading was too great to be satisfied by only original works, and the firm had recourse to reprints. In 1866, along with a new edition of D'Aubigné's five volumes, came a new six-volume 8vo edition of Glassford Bell's scholarly Shakespeare, followed two years later by a forty-volume set of single Shakespeare plays which was to stay popular for another thirty years. The *Complete Works of Robert Burns*, and the *Poetical Works of Sir Walter Scott* in two volumes with "numerous steel engravings" appeared in 1867. During the last seven months of the following year the sales of illustrated dictionaries reached more than a quarter of a million copies, and Herriot Hill was advertising yet another of the many Glasgow editions of *The Pilgrim's Progress*.

II

In the Collins family, traditions die slowly if they die at all. Just as William I had harnessed public service and private enterprise in a supply team, so his son was by this time devoting himself to the municipality of Glasgow, where several causes lay near his heart. His paramount interest remained temperance reform, an enterprise which he hoped to advance by reducing the hours for the sale of liquor, and restricting the number of licences. But being strongly Gladstonian in economy, he also believed that much of the city's expenditure was extravagant—to the detriment of town improvement schemes already in hand. It was on these two main planks and little else that he had been returned unopposed for the Fifth Ward of the City of Glasgow on 1st December 1868, to lead thereafter a most respectable double life.

Councillor Collins' conduct during his first year on the City Council was humorously related five years later in the lively but now long-defunct Glasgow *Bailie:*

"Such a tilting and fighting with windmills as he carried on during the first year of his Councillorship had never been seen since the days when Don Quixote made his famous onslaught on the plain of Montiel. And, extreme as he often was, Mr. Collins was yet an opponent not to be despised. Ungainly and gaunt as ' Agag-bind-their-kings-in-chains,' he was equally formidable in an encounter. With his figures noted down on a quaint little scrap of paper, he attacked the civic estimates with as much vigour and persistency as ever did Joe Hume the budget of a Chancellor of the Exchequer. Naturally, however, as is the custom of extreme folk of every kind, Mr. Collins gradually cooled down. He continued as keen an advocate for retrenchment as ever, but he chose his ground of attack with greater judgment. Naturally, too, he came to be listened to with greater attention, and assumed altogether a superior position to that of the mere carping critic. It is even rumoured that, upon a late occasion, when the local president was choosing his cabinet, Mr. Collins was offered a position wherefrom he might dispense judgment at the River Police Court. He, however, it is added, though a lover of water, declined to have anything to do with the element as a Bailie; and he therefore continues plain Councillor Collins still. Mr. Collins was right, and exhibited a just sense of the weight of his own claims. Such a clear-headed shrewd man of business, and one so anxious for the public weal, cannot be passed over; and in some future distribution of honours, he will doubtless attain to the dignity of a City Magistrate. Outside municipal life, Mr. Collins is the head of a publishing firm, which is one of the most eminent in its way, not only in Glasgow, but in the three Kingdoms. The name of their schoolbooks is legion, their issue is extraordinary, and they are assistants to tuition round the entire world. A man able to conduct the affairs of a gigantic concern of this kind, honours the citizens of Glasgow by assisting in their government."

Clearly there was no Bumbledom about the new Councillor. Nor, despite his civic preoccupations, was there any slackening in the flow of books from Herriot Hill. If he ever paused to look back on his past thirty years, he must have felt a stirring of pride. At the beginning of 1839, the bookshop and the retail side of the firm's stationery manufacture had given employment to one man, one advanced apprentice, three boys and a traveller who drove round the country in an open machine: in the printing works there were not more than eight or nine printers, and these worked sixty-six hours a week. But in the same year, he would remember, steam presses had been installed in more spacious premises; and ever since, the expansion had been so remarkable that in 1869 the book-printing plant consisted of sixteen single and double cylinder printing machines, seven litho presses, and a number of small complementary presses, including the old hand equipment from Candleriggs Court. Yet even this impressive forest of steel was barely sufficient for its purpose. In this very year the records show an output of 1,352,421 printed and bound works, a most surprising total which master and men must have regarded with pride, especially one or two old men whose memory went back to the firm's earliest days.

William Collins' consideration for these faithful old servants and indeed for all his staff is evident from the events of 1870. He had already, quite voluntarily, reduced the weekly working hours of his printers from sixty-six to sixty—an example quickly followed by the other master printers of Glasgow. By the end of 1870 he had reduced them again to fifty-seven—an announcement which his workers greeted, said a contemporary report, with "immense applause," and which we can now see was, for the time, an enlightened act of social justice.

In this harmonious atmosphere, the house entered the second half of the golden decade begun in 1865. In the 'sixties the main body of its advance had consisted of scientific texts, schoolbooks and the Scriptures—all marching in step. During the 'seventies, the advance was to be more rapid for three reasons—the effect on the business of William Collins' two lively sons as partners, the Education Acts of 1870 (England) and 1872 (Scotland), and a piece of strategic daring in the final decision to extend the sale of Collins books across the oceans on the grand scale.[1]

The part played by the sons was noteworthy. Alexander—like the rest of his family no pensive dreamer—greatly extended Bible sales, while William III applied his mechanical flair to the

[1] In 1872, also, the London office was moved from 17 Warwick Square, where it had moved in the late 'fifties from Paternoster Row, to 4 Bridewell Place where office and warehouse were combined.

144, Cathedral Street, Glasgow

technique of manufacture. Of the two, William III was the more outstanding. An intensely individualistic, scientific youth, as much enamoured of paintings as of his beloved pistons, and fitting readily into no prepared groove as will appear, he was still the child of his environment: and that was one where the spirit of Energy had always reigned supreme. The city's population in 1870 was in fact approaching half a million. Since mid-century the doubling of the nation's tonnage and the trebling of its railway mileage had hastened the building of furnaces and factories on Clydeside. Moreover in this very year, at the height of the Franco-Prussian war, steel manufacture came to the west of Scotland to herald a new ingot age. In the wake of steel came great ships, and again Glasgow's wealth multiplied. But all these stirring events of 1870 deserve closer study, since they illustrate the extraordinary capacity of these Victorian publishers not only to create but to capitalise opportunities.

For some years the demand for the house's stationery had been exceeding the supply. To solve this exasperating problem, William III invented a machine which by folding, gumming and drying envelopes in one operation produced, in 1870, one hundred and eighty thousand envelopes in one day.[1] The arrival of steel was signalised by still more books on engineering. The Franco-Prussian war, though Britain was not directly involved, raged on Britain's doorstep: within a few weeks of its outbreak, a Collins map was on sale showing roads, railways and fortified towns in the theatre of war. Public demand for dictionaries appreciated noticeably during the year: by its end the *Library Dictionary*, planned earlier, with more than one thousand pages and one thousand wood engravings, was being widely advertised at 10s. 6d. The Forster Education Act meant a steep rise in the number of schools: at once new schoolbooks were planned, and the existing output increased. Three years later it became clear that the effect of the Education Act reached farther than was at first realised. With lightning swiftness the Collins partners not only expanded their output of text-books, but also floated a

[1]Ten years later the daily output was half a million.

monthly illustrated penny *School Newspaper*—the first number of which described the proposed English Channel Tunnel, a balloon ascent, the diary of a North Pole expedition, and an account of Stanley's African explorations. This journal lasted into the nineteen-twenties.

There was also something for the children's mothers. In the early 'sixties, Mrs. Beeton's *The Book of Household Management*—the story of which, by her descendant Nancy Spain, the house was to publish three-quarters of a century later—had begun its historic career in London. In Glasgow, in 1872, the house produced *Domestic Cookery* (for which Mrs. Hind got £80) and *Domestic Medicine*, two long-selling forerunners of Elizabeth Craig's cookery books which Collins have published in our own day.

By 1875 the time was ripe for another revolution. It will be remembered that in the early 'sixties William II became publisher to the Scottish School Book Association. Since then he had produced 139 volumes for it. But finding the arrangements rather cumbrous—its members, incidentally, supplied schoolbook copy for an average royalty of fifteen per cent—he now bought the Association out and put its officials on his own pay-roll. This stroke, brilliant in its simplicity, smoothed out many difficulties, and production again rose. It was indeed so vast by this time that in 1875 there were 920 schoolbooks in the catalogue, compared with 571 ten years before. Meanwhile, the number of Collins employees had risen to more than 1,200.

Thus do sagacity and hard work bring their rewards. As he looked back over the years to the days when his father was grappling with adversity and he himself was a twelve-year-old apprentice, one wonders if William II ever read with special emotion the lines of his favourite poet, Tennyson:

> *The little seed they laughed at in the dark*
> *Has riven and cleft the soil, and grown a bulk*
> *Of spanless girth, that lays on every side*
> *A thousand arms and rushes to the sun.*

His own thousand arms were now about to rush to the sun in all the English-speaking parts of the globe.

III

It was, by this time, almost fifty years since the first consignment of Collins books had gone by sailing ship from Greenock to Nova Scotia. Since then, the overseas trade had developed so steadily that many another publisher would have been satisfied with the imperial gains already in the hand. Not so William Collins and his sons. As Scots, their eyes were traditionally on the ends of the earth, upon great prairies, gold-mining villages and schools in lonely outposts. As shrewd men of business, they realised, too, the intrinsic value of the markets shimmering under distant suns. And thus, no sooner had the Franco-Prussian war ended than they resolved on an overseas campaign to match their progress at home. This decision—a climacteric in the present story—was implemented by decisive action.

To the "long wash of Australasian seas" sailed John McLeod, an experienced salesman, to report on the advantages of direct permanent representation in Australia and New Zealand (1872). Already in both Dominions William Collins enjoyed a kind of favoured family treatment, partly because of the venturesomeness his travellers or agents had already displayed, but also because so many Free Kirk Scotsmen had emigrated to the Antipodes after the Disruption.

To New Zealand, for instance, in the year of Doctor Chalmers' death, had sailed from Glasgow the 550-ton copper-bottomed barque *Philip Laing* with two hundred and seventy Scottish emigrants on board. Among them was the Rev. Thomas Burns, nephew of Scotland's national poet, whose first act on landing among the native flax of Otago was to name the middle of the bay, on which Dunedin now stands, Port Chalmers in memory of the settlers' especial hero. Burns and his co-religionists— Disruptionists to a man—not only revered Chalmers but respected the honoured, and to them familiar name of the first William Collins as a giant of their old cause. Nothing could be more fitting than that in this Dominion—William I's descendants should now have a branch.

In the wake of these earnest pioneers had flowed a stream of books from their native land. Indeed, as early as 1865 the house had published a special edition of the Prayer Book for New Zealand and most of the Herriot Hill schoolbooks were to be found in New Zealand schools.

So too with Australia, which had developed rapidly after the discovery of gold at Bathurst and Ballarat in the early 'fifties. The Collins books entered Australia early; and for many years the firm of Bright Bros. in Sydney, acting as agents for the house, brought into the country varied and curious shipments— Bibles, schoolbooks, and household publications as a matter of course, but also, since stationery has always been part of the Collins production, wafers, sealing-wax, quill pens, pencils, writing papers, envelopes and ledgers. As the demand grew, especially for reference books and Bibles, the firm of McGreadie, Thomas & Niven were appointed sole canvassers for all part publications of the house in Australia and New Zealand; and the Glasgow output—12,000 miles away—took another forward leap. But the visionaries of Herriot Hill were still so dissatisfied that in 1874 another traveller, Thomas Walker, made a two-year tour, rewarded by large contracts for schoolbooks and stationery in Queensland, Victoria, South Australia, New South Wales and Tasmania. On his return to Glasgow it was decided to open a permanent warehouse and showroom at 69 York Street, Sydney under the family name.[1]

While McLeod and Walker were carving out these new fortunes for the firm under the Southern Cross, yet another trusted travel-ler, James Sherriff, was hard at work under an Indian sun, visit-ing customers in Bombay, Calcutta, Madras and Colombo, and seeking new markets in the Western Provinces.

The other side of the world witnessed the same imperative

[1] The first separate branch for New Zealand was not opened until 1888.

drive. In 1872 William Collins III, who had crossed the Atlantic to study both the American book market and the latest American printing and binding machinery, brought back a disc-ruling machine which ruled both sides of a ledger page. At the same time other representatives of Herriot Hill toured Canada, that vast Dominion into which domestic poverty had cataracted so many Highland Scots during the nineteenth century. But this was familiar ground. As far back as July 1825, the sailing ship *Mercator* had sailed from the Clyde with packages of Dr. Chalmers' works and the *Select Library of Christian Authors* on board for Messrs. Mackinlay of Halifax. Thereafter, William Collins' transatlantic connections grew fast among the welcoming population beside the Great Lakes and across the prairies. His books were bought by the Hudson Bay Company, carried by coach and buggy into remote fastnesses, and increasingly after 1836—as Canada lengthened her then sixteen miles of railway track—by rail. Thus when Canada was created a Dominion (1867), the house had already a healthy market for books and stationery in Newfoundland, Nova Scotia, New Brunswick and Prince Edward Island, and was gradually extending, on the mainland, to Quebec, Montreal, Ottawa and Toronto, where bookshops exist to this day which have been on the Collins list for a century. Much of the credit for this steady growth goes to " Ready Reckoner " Henderson, who roved about Eastern Canada in the early 'sixties; some goes also to Messrs. Briggs & Co. of Toronto (Ryerson Press) who handled all the Collins trade west of Winnipeg and as far as the Pacific seaboard until 1901; and some to the members of the firm who designed a set of Maritime Readers specially for Canadian schools, a Canadian Geography (first edition 6,500 copies), and a history of the Maritime Provinces which was to sell for thirty years.

In Canada, as in Australia, the house merited its success. Imaginatively it had scrutinised the text-books designed for export and perceiving that some were too rigid in form and matter, with illustrations too redolent of the Old World, it had been wise enough to stress in letterpress and pictures alike the

Dominion's surprising beauties and the expansion of its industry and agriculture. Dominion scholars were also recruited as writers and editors—a progressive policy which produced glittering results. To take only one example: of seven primers and readers, compiled by Australian teachers but printed in Glasgow, almost four million copies were sold within twenty years. Simultaneously the firm's long arm was reaching out to the West Indies, especially Jamaica, Trinidad and Barbados, for whose benefit special school readers were prepared by local editors, printed in Glasgow, and shipped across the Atlantic.

There remained Africa, which must have seemed at first a huge, inscrutable market. Collins religious publications, however, had penetrated to that dark vastness as early as the 'thirties; and from mid-century onwards, the founding of schools in the Gold Coast and Nigeria by missionary enterprise had opened up new and profitable channels for educational works, to be followed in the 'seventies by the printing of the Gospels in native tongues. Three decades later, permanent Collins representatives were to be appointed in South Africa to disseminate not only English books but readers and dictionaries in their own tongue among the Afrikander population.

IV

While his ambassadors were thus encircling the globe, the Great Mogul at Herriot Hill—fifty-six years of age in 1873—ruled his business in splendour and sustained his stubborn role on the City Council. Still panoplied with his "quaint little scrap of paper," we find him repeatedly demanding the authority of law to prevent young children of school age working in factories; denouncing enlargement of the city's boundaries as "large and useless expenditure"; calling for the exploitation of the coal under Glasgow Green and the devotion of the proceeds to extend the city's open spaces; appealing in and out of season for early-closing of public houses.

On all these counts he seems to have been most vociferous in 1873, which was for him a memorable year. During its passage he was elected, like his father before him, President of the Glasgow Company of Stationers; the lineage of his firm and family was further assured by the arrival of a grandson, William IV, in the house of his son Alexander who had married a lady named Cornelia Pattison; and at the end of the year—in the city of Bailie Nicol Jarvie—he became Bailie William Collins.

As a prominent local Liberal he was always on the City Hall platform when Glasgow's three Liberal members gave an annual account of their stewardship—an event eagerly anticipated by the noisier members of the community. On one occasion the crowd was so tightly packed, said the *Glasgow Herald*, that "the Bailies of the Second City squatted like Hottentots on the floor." On another it was noticed that when the Lord Provost took the chair—in accordance with tradition—he was "met with serpentine and other animal noises of the most hideous description." "I have been lately in America," started one M.P.—a remark greeted with "hear, hear," and laughter, and a voice "How is Emma?" (great laughter). "I did not go to America specially to study political or social questions" (hear, hear, and the usual voice: "To see Emma"), "but I can assure you that neither my ears nor eyes were shut to what was going on around me. . . . Well, when I was in the very far West, I had the pleasure of meeting a friend of mine—one of the hopes of the Conservative Party—the hon. member for Westminster." (A voice: "Sir Roger," and great laughter.)

It must have been difficult to combat this traditional technique. Fortunately for Bailie Collins, the Glasgow M.P.s were more obvious targets than the magistrates, though these active men were kept busy enough by many other noises and interruptions. Thus in 1875, pitched battles in the streets followed the Irish population's celebration of Daniel O'Connell's centenary. "To the exuberant Irish spirit," explained the *Glasgow Herald* on Monday, 9th August, "must be ascribed scenes of disgraceful rioting which occurred at Partick in the evening (of Saturday) and yesterday disturbed the Sabbath quiet of the Burgh." It appeared from the account that two hundred O'Connellites after hailing the Liberator were returning to the then burgh of Partick. Unhappily, one of them in a fit of enthusiasm punched a bystander on the face, a *casus belli* which started a free fight between the watching crowds and the procession. For two days the noise of battle rolled—with an interval for sleep after midnight on the Saturday—until, as often happens in war, the fighting became confused and what had been originally an Orange-Catholic affray became, since "the Irishman's love of fighting had been aroused," a trial of strength between the erstwhile processionists and the police. After many casualties due to sticks and stones, the police arrested sixty prisoners of war; and early on Monday, said the *Glasgow Herald*, "the streets were relapsing into the ordinary silence of the early morning." In the aftermath of such incidents, Bailie Collins had full employment.

A more pleasing event in his life this same year was the birth of his grandson Godfrey (in the Alexander Glen Collins family) —a significant arrival, for although he was to play a vital part in the business, Godfrey was to earn perhaps greater public distinction, in the twentieth century, as its first Cabinet Minister.

By this time William Collins' career as a Bailie was nearly over, but new responsibilities were on the way, though he was already a member of twenty-four committees and President of the Scottish Temperance League. His interests like his business were widely-ranging, his philanthropy far-reaching. Continually during this period, the Glasgow newspapers report his munificence —£50 to an Indian famine relief fund, £50 to relieve distress after the famous Blantyre colliery disaster, and so on. It seemed natural, therefore, in view of such manifold services to his community that on 10th November 1877, a fellow-Bailie should rise in the City Council to propose him as Lord Provost of Glasgow both for his own public-spirited qualities and as "the son of one who was conspicuous in the city of his day for the active interest he took in many good works." In accepting office,

William Collins II aptly defined his attitude to all affairs in his first sentences:

"It has been truly said that property has its duties as well as its rights. I think it may with equal truth be said that position has its responsibilities as well as its privileges."

Henceforward, for four years, he was the executive head not only of his own employees, then 1,300 strong, but of the six hundred thousand inhabitants of the British Empire's Second City.

CHAPTER XI

The Long Victorian Afternoon

1877-1895

I

JOHN GALT'S liquid satirical prose survives mainly in two unforgettable classics of early nineteenth-century Scottish literature—*The Annals of the Parish* and *The Provost*.[1]

The magistrate of his novel was Provost Pawkie of Gudetown, a whimsically corrupt municipality, where, said the Provost of his associates, "since the cloven foot of self-interest was now and then to be seen aneath the robe of public principle. . . . I had, therefore, but a straightforward course to pursue, in order to overcome all their wiles and devices." Provost Pawkie's course was not, however, always successful; and on one occasion when he faced the dissatisfied populace, a dead cat, "whizzing through the air like a comet," knocked him to the floor despite his exalted view of himself as an "instrument to represent the supreme power and authority of Majesty."

When Lord Provost Collins succeeded to the civic headship of Glasgow, these palmy days were over. Jeffrey's reform of burgh administration in the 'thirties, and his own persistent scrutiny of

---

[1] *The Annals of the Parish* is the first-person story of the thrice-married Reverend Mr. Balwhidder who ended his reminiscences with the pleasant thought that he had no more to say—"saving only to wish a blessing on all people from on high, where I soon hope to be, and to meet there all the old long-departed sheep of my flock, especially the first and second Mrs. Balwhidders."

the city's accounts, had left little room for municipal aggrandise-
ment. On the other hand, the people of Glasgow were gifted
with a candour which spared neither Provost nor Parliamentarian,
and in a hard-drinking city the first teetotal civic head in its long
history—" Water Willie " as he was known—was too big a target
to miss.

In the meantime thousands of fanatical temperance workers all
over Scotland were waiting expectantly for outward and visible
signs of their stubborn leader's principle. For they knew their
man. They knew that William Collins' make-up hid a nub of hard
courage—that order of courage which takes a man over a river
amid a storm of bullets, not in an heroic glow but cold-bloodedly
because the crossing is vital to his cause. It was in such a spirit
that within a few weeks of his election he decided on a public
coronation of his principles before an audience of one thousand
six hundred guests invited by himself to a " musical and scientific
conversazione." It was a resplendent occasion. To the music of
Handel, Beethoven and Brahms, the genial, unruffled Lord
Provost and his lady moved through a fine display of snowy
shirt fronts and sweeping dresses. Around the walls were displayed numerous scientific devices, including a newfangled
instrument called the telephone which excited very great interest.
The confections are reported to have been luscious and elaborate,
the coffee and iced liquids delectable. But, for the first time at a
civic entertainment on the banks of the Clyde, there was no
strong drink, neither whisky from the north nor sun-mellowed
vintages from the south. Nor indeed from that symbolic night
were alcoholic beverages ever served at civic functions for which
Lord Provost Collins was personally responsible.[1]

By strange coincidence on that same evening, the *enfant
terrible* of the City Council, Councillor Martin, addressed the
annual soirée of the Glasgow Wine, Spirit and Beer Trade.

[1]He went even farther the following year when, according to the *Glasgow Herald*
(30th March 1878), he gave similar entertainment to "a large party of ladies and
gentlemen, members of the learned professions and their friends, and others." Again
there was music, but this time a temperance lecturer was introduced midway in the
proceedings.

"There has been a great deal said," declared the Councillor, "about the evils of the drinking customs. But we are told that in ancient times there was both eating and drinking, and marrying, and giving in marriage, and the flood came and swept them all away. Yet here we are still pursuing the same practices. And when we cease to marry and be given in marriage, then will we cease to eat and drink. (Loud applause and laughter.) It gives me great pleasure to be able to stand here and to look upon so goodly an assemblage as is here met. I look around and I must say that I cannot for the life of me see the bloated faces and the brandy noses which are said to be the distinguishing feature of your trade. (Great laughter.) Your case is not like that of a clockmaker we have in the East-end who used to be asked how much it took to paint his nose. He could not tell, he said, but he thought it would have been much cheaper to have papered it. (Loud laughter.) The other night I was at a dinner at the Lord Provost's table, and I received a large card for his party to-night in the New Halls. I, however, elected to be here in preference to being there. (Loud applause.) The order of things at His Lordship's table will be understood when I say that we get that (holding up a tumbler partially filled with water). (Loud laughter.) We get a tumbler two-thirds full of water with a chunk or two of ice in it—(renewed laughter)— and that is food and drink for the month of December. (Continued laughter.) But it will keep you cool. (Roars of laughter.)"

Here surely was lack of taste, but time brought its revenges. The ebullient Martin eventually lost his seat on the Council: apologies for his misbegotten speech were made at a similar banquet the following year; and in any event, William Collins was much too preoccupied to waste time on his less busy critics.

There is no occasion to chronicle all the multifarious events of his civic reign. But several deserve note.

Almost his first official duty was to receive on behalf of the Corporation a statue of Thomas Campbell the poet. Now in his young days the Lord Provost had himself cherished literary ambitions. Of his prose the only record left is the diary of his 1837 trip to London: his prosody is memorialised even more briefly by the following stanza solemnly ascribed on the title

page of an old family album to "William Collins, Junior.
Gent."—

> *Life's a medley all agree;*
> *This Book's a medley you shall see—*
> *Sometimes grave and sometimes gay,*
> *Changing like an April day,*
> *To suit the taste, whate'er it be,*
> *From wisdom down to repartee;*
> *Or if 'tis pleasure to the eye,*
> *The varied charms of painting vie—*
> *The autographs of many a hand*
> *Of fair and wise throughout the land.*
> *Thus, while assistance we invite,*
> *The Pencil, graver, pen, unite*
> *To form of it a pastime meet*
> *To make a vacant hour pass sweet.*

There is, indeed, slender enough evidence here of "the quick
Dreams, The passion-winged Ministers of thought." Yet despite
the tenuous proof of aptitude, the author had so genuine a love
of the classical forms of literature that his compositors and
printers were at work on an ambitious series of poetry reprints
at the very moment their employer was reminding a large crowd
that Thomas Campbell—"secure in immortality"—was "sprung
from that merchant class whose integrity, energy, and enterprise
in the last century contributed so greatly to make Glasgow
flourish into the great city of to-day." These reprints deserve
honourable mention.

Some years earlier, Edward Moxon had begun to publish
Moxon's Popular Poets with critical and biographical prefaces by
William Michael Rossetti, talented brother of Christina and Dante
Gabriel, and a foundation member of the pre-Raphaelites. By
1871, however, Moxon's star was on the wane, and Ward, Lock
and Company bought most of his copyrights. In turn, William
Collins took over the *Popular Poets*, which he re-christened *The
Grosvenor Poets* and issued in nineteen volumes, all beautifully
printed and bound, and destined to have an immense vogue
until the 1920s, by which time their editors included John

Drinkwater and Alfred Noyes.[1] Our publisher thus spoke with a twin interest when he stood on George Square and recited:

> *The meteor flag of England*
> *Shall yet terrific burn*
> *Till danger's troubled night depart*
> *And the Star of Peace return.*

The rest of his public appearances were exceedingly various. We hear of him attending a ball given by the Duke of Hamilton at Hamilton Palace in honour of the Prince of Wales; accepting a statue of David Livingstone on behalf of the city; extending civic greetings at different times to the Crown Prince of Austria, Princess Louise, the Maharajah of Cooch Behar, the Grand Duke Alexis and the Chinese Ambassador; laying the coping stone of the Queen's Dock and the foundation stone of a bridge in Kelvingrove Park; escorting Lord Rosebery to an art exhibition; pleading before a House of Lords Committee that Glasgow public-houses should be closed earlier and the duty on spirits increased; and finally, after their marriage, toasting the Duke and Duchess of Connaught at a meeting of the City Council where he announced good-humouredly that the water of Loch Katrine—"that emblem of health"—was available for those who shared his own principles.

It was all very splendid. But the Lord Provost's stately progress was suddenly interrupted by catastrophe. On 1st October 1878 the City of Glasgow Bank crashed in one of the most tragic bank failures in financial history.

For some time there had been ominous suggestions that the Bank was in difficulties, though its outward habiliments seemed far from threadbare. Its deposits were reckoned to be more than £8,000,000, its capital £1,000,000; and for years its many shareholders had been enjoying dividends of at least nine per cent. By September, however, sinister rumours that the bank was unstable seeped through the city and eventually its directors

---

[1] The poets in the Series were—Burns, Byron, Cowper, Goldsmith, Hood, Campbell, Longfellow, Milton, Moore, Pope, Scott, Shakespeare, Whittier, Wordsworth, Shelley, Mrs. Hemans, Mrs. Browning, Lowell. There was also an Anthology, *Gems of National Poetry.*

appealed to other banks for assistance. These wiser institutions at once made their help conditional on an enquiry, which revealed —almost at a glance—that the City of Glasgow Bank's losses could not be less than £3,000,000. Any sort of accommodation was therefore refused; and soon after midnight on 1st October the newspapers were informed that the Bank's 133 branches had stopped payment.

To Scotland this collapse was a national tragedy. But so widespread was its effect that the whole of the British financial world reeled, when the losses of an institution always secure in public trust were seen to exceed £5,000,000, while many of its more recent balance sheets were so clearly falsified that the securities and gold reserves held by the Bank were respectively £1,000,000 and £200,000 less than they should have been. In due course the Directors and the Secretary were convicted in the High Court of Justiciary in Edinburgh. But long before that condign outcome of their villainy many families and industries were irretrievably ruined. For although the wiser merchant princes had shunned a financial institution which seemed to be overflamboyant, the less wary shareholders included a pitiful list of widows and spinsters, retired doctors and clergymen who had been enticed to invest their entire savings in the Bank by its consistently high dividends. In fact, the circle of distress widened so quickly that it soon became clear that only public philanthropy on a large scale could relieve the worst cases.

It was fortunate at such a moment that Glasgow had a philanthropic and energetic Lord Provost. William Collins immediately started a relief fund with several thousand pounds already collected privately from wealthy citizens—one recalls the great church-building campaign of his father—and then summoned a meeting of important citizens to float his fund publicly.

"I feel," he said, "as if I cannot trust myself to speak of the great calamity which has fallen on this community; and not on this community only, but in every district in our land. Hundreds, I might almost say thousands, have been reduced from comparative affluence to stern poverty, and that by no fault of their own. This is not the time or the place to dwell on the causes which have led to this national calamity. Neither can we realise the depth of the misery which it has brought upon many homes, dethroning reason in not a few cases, and hastening its victims to the silence of the grave. While we cannot but admire the expressions of strong resolve and the determination to face their difficulties bravely by standing shoulder to shoulder at the late meeting of shareholders, let it be our part, by an expression of our warmest sympathy, not in words only, but in generous deeds, to alleviate these difficulties by shedding some rays of light and hope over the gloom in which so many of our fellow countrymen and countrywomen are surrounded."

His own contribution to the fund was £1,000, and at the city Council he moved that the Glasgow Corporation should head the list with £5,000. By the end of the first week in November he had collected £80,000. Three weeks later, when the Scottish total was £280,000, the Lord Provost was throwing his net so much wider that his appeal was read in London at a meeting of "gentlemen connected with Scotland." By Christmas Day, when Scottish contributions alone amounted to almost £343,000, the Lord Provost was also running a relief fund for the benefit of Glasgow's 4,000 unemployed to which he gave £200. Nor was this the limit of his generosity. He made special arrangements at Christmas for thousands of the poorer victims of the bank crash to be entertained at his own expense at a chain of "treats" in five of the largest halls in the city—with tea, presents and a concert.

In furtherance of his Bank Fund the Lord Provost showed both energy and ingenuity. Not only did he make personal appeals to wealthy industrialists, but he also raised £470 from public Shakespeare readings by the famous actress Helen Faucit, and he even urged the celebrated author of *The Cloister and the Hearth* to stir the public conscience with a novel on the bank crash theme.

Charles Reade's reply was characteristic:

"It is most proper that the pen should take up the cause in this case, should expose the iniquity and paint the misery of the

William Collins, 1846-1906

sufferers so as to excite universal sympathy if possible. But I do not think fiction is the proper form. The reader of fiction is narrow and self-indulgent. He will read no story the basis of which is not sexual. I feel I could not write a good fiction or command readers on such a subject. Indeed, I have made a trifling experiment in that line already. Guided by the deaths and lunacies that followed the stoppage of the Leeds Bank, I endeavoured in my novel *Hard Cash* to impress upon the novel-reader that a fraudulent Banker is a murderer as well as a thief. I even wrote a list of victims to prove it. It was wisdom wasted. Neither the novel-reading ass, nor the criticism ass received it. It was never commented on, and I believe everybody skipped it. Besides this there are other difficulties. A story—such as I write—can only be founded on a plot, and the distresses of several shareholders and depositors are not a plot. They are mere (——) facts. To all this I must add something personal. I am old, and afflicted with a cruel cough, which subdues my energy so that for many months I have been obliged to decline all commissions of that serious kind."

In the end William Collins and his coadjutors collected the impressive sum of £400,000. He also, in the same year and with the help of his son Alexander, collected £3,500 from an art exhibition in aid of Glasgow's Royal Infirmary.

II

Municipal office, burdensome though it may be, has of course its own rewards. On 6th December 1879 William Collins had the satisfaction of presenting on behalf of his native city a municipal address to his great hero. His speech, which followed the rhetorical fashion of the day, was not only a heartfelt tribute to a towering political figure but also in the light of history a remarkably accurate estimate of the man.

"We believe," he said to Mr. Gladstone, "that most of your fellow-countrymen, to whom your name is a household word, look up to you as a representative of all those qualities which go to make up what has been described to be the noblest work of God, ' an honest man.' We recognise in you a statesman of commanding intellect— of brilliant genius and of high-toned principles—a born leader of your fellowmen. A financier who has with almost magical skill dealt with the many-sided phases of national taxation in such a manner as to minimise the burdens imposed upon the British ratepayer, while at the same time securing the maximum of good from the national expenditure. An orator who can with unequalled power sway at will the hearts and carry conviction to the intellects of all classes of society. A scholar who has illustrated the choicest treasures of the literature of Greece, and contributed in an eminent degree to the political, ecclesiastical and social literature of our times. A philanthropist, whose time and talents have been unreservedly devoted to promote the happiness and ameliorate the conditions, not only of your own countrymen, but of the suffering and oppressed of every nationality."

It is not surprising that the Lord Provost had a special affection for the statesman with whom he had a close temperamental affinity, and who had done so much to forward so many of his own pet causes—literature, philanthropy, retrenchment, and above all Liberalism, of which he himself was now a frequent advocate on the hustings. Thus, amid the winter snows of 1879-80 when Gladstone embarked on the Midlothian campaign, his chief lieutenant in the West of Scotland sloughed off the robes of office and plunged into the hurly-burly with equal ardour. At a meeting in the City Hall he outspokenly introduced the Liberal candidates for the City. Lord Beaconsfield's policy he thought "reactionary, wasteful, and unconstitutional," while his Ministry had "imperilled, if not sacrificed British interests in almost every part of the world," and "neglected, even opposed legislation for the social improvement and political elevation of the vast masses of the people in our kingdom." Many similar utterances are recorded in the public prints of the time.

But in that winter his duties as active politician and Chief Magistrate were nearing their end, and varied recognitions of his public services began to pour in upon him. In January 1880 he received an elaborate address on vellum from the Glasgow Company of Stationers, which he acknowledged with a tribute to his father:

"I received from my revered parent," he said, "the inheritance of a business it has been part of my life-work to build up, and now to seek to place on a basis of permanence; and I also received, what I value still more, the legacy of the fragrant memory of his good name, which I hope I shall carry to my grave without dishonour or disgrace."

A month later 1,500 of his employees assembled in the City Hall to celebrate his business jubilee; and in October, when he appeared at the City Council for the last time as Lord Provost, member after member spoke of his "devoted and constant attention to the duties of his office," his "amiable disposition," his "great experience" and his "natural modesty." He was to remain on the Council and later the Glasgow School Board for some years as a private member; but further honours were still to come in a larger sphere. When the Glasgow Town Council met in September 1881 for its usual monthly meeting, the new Lord Provost began its business by saying: "I observe, gentlemen, our esteemed colleague, Sir William Collins, present"—a remark greeted with prolonged applause. For the publisher had been summoned to Holyroodhouse on 26th August to receive the accolade from Queen Victoria, and Glasgow was genuinely delighted.[1] Many of its citizens differed profoundly from "Water Willie," but they respected his stubborn honesty of purpose. *Quiz*, a humorous periodical which mercilessly lampooned every public character in the city, forthwith published a cartoon of Sir William—he was now sixty-four years of age—drinking water from a pump, with the following malicious parody for caption:

> *A SOMETIME down-cast old man,*
> *A knighted at last old man,*
> *A feeble and watery*
> *Carriage and yacht-ery,*
> *Troubles all past old man.*

But such pleasantries could not detract from his prestige. He remained on many public committees, presided over the City Improvement Trust which for years, like an eroding sea, had

---

[1] The ceremony was attended by Mr. Childers, Secretary of State for War, as Minister in attendance.

been eating away some of the worst slums in Glasgow's old region, and continued to press for the acquisition of open spaces. It is to his negotiations that present-day Glasgow citizens owe the handsome Cathedral Square, only a bow shot or two away from the present Collins printing works in Cathedral Street. His temperance enthusiasm was of course as keen as ever, in witness of which the Collins' Memorial Drinking Fountain, erected by his admirers, stands to this day at Glasgow Green.

The unveiling of this fountain in the presence of some fifty thousand people on 31st October 1881 led to astonishing scenes, when a procession of ten thousand enthusiasts with bands, flags, mottoes and emblems of temperance societies from many parts of Scotland marched from the centre of the city through crowds so vast that all traffic came to a standstill. This long procession then merged into another waiting crowd of at least forty thousand people on Glasgow Green, where unfortunately the noise was so great that most of the speeches were imperfectly heard, though the speech of Lord Provost Ure, who received the fountain on behalf of the City, has been preserved in fragments:

"I am not here," he said in one passage, "to give my unqualified approval of the strict abstemiousness which many of those around me practise and would like to see others practise, but I am here to say that the manner in which Sir William Collins held so faithfully to his principles had the admiration of nearly all the members of the Town Council. . . . He neither takes strong drink himself nor puts it in the way of others, but in every other respect his hospitality is unbounded."

Even the satirical *Quiz* was a little mollified, addressing the following lines to those with " drouthy throats ":

> Say to them the day is dawning
> When our pubs will close their doors—
> When the idle bobby, yawning,
> Finds the caseless Bailie snores.
> Then no spreeing, fighting, killing,
> Men will not their wives bethump;
> All will seek the wine that's filling,
> Flowing from Sir William's pump.

III

The founder of the firm had now been dead for more than a quarter of a century. During that time progress had been remarkable. But Sir William's expansionist urge was still to be untiring for many years to come.

Already, in 1879, he had turned aside from his civic cares to buy a paper-mill at Bowling in Dunbartonshire for his third son John, and to convert the concern into a Limited Company. For some years the business, with total assets worth not less than £300,000, had been run by a co-partnership consisting of himself and his two sons, and several extra-family partners from inside the business. By the end of 1879 all the partners had been bought out—Morrison (who retired) for £39,000, Walker (who started his own business) for £8,000, Donald (a clever accountant) for £4,000, Matthew Riddell for £2,400, William Collins III for £12,600 and Alexander Glen Collins for £9,600. A new Limited Company was then floated and the old-time partners, excepting Morrison and Walker, but with the addition of two new directors from the business, were allotted shares and became the new Company's first Board.[1]

William I would have watched these events with admiration and astonishment. By this time the firm's notepaper had a London, Glasgow, Edinburgh and Sydney address. The house's travelling salesmen at home and abroad were about to be increased in number—a step commensurate with Herriot Hill's now tremendous output. Within twelve months, the stationery side of the business alone had issued 10,000,000 copy and drawing-books, 120,000,000 envelopes and 150,000 ledgers; while the twenty-eight letterpress and lithographic machines in the printing house had produced about 2,000,000 bound volumes of the printed word. There seemed no end to Sir William's unflagging dynamism.

[1] The new Directors were W. Penman, manager of the London House, and J. B. Craig of the Counting House.

The year 1881 saw an important new undertaking—the first of the famous Collins Diaries.

"We converse with the absent by letters and with ourselves by Diaries," wrote Isaac Disraeli; and both methods of recording our thoughts and actions are as old as civilisation itself. But the modern diary is not adapted for introspective or social tittle-tattle. It is primarily an almanac, a miniature book of reference, and finally a note-book in which one records business or social engagements. The Collins diaries of 1881 were adapted for all these purposes, but they were by no means the first of their kind to be published in Scotland. Sixty-five years earlier James Lumsden of Glasgow had issued *The Glasgow Commercial Memorandum Book*—the first business diary, as distinct from the almanac, traceable north of the Border. The firm's triumph in this field was not, therefore, that of the pioneer. But it did succeed in making people more diary-minded; for although less than 10,000 copies of the first three Collins diaries were sold, the house was quick to attack the market again with a Pocket Diary which, because it contained one day to a page, immediately trebled the sales. Then came diaries with "sea-green sight-preserving paper." These were adopted by Queen Victoria's household. Thereafter, with regal cachet the publication of diaries from Herriot Hill grew so rapidly that by the end of the century twenty-five different diaries were being published in sixty-four different bindings. To-day the firm's annual sale of diaries is reckoned in millions.

To cope with this ever-widening production, additional printing machinery now had to be installed. By 1882—a year in which the house advertised ninety-one different Bibles, Testaments, Psalm Books, Hymn Books and Prayer Books (in six hundred bindings)—the heavy printing plant had been increased to twenty double-cylinder machines and fourteen cylinder litho presses. It expanded again the following year, and yet again in 1884 when the house undertook a new series of twelve school readers and primers with larger-faced type and a brighter text, of which 2,700,000 copies were sold in ten years.

What were the main reasons for such stirring progress? They were of course many: Sir William's own relentless driving force, the new Board's acumen, the long-established reputation of the house for good workmanship, the winning of trans-oceanic markets, and the loyalty and cordial co-operation of the men and women engaged in every branch of the business. All deserve a closer look, starting at the top.

The joy of work, as we know, was a gospel which William II preached in and out of season to everyone in the business. His own sons he sometimes treated with a rigour which the average Victorian industrial worker might have expected from the toughest of employers. No sooner had the limited company been formed than he introduced a bye-law that no director was to absent himself from business for more than twenty-one weekdays a year. At one Board meeting, William III, who in 1881 had made a business tour of the world including Australia and Japan, applied for "permission to visit the Colonies." Smelling a fragrant rat the Board on Sir William's recommendation decided to delay consideration of the request. But the application was re-newed a month later, with the United States of America added to the itinerary. Sir William then moved that his son should have leave of absence for five months only "on condition that the Company bear no part of his expenses, and that he pay for a substitute to take his place in the warehouse." Later, he even moved the suspension of directorships held by members of his family on the grounds of "inattention to business," so determined was that resolute old man that no adverse tides should seep into the structure he had built up, through fissures left by his able but oft-times rebellious sons. As the result of this attitude William III, who conducted all his affairs with enormous *brio*, suffered some searing experiences towards the end of his father's life. One Board minute reveals that with his usual haste he had altered a paper order without consulting his fellow directors. When the paper proved on delivery to be unsuitable the Board decided that he must defray its cost out of his own pocket. Within a few weeks of this mishap, William III was again in trouble.

He had arbitrarily dashed off an order for a new dictionary. The minute book records:

> "The Board instructed Mr. William Collins, Junior, as to the impropriety of his conduct and again enjoined him to conform to the resolutions and instructions of the Board with certification that if he persisted in setting aside or over-riding these, his conduct would at once be brought under the notice of the Company in General Meeting and be dealt with under Article 82, paragraph 'D' of the Articles of Association of the Company."

William III was not the only family culprit. His brother Alexander—a cheerful character with a passion for roses, paintings, golf, his own private schooner, and Bible salesmanship—planned a cheap store on Woolworthian principles; Sir William said nay, and the project lapsed.

Despite this rigid discipline, always more stoutly directed to his family than to his staff, his workers had a marked pride in the business and a growing satisfaction with the welfare measures which his high sense of social justice dictated. Annual festivals of song and dance (always teetotal) had been held since mid-century; and at these, as an old 1884 programme shows, the firm's employees danced Quadrilles (later to be nicknamed "Clear-type Quadrilles "), Waltzes, the Petronella, Scotch reels and Schottisches, Polkas, the Guaracha Waltz and the Galop. A Friendly Society inside the works had been flourishing since 1865. Since 1870, and they both continue to this day, there had been two annual excursions—one down the Clyde from the Glasgow works and the other up the Thames from the London office. The Thames trip has now taken on certain notable characteristics, not least the famous cricket match between Authors and Publishers, and the frequent attendance of Collins authors from the Dominions and the United States. Of the Clyde trip detailed records have been faithfully kept.

On the first occasion an army of Collins workers, heralded by waving banners and a brass band, marched to the Broomielaw to board one of the famous Clyde steamers. This was the procedure for many years. For example, in June 1883 (the year

in which Sir William retired from the City Council) almost 1,000
members of the firm sailed in S.S. *Bonnie Doon* for Kilchattan
Bay. The ship cost £40 to charter, but in view of Sir William's
teetotal principles, an additional charge of £2 was paid to the
ship's owners for keeping the bar closed during the voyage. It
seems a modest fee, unless—the hypothesis is doubtful—Sir
William's principles had already achieved a complete triumph
over his employees. "Organisation," a committee item, cost
19s. 9d. Music for the choir came to 9s. 8d. The cleaning of
three flags—torn and salt-encrusted after a previous trip—cost
3s.; the committee's flag-bearers were paid half a crown each;
and the committee even had a private dinner to celebrate its own
efficiency which cost £8 5s. In all, there was a deficit on this
happy day of £42 3s. 9d., a sum, the report says, which the
directors "paid with pleasure." It is noticeable, however, that
the cost of the committee's dinner the following year—due
perhaps to aquarian circumstances over which Sir William had
some control—had slumped to £3. But the over-all deficit was
greater. Nevertheless, in appreciation of the committee's labours,
its members were allowed cigars to the value of £1 5s., and once
again the directors redressed the adverse balance.

William II deserves a tribute here. For of all the many
benefactions of this generous man—a man decades ahead of his
time—his treatment of employees was the most remarkable.
Though he did not know it, he was a pioneer of personnel
management (which a few employers even to-day regard as an
unnecessary luxury); and his schemes of works welfare compare
favourably with the practice of the most forward-looking modern
manager. He founded and endowed the Collins Institute, a red-
stone building near the printing works (believed to be the first
of its kind in Scotland), which contained dining-rooms, a concert
hall, games rooms, a library and other amenities (1887). But
this munificent gift was in keeping with his general humanity,
though many other employers of the time must have thought it
just another of Water Willie's eccentricities. In fact, he was one
of the very few nineteenth-century industrialists who did not

share the fallacious but then almost universal view of workmen as "hands" or "labour," as a mere component of production to be acquired or dispensed with as easily as machines or raw material. His penetrating eye had recognised the obvious fact that "labour" consisted of human beings: more, to him they were first and foremost Christian souls. It was in this spirit that he even employed deaf mutes at Herriot Hill as a practical sign of his sympathy with the Glasgow Mission for the Deaf and Dumb. If there had been more employers like William Collins in the nineteenth century, the winter of our twentieth century discontents would have been less rigorous.

In this friendly internal atmosphere the house continued its progress through the 'eighties and early 'nineties. A New Zealand branch was opened at Auckland in 1888. Sir William purchased two more paper-mills at Denny in Stirlingshire, which along with the Bowling mill he converted into a limited company under his son John's chairmanship (1893). He introduced, or at least his sons and lieutenants did for he was now old, the innovation of coloured illustrations in school readers, using a newly invented process block to produce "composite" pictures, that is half-tone blocks with litho colour overprinted to resemble a colour drawing. From 1891 onwards for many years this new method was used to advantage in the popular *Graphic* schoolbooks. These had a vast sale.

The firm's sale of the Scriptures was equally impressive. By the early 'nineties, Sir William Collins had overhauled so many formidable competitors in this field that his *de facto* monopoly of Bible-printing in Scotland was virtually complete and the way paved for the first appearance in 1892 of Bibles and a dictionary in Clear-Type, a name which has long provided the printing plant at Herriot Hill with its subsidiary title—*Collins Clear-Type Press*.[1] With this innovation the sales again soared, and soared again when the demand for Clear-Type Bibles, elegantly bound in

[1] The Scottish monopoly was not *de jure*. Occasional Bibles and Testaments were and are still produced in Scotland, under licence, by other publishing firms for special purposes. In England, the Patent prevents anyone from printing the Bible except Eyre & Spottiswoode, and the Oxford and Cambridge University Presses.

morocco, calf and russia with gold toolings, was accompanied
by a sudden craze for Teachers' Bibles.

Why Teachers' Bibles—Bibles, that is, with reproductions of
ancient manuscripts and monuments, maps and accounts of
Biblical history by famous scholars—spread so rapidly across
the English-speaking world in the late years of last century, is at
least a half-mystery. It may be explained by mere change in
fashion, for even the Bible publisher cannot resist the impulse
to create something new for the sake of its novelty. Or it may
have been the joint result of the pulpit's permeation by the
higher criticism, and the widespread religious revival in the
'eighties when evangelists roved perfervidly about Britain and
America. What is quite clear is that suddenly a great many
church-goers on both sides of the Atlantic became obsessed with
the idea of owning a Teachers' Bible, and that of the first one to
be issued from Herriot Hill (1878) with engravings and maps,
10,000 copies were sold. Fifteen years later when the fashion
had reached its apogee there came a new edition of the Bible
adorned by sixty-four composite coloured plates, of which not
less than 75,000 copies a year were printed at the height of the
demand. But this was a temporary mode. Soon came half-crown
Bibles—an immensely popular development especially in America
where the sales were stimulated, firstly by the creation of the
International Bible Agency at 150 Fifth Avenue, New York, to
act as sole American agents for Collins Bibles, Testaments and
Prayer Books (1892); and secondly by William III's visit in the
same year to supervise the start of the new drive on the spot.[1]
Again the results were heartening. In one year the International
Bible Agency imported £20,000 worth of Bibles, while the
Collins American catalogue pointed to 337 different bindings
of Bibles and New Testaments.

Though the diary of history shows that in 1895 the long
Victorian afternoon was quickly fading into twilight there is no
hint of twilight in the contemporary view of the typically

[1] In 1881, W. L. Allison of New York had been appointed agent for Collins Bibles.
A few years later, the agency passed to A. D. McLachlan of New York and Boston.

Victorian business. In that year the Collins wage bill had risen in fifty years from about £2,200 to more than £70,000, distributed among 1,900 workers working 52½ hours a week. Its total annual production of books printed and bound at Herriot Hill was nearing two and a half million. The printing plant consisted of 40 cylinder machines, 25 commercial jobbing machines, and 20 cylinder litho presses—which must have seemed armament sufficient for the battle of the twentieth century. But there was one subaltern who was not satisfied. Floating in and out of Herriot Hill with the feverish impatience that ruled his life and caused his death, William III had already sensed the new century's atmosphere.

IV

If Sir William Collins solemnised New Year's Day of 1895 by looking back to 1837—when he made his first visit to London and his father bowed to the young Queen Victoria—he must have reflected on the profound social changes in the six decades during which he had forged his fortune. At the time of his first visit to London, the population of Great Britain was little more than 25,000,000: now it was more than 40,000,000. His father had used flint and tinder: he now used lucifer matches. The first Collins books were conveyed from Glasgow by coach or horse wagon: by 1895 trains were travelling as fast about the country as they were to do in the middle of the twentieth century. He had seen crime and the death rate decrease steeply and the school population rise from 60,000 children to 5,000,000. In the span of his adult life he had seen the arrival of the railway train, the telegraph, the telephone, chloroform, the iron-clad steamship, and colour printing.

Looking into the future Sir William Collins would have been less confident; for the currents and cross-currents which were to make the twentieth century an era of tremendous social change were already flowing, though their strength could still only be appreciated by realists with something like clairvoyant vision. For a year or two these currents were to eddy below the stately Victorian feet of the Queen herself and Mr. Gladstone. But, as Professor Halévy has pointed out in his *History of the English People* and Mr. Churchill in *The World Crisis*, the Victorian epoch historically ended while Queen Victoria was still on the throne. In 1895 Mr. Gladstone officially ceased to be a member of Parliament. It was the year of a General Election in which twenty-eight Independent Labour Party candidates addressed fiery words to the electors; the year in which Sydney and Beatrice Webb produced a work of quiet but profound political influence, *The History of British Trade Unionism*; the first full year of Sir William Harcourt's graduated death duties on large estates. It was in 1895 that Alfred Harmsworth first began to plan the *Daily Mail* whose appearance the following year not only ended the almost Gibbonian roll and resonance of Victorian daily newspapers but blazed a new path for the popular journalism of to-day. Equally significant in 1895, and in striking portent of the future feminist movement, three women were members of a Royal Commission on secondary education, and the National Union of Women Workers was formed.[1] Above all, 1895 saw the Jameson Raid which began in the last few days of the year, overlapped into 1896, and left what Mr. Churchill almost thirty years later called in *The World Crisis*—"the rapids, in whose turbulence we are now struggling."

It seems fitting therefore that Sir William Collins' long life should have ended in this year. He had been born two years before his Queen, and while still young had seen his father embark on expansions of the business which miniatured perfectly the increasing glory of the Victorian age. For just as the nation as a whole had increased its population, wealth, and its influence overseas, so too had the Collins family increased the number of their employees, the capital value of their firm, and their home, foreign and Empire markets. Truly, Sir William Collins could be

[1]The *Confédération Générale du Travail*, the French T.U.C., was also founded in 1895.

called a true Victorian. But the Victorian era was over, and like his Queen he was already a monument of a departed age.

For a year or two he had been visiting Herriot Hill less frequently; but he was still fairly active. In 1893 he had laid the memorial stone of the jubilee buildings of the Scottish Temperance League which he had supported for half a century. The following year, he had heard one of the speakers at a dinner of one thousand of the firm's senior employees say: "Although we are an old house, we cannot, like Alexander the Great, sit down and weep because there are no more worlds to conquer."

He still went to sea in his handsome steam yacht the S.Y. *Mera*, but in June 1894, he instructed the *Mera's* captain to bring the ship from Cowes to the Clyde, and it was from the Clyde that the *Mera* took him on his last pleasure voyage. He then went to winter in Edinburgh pending the completion of repairs on his Glasgow house. And there he died, peacefully, on Wednesday the 20th February 1895, leaving munificent bequests totalling some £10,000 to the many public institutions he had generously supported in his lifetime. So passed a man of great worth and spirit to the regret of many admirers far beyond the confines of Glasgow. It was, however, Glasgow which showed its regret and respect most keenly when his body was brought back to his native city. He was buried high up on the Necropolis, near the grave of his father and beside the gigantic statue of John Knox which towers over even Glasgow Cathedral, and beyond it in the city smoke, the printing works which bears the Collins name.

CHAPTER XII

The Wise Eccentric
1895-1906

I

LONG BEFORE the twilight of the 'nineties the third William Collins had already emancipated himself from Victorianism: it was fortunate that he also possessed the qualities to emancipate the firm.

In startling contrast to the driving zeal of his grandfather and the solid, ineluctable faith of William II, he had a natural bravura, a liking for the roses of life, and a mechanical bent so marked that in the middle of the twentieth century he might have invented a jet engine or the world's fastest printing machine. As it was, he applied his adroit inventions to the machinery around him and was one of the earliest owners of a motor-car.

To his fellow citizens this third William appeared eccentric because his energy and common sense were woven in such an unusual pattern that for half a century the very mention of his name in Glasgow has revived a medley of credible legends and almost incredible facts. Fortunately for the record his chief qualities are not in doubt. He was kind and generous, though capable of robust opinions in the presence of carelessness or inefficiency. His main cultural tastes were old masters, music and literature. But he also liked sport and the countryside. Above all, he had a dæmonic impulse to extend the business, sprung partly from natural ambition and partly from the nervous energy which made him run when other men walked.

To follow his flying footsteps during the early hours of a busy day is to be reminded of an old Edwardian film played in quick time. If he was in a greater hurry than usual to reach Herriot Hill, his servants witnessed (or heard) the released force of an avalanche, fast-moving and sweeping up in a continuous movement the bare necessities which time, though not convention, had ordained as reasonable covering: a woollen vest with long sleeves (why waste time searching for a shirt and its fittings when urgent affairs were calling?); trousers certainly, but a jacket?—not if it lay beyond the reach of those darting fingers. Perhaps the day was cold; then he covered himself for the journey with a greatcoat lined from top to bottom with Shetland shawls.

With the same lack of self-consciousness he travelled now and then by night train to his hunting-box near Rugby where the dawn provided few better spectacles than Mr. Collins in pyjamas and dressing-gown, running from the station platform to a brougham and fast trotter waiting outside. At his London flat one winter afternoon a caller saw him garbed in dressing-gown, Shetland shawl and skull-cap—proof picturesque that while warmth and covering were essential, anything unusual in his appearance must be a figment of other people's imagination. Once, too, he was spotted leaving home for his office in all the glory of an opera cloak surmounted by a bowler hat swept up on his headlong rush to his front door. But these admittedly were occasions when time pressed hard and the shortest cut made common sense. Usually, his attire was conventional and often, indeed, as smart and fashionable as his winter brougham or his summer victoria, two equipages in which he took especial pride. For this being a carriage age, Glasgow's merchant princes vied with each other in cutting a splendid dash in the city streets, and William III was not a man to be easily eclipsed. By command of their owner, his coaches glittered like glass; his horse had to be a high-stepper; while his coachman, Ballantyne, was required to

W. A. Collins, C.B.E., D.S.O., 1873-1945

appear in a three-quarter length blue coat and white breeches, a shining silk topper with black cockade, and three-quarter top-boots surmounted by brown cuffs. It is not at all surprising in view of this Glasgow glory that sometimes when William Collins went to London or even to the Riviera for a periodical flutter at the gaming tables, his coachman, carriage and cob travelled immaculate on the same train.

But we left him preparing for his morning journey to the office. This event seems to have grown more breath-taking as he gathered momentum, plunged into the waiting carriage, and raised at intervals the anguished cry: "Faster, Ballantyne, faster!" Then came the morning stream of traffic in Sauchiehall Street and the inevitable traffic jam. But even such a sinister, devil-designed obstruction as this caused no delay. Within seconds the carriage's restless occupant had surged into the street, to speed irresistibly forward while slower citizens observed sagely to each other that Mr. Collins was in his usual hurry. Sometimes he was picked up again. Whether or not, he was soon leaping up the printing house stairs to his room three steps at a time; and there, for a few minutes at least, he had to stay like a suffering Prometheus, chained to his desk.

Some of these oddities shed revealing light on William III's character. Onlookers thought them eccentric; to William Collins they were common sense. When a clock's ticking disturbed his concentration, he rang a bell and ordered its removal. In the smartest of restaurants he would produce, from his pocket, a couple of cutlets or a saddle of hare and send them out to the chef to be cooked—a safe insurance that his meal should be as he liked it. But perhaps the most memorable of these very individual short-cuts to sanity was his purchase one day of a bunch of grapes from a fruit barrow. Being thirsty he ate the grapes while hastening along the pavement until his hands dripped with the juice. However, not even this sticky problem was insoluble. He spied a fishmonger's shop, dashed in, rinsed his hands under a cold-water tap, and dashed out again.

That a man with so few inhibitions should burst through

most of his family's century-old dykes was inevitable. Along with his love of music, which meant the lashing of a piano on board his yacht when he went to sea and the occasional engagement of a well-known string band leader to play to him at breakfast, went a penchant for brocades and beautiful women. "Why," he was once asked, "do you have a dado at head level in the sitting-room of your London flat?" "Because," he confessed like a flash, "I like to see pretty girls sitting with their heads against rosewood." He also liked to see pretty girls in the printing works. His addition of women—"Collins Paper Angels" as they were called—to the counting-house staff so delighted him that he extended the experiment to the bookbinding department, only to find himself involved in a lengthy strike of protest by his men employees who admittedly had certain other grievances about piecework. Still, not even this setback could damp his knight errantry. He once ordered a pneumatic chair for every woman in the factory; and one day, after noticing that in wet weather many of them arrived with rain-sodden shoes, he sent off messengers to ransack Glasgow for thousands of carpet slippers.

He was married to a lady named Annie Leask but had no children. By a queer coincidence his wife, too, had her whimsies. An inveterate church-goer herself, she used to fine her husband £5 for failure to attend divine service—an exaction which must have been frequent, since William III's quicksilver temperament could not easily have tholed the lengthy assize of an old-time Scottish service. Nevertheless, when in Glasgow he often drove his wife to the church door, raised his hat there in a sweeping farewell embracing both his wife and the sacred edifice, and drove happily away.

Those who knew him well were certain that such a fiery charger (and such a good business man) would not remain long in the one stable. Their view was quickly justified. Within a few months of his father's death he was in the United States, studying the booksellers' market, investigating new printing devices, and inspecting the house's International Bible Agency at 150 Fifth Avenue, New York, as a matter of course. On his return he carried out a similar inspection at home—with results as far reaching as his own travels.

The firm's earlier *Graphic* readers for schools were already selling in hundreds of thousands: he added a handful of *New Graphic* readers, the first of their kind to be illustrated with three-colour pictures. Within a year or two at the behest of the London County Council, he also designed the *Wide-World Readers* in quarto (a new size for schoolbooks), set up in bold type with reproductions of historical paintings from British and Continental Art Galleries. But even earlier than that he had produced an imposing edition of Shakespeare prefaced by Henry Irving's critique on the Bacon controversy. This volume became so popular—its sales were to exceed 1,000,000 copies—that one American publisher reproduced it by photography, and battened happily on the proceeds till a rash shipment to Australia, where the British copyright law ran and where the firm was already entrenched, brought his piracy to an ignoble end.[1]

William Collins had several other impressive achievements to his credit before he raced into the twentieth century. He floated £150,000 of debentures which at five per cent were over-subscribed. He drew up plans to extend his printing works and bindery. He also bestowed directorships on his three nephews—William IV, Godfrey, and William Collins Dickson, son of Sir William Collins' eldest daughter Annabella.

William IV, a young man of great charm, had been educated at Harrow, where he was contemporary with Mr. Churchill. To his great regret, he was unexpectedly removed from school on the initiative of old Sir William, who doubtless with memories of his own apprenticeship in the Candleriggs, declared that this promising grandson of his must enter the business at once. His father Alexander Glen Collins differed—having other visions for

[1]Over the years there have been many Collins editions of Shakespeare including the 40-volume Stage edition which included portraits of famous Shakespearian actors, and a John Barrymore edition for the U.S.A. Most of these were intended for a big public rather than for scholars. In 1951 the firm published a new edition of Shakespeare's complete works, brilliantly edited by Professor Alexander, Regius Professor of English Language and Literature at the University of Glasgow.

his son—but bowed in the end to the imperial edict; and so, at the age of seventeen, the fourth William started his apprenticeship in the London warehouse at Bridewell Place, with a wage of five shillings a week. But his bad luck, as he then saw it, continued. Not only did an apprentice's life after Harrow seem at first rather austere, but also, having started work on a Wednesday, he found that his first weekly pay packet contained only 3s. 6d. Quickly his natural enthusiasm overcame his initial doubts, and in 1896, after completing his indenture, he donned the top hat and frock coat of a professional traveller and began to drive in a brougham round London bookshops and stationers. As it turned out, all this was valuable experience. He made headway, and got his reward one day when his uncle remarked: "Go to Australia, New Zealand, India. Take a good holiday—and a box of samples." A year later he was elected to the Board at the age of twenty-four.

The second nephew came to the business from the sea. Trained in H.M.S. *Britannia*, Godfrey Collins had entered the Royal Navy in 1888, but had to retire through illness after serving three years on the East India station. It was perhaps fortunate that his naval career had this end, for he turned to printing, quickly mastered the intricacies of that skilled trade as a compositor and machine-room minder in London, and thus brought practical experience as his first contribution to the firm's management. By 1899 he was a director. A year later he married a lady named Faith Henderson, and was put in charge of the Glasgow printing office.

The third nephew, William Collins Dickson (born in 1876), was a product of Fettes College and Glasgow University, where, like his uncle, he had studied Natural Philosophy under Lord Kelvin. He, too, became a director in 1899, after visiting New York to study Bible salesmanship. But this was not his real bent. Like his uncle again, he had strong mechanical and mathematical leanings and was, therefore, made responsible for the engineering and costing rather than the scriptural side of the business.

Clearly, then, the Board had been reinvigorated.[1] But its

[1] The full Board of Directors from 1900 to 1903 was: Williams Collins III (Chairman), W. A. Collins IV, Godfrey P. Collins, W. Collins Dickson, Hugh Allan, Frank Atkinson, James M. Hay, Thomas Hislop, Robert Leask, John Mitchell.

chairman was still dissatisfied. For too long, he told his nephews, the family had concentrated on mass production of Bibles, non-copyright classical works, schoolbooks and reference books, and on the manufacture of stationery: had the time not come to publish more original works as the first William had done? No suggestion could have touched the ambition of his nephews more closely. The result was an entirely new list of children's fiction which we must consider as part of the policy, now taking shape, for book publishing and printing on a multi-million scale.

II

To look back at the early Collins lists of this century is to sense the firm's zest for its new enterprise. The covers and the illustrations for its boys' adventure books sparkle with gleaming cutlasses, while its school stories ring with the old fifth-form excitements which seemed to make Edwardian youth a jolly carefree adventure. Yet their preparation could not have been easy.

For several centuries authors and publishers of varying accomplishment had tried, with as varying success, to enter the charmed world of the child mind. The ancient fables of Æsop were extensively published in the seventeenth century. In its successor, children were given Defoe's *Robinson Crusoe* and Swift's *Gulliver's Travels*. Later still, two Frenchmen, Charles Perrault and his son, brought to life Bluebeard and Cinderella and other enchanted beings. But by this time not only had the children's chap-book also arrived, with quaint woodcuts and spirited accounts of *Jack and the Giants* and *Red Riding Hood*, but John Newbery of St. Paul's Churchyard, who is generally regarded as the real father of juvenile literature in our modern sense, had produced Nursery Classics with pretty illustrations designed to catch a child's interest. He evidently realised, as Janet Adam Smith has recognised since, that picture-books offer one of the earliest ways in which a child can extend his experience of the world:

> "Arabia, kettledrums, emperors and elephants, a mumbo-jumbo of syllables when received by the ear alone, take on shape and reality in an illustrated *Arabian Nights* or *Hans Andersen*."[1]

After Newbery the eighteenth-century chap-books were gradually ousted by Charles and Mary Lamb, Hans Andersen and the Brothers Grimm, and by the evangelical upsurge which encouraged such literature as William I's religious books for children, cloying annuals more suitable for the sentimental adult than the inquiring child, and the spirit of censorship which tempted Dr. Chalmers to hide his volume of Byron from his daughter. Luckily the sterner moralists, who did not always appreciate the fierce reaction they bred, succumbed in the end to *Alice in Wonderland* and the adventure stories of Henty and Ballantyne.

By this time the house of Collins had unaccountably forsaken books designed for children's entertainment; and in the twenty years before 1895 only a few toy books were published. William III soon stirred up this slumbering branch. Two years after assuming the chief direction of the business he issued the *Graphic Story Books* as a kite to test the air currents, saw that it flew well, and in 1900 started a catalogue of juvenile literature, known to booksellers as Reward Books—the first series of children's fiction, it is believed in Glasgow, to be illustrated throughout in colour. It soon achieved an annual sale of more than one million copies.

This gratifying success was due not only to a careful combing of old-time children's classics, but to the enlistment of skilled contemporary writers for children under the editorial guidance of a well-known writer of boys' stories, Herbert Hayens. Hayens was admirable for such a purpose. He came of Devonshire seafaring stock, and with his blue eyes, flowing moustache and greying hair looked more like an old-time Devonshire sea captain than an editor. Even his room, high up in the Glasgow office,

---

[1] *Children's Illustrated Books* (*Britain in Pictures* series): Collins, 1948.

was a glass-topped crow's nest approached by steep and narrow stairs which resembled a ship's companionway sufficiently to strengthen the general nautical illusion of his surroundings.

Apart from the long toil of editorship his own considerable literary output for the firm—mainly adventure stories—carried on the Henty-Ballantyne tradition and bridged the gap to the more modern mechanistic tales of Percy Westerman; while his school stories, in the *Play-Up* series, catered as successfully for boys as Elsie Oxenham did for girls in her companion *Abbey Girls* series. He recruited many other popular juvenile authors— Manville Fenn, Bessie Marchant, Mabel Quiller-Couch, and Mrs. L. T. Meade (one of whose girls' stories the authorities thought suitable reading matter in Brixton for Ford Madox Ford, the intellectual founder of the *English Review*, who had been committed to prison on what he considered to be an issue of principle). Most of Mrs. Meade's books were published, however, with the imprint of Collins' very near neighbours and friendly rivals Messrs. Blackie. There was also Florence Dugdale whose gentle *Old-Time Tales*, *Cousin Christine* and *Country Life* were far removed from the great and sombre tragedies of her future husband, Thomas Hardy. Finally, there were two other contributors to the list still better known—Katherine Tynan and Andrew Lang.

Lang was a most prolific writer, with an output ranging from history, biography and poetry to leading articles in the *Daily News*, a share of Butcher and Lang's classic translation of the *Odyssey*, and, although he was not naturally genial, a great many fairy stories for children. Of these the first Lang contribution to the list—by a special arrangement, since Collins were not his usual publishers—was one of the *Tales of a Fairy Court*, *The Story of Prince Prigio*.

Katherine Tynan, whom Æ described once as "happy in religion, friendship, children, instantly kindling at any beauty in gardens, flowers, in sky and clouds," and, more importantly, as "the earliest singer in that awakening of our imagination which has been spoken of as the Irish Renaissance," had already achieved Victorian fame for her poetry with its many tender sentiments about children:

> *What shall hurt me or harm*
> *With all Heaven in my arm?*

Now, in the Edwardian age, she began to write children's fiction, notably *The Luck of the Fairfaxes*, which remained popular for many years. But then, as she herself once wrote: "I was born under a kind star." For the firm it was encouraging that an equally kind star was already shining on the new venture when Katherine Tynan gave it her own kindly impetus.

III

We must return to 1900. For this was the year which saw the birth of the house's present chairman, William Collins V.[1] Son and heir of William IV whose wife, formerly Miss Grace Brander, was to endear herself to countless Collins employees by a warm personal interest in their welfare, the fifth William was born in London on Mafeking night and not, like most of his ancestors, in Glasgow.

That city, still the hub of the Collins fortunes, was as unwearied as ever despite two centuries of tremendous growth. Its population by this time exceeded three-quarters of a million, its area eight square miles. Perhaps the West Highland sunsets over the city, where they could be seen, had become murkier; for its famous dockyards, furnaces and foundries were still spreading fast, and almost eleven hundred vessels were now using Glasgow as their port of registry. Electric cars, too, were running about the streets, though here and there a few horse-drawn trams still reminded the citizens of a bygone age, and the drivers of horse-drawn lorries, including the firm's own, persisted in moving

---

[1]Both his brother Ian Glen Collins, now vice-chairman, and Godfrey's son, William Hope Collins, another present-day director, were born in 1903.

slowly along the tram rails in feigned ignorance of the tram-car gong behind them until fines were imposed for the offence.

This eventful year also saw a new drive to increase sales overseas. A family relative, Alec B. Glen, was dispatched to the South American republics to study the book market and appoint agents in Argentina, Brazil, Peru and Chile. Within a year, Alec Glen, who was later to take over the house's Australian business, became the first Collins salesman to travel across Canada to Vancouver, then on to India and Ceylon. He also visited the West Indies where, especially in Jamaica and Trinidad, the house for a century has enjoyed a sure foothold. Simultaneously (1901), William Collins Dickson, after touring New Zealand and Australia, reported the need for a stationery manufactory in Sydney to combat the high protective tariff imposed by the Australian Government. The consequence of that report was yet another addition to the firm's properties—a seven-storey building at 105 Clarence Street, Sydney (1903). Meantime one of the firm's travellers was roving South Africa.

At home, William III showed the same expansive spirit. For some time he had been contemplating a bold and costly modernisation of his printing plant before embarking on a new enterprise which was to prove one of the most constructive (and popular) social changes of our time. The printing machines he chose were the then latest type of German rotary printing presses, which young Mr. Godfrey had examined three years earlier at Leipzig—on his honeymoon—at the request of his uncle. As in fact they were able to print 128 pages at a revolution from the reel and deliver the sheets folded and ready for the binding shop, it was, for the time, superb equipment; and so much importance was attached to it that Godfrey Collins returned to Germany for a stay of nine or ten weeks while the first great press was completed by the manufacturers. No step perhaps could have been more typical of William III's thoroughness, for it ensured that one executive at least would have complete knowledge of a machine on whose speed and efficiency was to depend that now familiar enterprise—the *Collins Pocket Classics*.

IV

The roots of this highly successful series lay far back in the nineteenth century.

One spring evening at Abbotsford, when Sir Walter Scott was entertaining some of his literary friends, Constable, already planning a miscellany of shilling volumes, startled everyone by saying:

> "Literary genius may, or may not have done its best; but printing and bookselling, as instruments for enlightening and entertaining mankind, and of course, for making money, are as yet in mere infancy."

Three-quarters of a century later, William Collins and his nephews, and some of their rivals put the prophecy into ambitious practice. They had the glittering vision of the world's great classical works brought together in an endless series of *illustrated* shilling volumes—a vast porch, as it were, through which poor and rich alike would have simple access to permanent literature. To turn this dream into reality required painstaking organisation; for although between Constable and Collins there had been other shilling libraries—Bohun's, Morley's and Routledge's for example —this was the first to carry illustrations, and these had to be commissioned. Then the volumes for such an elaborate series had to be planned a long time ahead; the enormous output foreseen had to be maintained without detriment to other publications; and somehow the series had to be harnessed economically to the talismanic shilling.

By the autumn of 1903 the prospects seemed favourable. Popular education had spread rapidly enough during three decades to guarantee a good market. The 1842 Copyright Act, by limiting the period of a book's copyright either to the life of its author and seven years after his death, or for forty-two years from the date of publication, whichever was the longer, had thrown many of the mid-Victorian classics on to a free market. Finally, the new rotary presses were in action. So William III waited no longer. On 1st October he launched the *Collins Handy Illustrated Pocket Novels* (the only fully illustrated series of classical works on the market in pocket size), soon realised the unwieldiness of the title, altered it within three years to *Collins Illustrated Pocket Classics*, and made the series as familiar to booksellers as the coinage of the realm.

The first six volumes to appear were *David Copperfield* by Charles Dickens, *Kenilworth* by Sir Walter Scott, *Adam Bede* by George Eliot, *Westward Ho!* and *Two Years Ago* by Charles Kingsley, and *John Halifax Gentleman* by Mrs. Craik. By the end of the year four more titles had been added—*Shirley* by Charlotte Brontë, *Tom Brown's School Days* by Thomas Hughes, *It is Never too Late to Mend* by Charles Reade, and *East Lynne* by Mrs. Henry Wood. Within six months these ten books had made a fair start with a joint sale of some eighty thousand copies.

Perhaps *David Copperfield* illustrates best why the *Classics* speedily became popular not only here but in the United States where their sales through the firm's New York office have always been considerable. "The size is small, 6¼ ins. by 4 ins.," said the advance notices, "the type is bold and well leaded; the half-tone illustrations are from original drawings and many in number; the price is low." Even more remarkable, *David Copperfield* consisted of 876 Bible-paper pages with 16 illustrations and a binding of maroon cloth with full gold back. All for one shilling![1] Booksellers generally were surprised, and one London publisher even observed publicly that the Collins *Classics* could not pay—a gentle touch of prejudice which the *Westminster Gazette* brushed aside with the cold comment: "They have in hand for early publication a very large number of new titles." *They* also had by good fortune their own printing machines, their own paper, their own bindery, and the whole rich granary of the world's literature at their threshold.

[1] It is worth noting here that for many years the house had produced a Pearl 24mo Bible of 850 pages for less than 1s. The secret lay in highly organised production, cheaper raw materials, and lower wages costs than are now the rule.

The new undertaking went forward swiftly. Within two years fifty volumes were on the market, and the sales for 1906 alone were 405,000 copies. But here we must outstrip the calendar and trace the series' subsequent fortunes.

Competition with other publishers naturally became severe, as *Everyman's Library* (Dent's), the *World Classics* (Oxford University Press) and the *Nelson Classics* joined in the fray. But the challenges were met. By 1908 the first 100 titles were completed, and the firm had even devised an ingenious publicity plan which must have raised the lighting costs of all the large station hotels throughout the British Isles. In every hotel bedroom one day there suddenly appeared a Pocket Classic, blocked in gold with a local bookseller's name to discourage misappropriation by those who either had an overweening passion for literature or who—like most book borrowers—imagined the printed word to be exempt from the moral law. Needless to say, this spread the fame of the series farther; more volumes were sent to the presses; and by the end of 1911 the year's sale was almost 660,000—an annual total which remained practically stationary until the First World War and its effects compelled a rise of price to 1s. 3d. in 1917, 2s. 0d. in 1918 and 2s. 6d. in 1920.[1]

Meantime, the public's "classical" tastes were changing in the post-war years. True, Charles Dickens' pre-eminent position seldom altered, his *David Copperfield* heading the list nearly every year after 1904. But Scott was slipping down the ladder, and Stevenson was climbing.

By 1934 more than £100,000 had been spent on the series' production. There were 320 titles, mainly novels, and each one was reprinted at least once every eighteen months. To describe such a wide panorama in detail is of course impossible; but it is noteworthy that by this time the *Pocket Classics* had begun to include books by living authors such as Walter de la Mare's *Memoirs of a Midget* and a dozen novels by H. G. Wells. It is also of interest that surprisingly few changes in format were found

[1] The price was restored to 2s. 0d. in 1922 and remained so until 1939, when the impact of the Second World War compelled a rise to 3s. 0d. Higher production costs in 1949 necessitated a further increase to 3s. 6d. for each cloth Classic, and 7s. 0d. for leather.

necessary until 1936 when the maroon cloth, so dear to the faithful early subscribers, yielded temporarily to art cloths in red, blue, green and maroon, with a classical design by Eric Gill and a new title page.[1]

Owing to the Second World War the fateful year of 1939 was the last to see a full list of titles. Out of more than 300 books then in the series, and almost all in print, the following were the ten best-sellers:

1. Wuthering Heights	6. Lorna Doone
2. David Copperfield	7. Pride and Prejudice
3. A Tale of Two Cities	8. Pickwick Papers
4. Vanity Fair	9. The History of Mr. Polly
5. Jane Eyre	10. The Golden Treasury

A living author, H. G. Wells, had thus arrived among the "upper-ten." Poetry, too, was there for the first time. Dickens was as popular as ever, being ousted from first place only because the current film of *Wuthering Heights* revived interest in the book and its author. But Sir Walter alas! had dropped out altogether.

Through the late war, the *Pocket Classics* still sold in hundreds of thousands, though at least 200 titles had to be shed for lack of paper. However, by 1948, though the list was still compulsorily limited—to a level below that of rivals with perhaps fewer other commitments—the annual sale increased to almost 650,000, thus bringing the sale of Collins *Pocket Classics* since their inception to more than 25,000,000 copies.

[1]The year 1936 also saw, on 15th December, an English Classics Luncheon organised jointly by the house and Messrs. Foyle, with the Lord Mayor of London in the Chair. At this luncheon John Drinkwater, speaking from his own experience, repeated the Lord Mayor's thanks to Messrs. Collins for placing great literature within the reach of his impoverished youth. The climax of the function was reached when descendants of great British classical writers were announced under a spotlight—a new and pleasant form of ancestor worship.

V

The founder of this venture, while still in his prime, was not to see more than the first glimmerings of its future success. When the *Pocket Classics* came into being he had only three years to live—a triennium distinguished by what *The Times* called after his death "great energy and enterprise." He still contrived to yacht, hunt and ride, appeared frequently in his box at the opera, visited Ascot and the Riviera, acted as a Justice of the Peace, and once knocked down a telegraph post with his motor-car. Yet he seldom seemed out of Glasgow, so swift were his departures and returns, and these varied interests of his were always kept subordinate to the firm's expansion.

This seemed never ending. During the last two years of his life he founded Collins Brothers and Company to operate the Australian and New Zealand businesses (1904), extended the Glasgow factory (1905), and saw the incorporation of the William Collins Company at 27 East 21st Street, New York (1905), to facilitate his transatlantic Bible sales and those of the new *Pocket Classics*. This last move was timely. The tide of Collins printed Scriptures was rising; and one new pocket volume in particular, the Brevier Antique Text and Reference Bible described as "the smallest large-type Bible in the world," was becoming well known on both sides of the Atlantic.

But William III's vivid career was over. On 15th July 1906, at the age of fifty-nine, he died tragically in a way which seems almost in keeping with the pace of his life. Speeding through the entrance to the block of flats in Westminster, where he lived when in London, he made for the lift. The hall was dark, for the lights had fused and the lift porter was mending the fuse at the top of the building. But William III, inveterate mechanician to the end, had made his own lift gate key which, to avoid awaiting on the porter's pleasure, he promised to change as often as the management changed the lock. With it he opened the gate, failed to notice that the shaft was empty, and fell to the basement. During the night an emergency operation was performed. But his injuries were too severe for recovery; he died in the early morning; and British publishing thus lost one of its most ambitious, able leaders and the Collins family one of its most colourful and endearing kinsmen.

CHAPTER XIII

Books for the Million

1906-1917

I

WHEN William Alexander Collins succeeded his uncle he became the fourth William Collins in succession to guide the company's fortunes. He was then thirty-three years of age; and as his brother Godfrey was only thirty-one, and his cousin William Collins Dickson thirty, the new order was evidently to be one of youthful vigour. But vigour alone would not have brought the business through the coming storms. It was to prosper because William IV and Godfrey especially were knit together by fraternal affection and a strong community of aim and interest. No jealousies ever arose between them to undermine the sense of loyalty without which any family endeavour must perish. Nor did either ever lose the gift of inspiring subordinates with his own enthusiasm and instinct for teamwork. Thus in 1906 it was easy for them to carve out their respective spheres of influence. Godfrey took over publications, a branch now bigger than it had ever been; while William, in addition to a chairman's normal wide-ranging duties, supervised the home and overseas offices and the manufacture and sales of stationery.

As these words appear William IV has only been dead for seven years, and the true picture of a man can seldom be written at

The Rt. Hon. Sir Godfrey Collins, K.B.E., C.M.G., LL.D., M.P., 1875-1936

such close range. Even so, any historian would at once acknowledge his efficiency, his optimism, and a kindliness which found
particularly happy expression in friendly encouragement of
younger members of the staff, both apprentices and girls. "Is
your staff happy? Are we doing enough for them?" were
queries he frequently put to heads of departments; and in the
same warm-hearted way a humble wan-looking member of the
firm might suddenly hear his employer say: "You're not looking
well. It's a sunny day. Take the afternoon off." His business
capacity, founded on the family's indestructible zest for work
and its natural swiftness of movement and decision, was as
notable as his generosity. His speed, certainly, was a byword in
Glasgow where commuters to Ayrshire were awestruck at the
precision with which, after a headlong rush, he could smilingly
board a train with a few seconds to spare and set to work, as if
at his desk, on manuscripts or business papers. Once—so the
story goes—he found the nearest carriage door locked and the
train moving. Even then, after a precipitous dive through the
open window, he immediately opened his brief-case in the
manner of one pursuing his normal avocation. But this refusal
to be ruffled was in keeping with his general deportment. He was
a handsome cavalier in the romantic sense of the word. His
very dress was as immaculate as his manners were punctilious.
And though he could be firm over matters of business and stern
to malingerers, his warm-heartedness was transparent.

Young Mr. Godfrey shared these generous qualities. But
eight years of hard naval training and a deep veneration for the
courage of the first two Williams had made him unusually
purposeful and puritan. He was admittedly at an age when
youthful earnestness requires a vigorous outlet—in his case
boys' summer camps and Bible classes, and an active part in the
Glasgow Parliamentary Debating Association. Once, even,
having convinced himself that they were "instruments of the
devil" he hurled his pipes and tobacco pouch, inseparable companions of his later years, into the Thames.

As time went on Godfrey became much broader-minded,

though his wholehearted adherence to the family evangel of hard
work tended on the other hand to become more individualistic.
"If tired of work," he once told a member of his staff, "refresh
yourself with work of a different kind "—a precept which he
himself put into daily practice. Sometimes, too, he could be
laconic to his business employees. Yet this left no scar, his
forthrightness being recognised everywhere as the honest
expression of a friendly but resolute man.

Both brothers—and the tradition has been continued by their
sons—played as hard as they worked. William IV's wide range of
sports included golf, tennis, polo, hunting, ski-ing, and yachting
on the Clyde where in seven years before the First World War he
won more than a hundred and forty flags. Godfrey, who also
played many games, was a little less successful than his brother
as a competitive yachtsman, but in 1921, with his son W. Hope
Collins as a member of the crew, he represented Great Britain
victoriously against the United States in the British-American
Six-Metre Cup Races.

In 1906 these pursuits were naturally of much less moment
to the brothers than the exigencies of the business. In the last
few years of their uncle's reign that mature organism had borne
all the outward signs of prosperity. Yet despite its output,
goodwill, large assets and flourishing appearance, William
Collins Sons & Company were not really so prosperous as they
seemed. William III's ambitious machinery improvements had
proved costly, while his building extensions and his development
of the overseas branches had not yet brought compensating
dividends. For a time, therefore, economy became the firm's
watchword. It was a short-lived phase. The brothers had new
dreams of books for the million; and in 1907 they began a new
and startling experiment in that field.

II

For some time various publishers had been issuing rival libraries of celebrated novels out of copyright, the Collins own *Famous* sixpenny library being a good instance. But the brothers now had the more ambitious dream of reprinting cheaply *copyright* novels by *living* authors which had already been published at standard prices.

At first this new vision was clouded by the prejudice of most authors and publishers against low-priced reprints of high-class works—a prejudice as old as Dr. Johnson's censure of the London bookseller, Donaldson, who sold cheap editions of popular books with scant regard for the common law right of literary property:

> *Dr. Johnson:* He is a fellow who takes advantage of the law to injure his brethren.
> *Dempster:* Donaldson, sir, is anxious for the encouragement of literature. He reduces the prices of books, so that poor students may buy them.
> *Dr. Johnson (laughing):* Well, sir, allowing that to be his motive, he is no better than Robin Hood who robbed the rich in order to give *to* the poor.

There was now no question of piracy and the brothers were hardly Robin Hoods, but the prejudice against cheap editions remained. None the less, by the New Year of 1907 they had acquired a few titles from Chatto and Windus and others, though quite a number of publishers turned a frigid shoulder. One wrote: "We regret we are unable to agree to you re-issuing a cheap form of any of our copyright works." Another was even icier: "To use your own phrase, we are not by any means ' open to consider this principle.' " In spite of these set-backs, which time was to remove, sufficient titles were forthcoming to justify a start—at sevenpence per volume.

It was a gallant endeavour, but an unwelcome surprise was in store. Nelson's had hit on the same idea at the same time, made the same approaches to authors and publishers, met presumably with the same rebuffs, stuck to their plan with the same native pertinacity, and eventually had begun to print their own *Sevenpennies* with the same sense of timing. Thus a race was in progress which the brothers lost. The first Nelson *Sevenpenny* appeared on 15th May 1907, its Collins namesake three days later.

The popular appeal of the Collins *Sevenpennies* was certain from the start. Issued in pocket size, they were cloth bound, with gold title, coloured frontispiece and title page; and they had a full three-colour wrapper. Moreover, when the project got under way, the new rotary presses and binding plant guaranteed rapid mass production, and this in turn evoked a response from many poor people who, because they could not afford six shillings— then the usual price of a novel—agreed with Arnold Bennett that the *Sevenpennies* were "as great a boon as cheap bread."

Imagination boggles nowadays at the extraordinary cheapness of Edwardian reprints. It may have been forgotten, for example, that while the *Sevenpennies* were securing a sale of many millions, the house of Collins even published a *Penny Library* for schools— a series of books, with coloured wrappers, varied enough to include *Gulliver's Travels*, *The Water Babies*, and some of John Ruskin's works. There was also the 3½d. *Pocket Library* of 80 full-length novels, well printed, strongly sewn and bound. These achieved a sale of several million copies before the First World War brought them to an untimely end.

III

During these remarkable essays in mass production the main business in Glasgow and its branches overseas continued to grow so rapidly that by 1910, when the sombre meaning of the gathering war clouds was seen only by a few and not even suspected by the many, William IV and his brother could have seen no unsurmountable obstacle in their path. In Australia they were supplying educational texts and stationery on a large scale. Sales in New Zealand were also increasing, and a new stationery factory and warehouse in Auckland (1908), with branch offices at Wellington, Christchurch and Dunedin, had just been visited by William IV. Canada and South Africa were being extensively toured by experienced representatives. At home the staff, well over two thousand (including London), was producing about 89,000 bound volumes a week.

Not unnaturally during a phase of such rapid expansion, the brothers began to strengthen the Board of Directors. The newcomers were James Paterson who had been twenty-seven years with the firm and whose long managerial experience in charge of the binding works had given him special knowledge of labour questions; Ebenezer Dow, an unrivalled expert in diary sales and production; and Alec B. Glen whose many visits to the Dominions had given him specialised knowledge of overseas markets.

With such skilled lieutenants and in view of the firm's headway it now seemed a suitable time for Godfrey, with his brother's warm approval, to honour the family's tradition of public service. As his aim was Westminster, and he had always been a keen Liberal supporter of the social reforms which Asquith and Lloyd George were then carrying through Parliament, he gladly accepted an invitation from the Greenock Liberals to carry their standard at the 1910 General Election. It was a hard-fought contest, but Godfrey got home by a majority of 1,601 votes over his Conservative opponent, though lacking the assistance of his wife, whose absence he explained immediately after his election. "This," he said, "has been a doubly interesting day to me. I have had a double event. My wife presented me with a daughter about five o'clock this afternoon."[1]

Within a year the birth of his daughter was followed by the death of his father, Alexander Glen Collins, who after a long career devoted to the production and marketing of new editions

[1] His third child, Elspeth to whom he gave the middle name of Grianaig (Gaelic for Greenock) to commemorate her birth and his political victory. His eldest child was Alexander Godfrey Crosbie Collins who was born in 1901, joined the business in 1923, and died nine years later.

of the Scriptures had been living for some years in semi-retirement.

In this narrative Alexander Glen Collins, who never played quite the same decisive part in the firm's direction as the other members of his family, has been a remote figure. But in great measure the firm's large output of Bibles and schoolbooks was due to his zestful salesmanship in earlier days. For example, old W. H. Smith employees—in the days when that company was pledged to display a Collins Bible on each of its bookstalls—may remember a gentleman of impeccable courtesy asking if they had such a thing as a Bible among their wares. If it were not immediately forthcoming, A. G. Collins would suggest that surely there must be at least *one* Bible somewhere in the bookstall: after all, was not the Bible the world's best-seller? This delicate reminder usually stimulated a fresh search. If still unsuccessful, its instigator never failed to suggest with great charm that the Bible, and especially a Collins edition, was really a very good book and should in future be displayed prominently on the counter. But these were the days of keen competition among Bible printers. So keen was it, indeed, that a young Scots bookseller arriving in Paternoster Row about this time noticed the following advertisement in a publisher's window:

> Holy Bible,
> Writ Divine—
> Bound in leather,
> 1/9.
> Satan trembles
> When he sees
> Bibles sold
> As cheap as these.

The firm was not responsible for this original publicity, but A. G. Collins would have chuckled with delight at the spirit of salesmanship which prompted it, and would have intensified his own efforts. At Cathedral Street, as Herriot Hill was by this time known, he was so liked that when he died the factory girls subscribed threepence each, in what must have been a universal subscription, to lay a great pyramid of commemorative red roses on his grave.

A. G. Collins unfortunately did not live to see his son achieving distinction in his dual role as publisher-politician. As politician, Godfrey soon became Parliamentary Private Secretary to the then Secretary of State for War, Colonel "Jack " Seely (the future Lord Mottistone), and a member of the War Office Supplies Committee. As publisher he never failed to keep an attentive eye on his favourite series; and sometimes his two callings were agreeably intertwined. Thus in 1913 it was Godfrey Collins' political grasp of the reasons for industrial unrest at home and diplomatic uneasiness abroad which gave rise to *The Nation's Library*.

The aim of this series was to explain the burning questions of the day in a series of new full-length cloth-bound volumes, specially written by acknowledged authorities and published at the low price of one shilling. It is interesting now, after almost forty years, to look at some of the early titles and authors. In the first batch came *The Case for Railway Nationalisation* by Emil Davies, *Aviation* by Claude Grahame White (described on the wrapper as "Britain's Foremost Aviator "), and *Socialism and Syndicalism* by Philip Snowden. Then came a book on the feminist movement by Ethel Snowden, written in days when women were voteless. J. M. Robertson-Scott, famous founder and editor of *The Countryman*, wrote on *The Land Problem*, Hamar Greenwood (the future Lord Greenwood) on *Canada as an Imperial Factor*, and Walter Layton (now Lord Layton) on *The Relations of Capital and Labour*. Unfortunately this promising venture was an early casualty of the First World War.

Another experiment of the time, the first Collins *Children's Annual* (1914), survived the war and became the forerunner of a long series of similar publications. This type of volume was not of course a novel idea. Far back in the Candleriggs days, the country had been flooded with annuals, many of them strongly religious in flavour like *The Amulet* (William I's usual Christmas present to Mrs. Chalmers), *The Keepsake* (an annual which Sir Walter Scott was invited to edit during the debt-laden phase of his life), *Miss Sheridan's Comic Offering* or *Lady's Melange of Literary Mirth, Hall's Juvenile Forget-me-Not, The Winter's Wreath,* and *The Amethyst.* By 1832 the first William who had a deep affection for those curious productions was acting as Scottish agent for many of them; but, his distribution channels being still inadequate, he was reluctant to start his own. Now, more than three-quarters of a century later, his great-grandsons, like several other publishers before them, were to bring out annuals, specifically designed for children, but fortunately more bracing than *The Amethyst* and its languishing companions.[1]

They had other ambitious plans in view. But these had to be laid aside when the outbreak of the First World War in August 1914 darkened the whole future of British publishing and took the brothers far afield.

IV

From the outset the brothers had a clear view of their duty. With 275 of their employees, including twenty-one from Sydney and Auckland, they were soon in uniform; and William IV allowed his Ayrshire home, Grey Gables, to be run for a time as a hospital. Then he went to France, where he served as an officer in the Royal Army Service Corps, won not only the Distinguished Service Order and a Portuguese decoration, but rose to the rank of Lieutenant-Colonel. It was characteristic of his thoughtfulness that while the war lasted he remembered to write every year—as he was to do in another war—a Christmas message of greeting for his Cathedral Street brothers-in-arms, and that for every £1 raised at home to supply comforts to Collins employees on active service the directors contributed an equal sum. Godfrey who likewise joined the R.A.S.C., served with distinction in France, Egypt, India, Gallipoli and Mesopotamia

---

[1] It is noteworthy that between 1903 and 1914 the firm published and printed more than 500 different colour books for small children.

from 1915 to 1917, when he was made a Commander of the Order of St. Michael and St. George—a prelude to his later knighthood.

The war meanwhile had faced those left at home with many critical problems— shortage of raw materials, for instance, and the loss of printers, compositors, binders, stitchers and all the other skilled tradesmen who make books. The whole story of these harassing problems need not be detailed as they have become only too familiar from more recent experience. But it must be recorded here that for more than three years the firm owed a great deal to James Paterson, who was luckily a director of resource and tact. If an untidy, ill-mannered youth slouched into his office, he would be met with the utmost courtesy. "Was it wise to ignore such gross bad manners?" asked an eye-witness after one incident. "That lad," Paterson replied, "is one of the most important people in the business. He is all we can get to drive our lorries. We must keep him at any price." On the other hand, there were series like *The Nation's Library* which rising costs and shortage of paper made it impossible to keep. But despite this, a few up-to-date schoolbooks were devised; and a very large number of Bibles was printed for men in the Services who had in their turn become the heroic characters of a new and stirring type of children's fiction. It was hardly surprising that elderly peace-time dowagers like *Juliette the Mail Carrier* yielded place to *Hunting the U-boats*, *With Beatty in the North Sea* and *'Midst Shot and Shell in Flanders*.

By 1917, a new situation confronted Godfrey Collins when he completed his soldiering abroad and resumed his publishing and Parliamentary duties. He noticed at once that the supply of paper and other raw materials was in jeopardy, that labour, actual or potential, was draining away into the fighting services and the munition factories faster than ever, and finally that costs were soaring. He therefore made a swift, dramatic change in publishing policy.

It was obvious that such series as the *Sevenpennies* were no longer an economic proposition in view of the stark rise in costs and the increasing scarcity of paper. The *Sevenpennies* were accordingly jettisoned, leaving any titles thought worthy of retention to be published later at an increased price—at first 1s. 3d. and later 2s. But it was also evident by this time that competition with other publishers in this field had diminished the sources of supply of good fiction by popular authors. And so, after weighing these issues carefully in the balance, Godfrey Collins decided that the time was ripe for putting into action a long-cherished plan. As regards the supply of titles for the cheap reprint market, he would make the firm quite independent by publishing his own original fiction. But also, having entered the field for the best available novels, he would by no means rule out reputable books in other fields such as history and biography. He would in fact return to the ideals of the first William and concentrate on developing an original list.

For this purpose a London publishing office was essential. London after all was the acknowledged centre of the publishing world and only there, he felt, was it possible to maintain close contacts with authors, literary agents and on the trade side with the lending libraries and other important customers. It was with all these considerations in mind that he secured a new London office at 48 Pall Mall, began an urgent search for original fiction, history, biography and poetry, found them at surprising speed and so, under the harsh pressure of war, reshaped the firm's destiny.

CHAPTER XIV

A New Destiny

1917–1932

I

IT IS an irony of history that one of the largest lists of original works in modern publishing should have been started in response to the exigencies of war. Yet, like the modest children's annuals, it was no more than the revival of an old idea. The first three Williams had from time to time published original literature along with their Bibles, schoolbooks, and reprints; and William I in particular had helped to found the house's fortunes by publishing original manuscripts by Dr. Chalmers, Wilberforce, Edward Irving, Pollok, James Montgomery, and other theologians. Now, in altered circumstances, the "ancient good" was to be fashioned in fresh forms.

The 1917 autumn list contained fourteen works by authors whose names are still remembered. But if their selection was a tribute to the firm's discernment, their publication severely taxed its traditional pertinacity. "Godfrey Collins and his editor (Gerald O'Donovan) found the manuscripts all right," said an old member of the firm in later years, "but they soon discovered that to print them in time would seriously interfere with the firm's existing commitments. And these were pressing. Orders for Bibles for the troops and school texts were pouring in, and a hundred and thirty-two expert printers and bookbinders were on active service. An obvious solution was to place the contracts with other firms; but these like ourselves were short of technicians. For several anxious weeks the fate of the new list hung in the balance until Godfrey, by skilful diplomacy, combined several famous printers and binders in an all-out effort. This succeeded in producing 80,000 copies of the fourteen books by the promised date."

Godfrey began his young list with an old master—Henry James. It was a shrewd choice. In his lifetime the "Grand Literary Panjandrum" had enjoyed great prestige; and though this was followed, after his death (1916) by public indifference, that almost inevitable penalty of successful talent was still to come when the house bought four posthumous works from his executors—*The Ivory Tower*, *The Sense of the Past*, *The Middle Years* (autobiographical) and *Within the Rim*.

Along with Henry James came another famous old Victorian —Mrs. Humphry Ward, whose later books the house published, beginning with *Missing*.[1]

But though the 1917 list thus began with eminent Victorians, it was also notable for younger writers like Francis Brett Young, a gifted poet and prose writer, most of whose important work was to be published from Pall Mall during the next ten years or so. During the war Brett Young had served as a medical officer in the East African campaign: hence *Marching on Tanga*, a book which paved the way for his subsequent better-known novels— *The Black Diamond*, *Red Knight* and *Cold Harbour* for instance— and a volume of poetry entitled *Poems 1916-1918*. Among the other 1917 books was *Turgenev* by Edward Garnett, with a preface by Joseph Conrad.

The 1918 lists included works by such well-known authors as Sir Arthur Quiller-Couch and J. D. Beresford, the firm's literary adviser. Of Beresford's novels the house published about a score in the 'twenties, though their dissatisfied author thought they were written too quickly, under the dire compulsion of making

---

[1]Her subsequent Collins books were *A Writer's Recollections*, *The War and Elizabeth*, *Harvest* and *Cousin Philip*.

ends meet. His special virtue was that despite his preoccupations he could still find time for a quite selfless search for novels by young writers.

During the next two years, with Beresford's guidance, Godfrey Collins continued to add variety and distinction to the list. He also earned personal honours of his own—a knighthood like his grandfather before him (1919), and a political appointment as a Junior Lord of the Treasury, which he soon had to resign owing to an unlucky fall which damaged his knee-cap and, following an operation, gave him a permanent stiff leg. Except for his constituency duties, he was thus to have no political cares until 1924 when he became Chief Liberal Whip.

In the meantime several authors of note were added to the list. These included Victoria Sackville-West, an authentic poet whose first three novels *Heritage*, *Rebellion*, and *The Dragon in Shallow Waters* the firm published, and Sarah Gertrude Millin, the South African writer, who brought four books in all (*The Dark River*, *Middle Class*, *Adam's Rest* and *The Jordans*). Katharine Tynan, whose novels Collins published until her death in 1931, St. John Ervine three of whose novels were issued from Pall Mall, and John Middleton Murry (*Aspects of Literature*, *Countries of the Mind*, and *Discoveries*) were other well-known names of the period. There was also Rose Macaulay.

Rose Macaulay's first contribution to the list was *Potterism* (1920), precursor of those outstanding novels of hers which the house has published ever since. *Potterism* was an immediate success. Stretched out before her humorous eyes lay the whole of British society with all its post-war follies—a target impossible to miss, and one which enabled her, while England laughed loudly, to do for the English Potters what Sinclair Lewis did for the American Babbitts. The critics may have differed about her satirical style. Some thought that her mission of stripping away the veils of stupidity and social hypocrisy was overcast by the very cleverness and sustained swing of her satire. But though on this the critics differed, their variance did not prevent the public from chuckling with Miss Macaulay through the years as she continued to expose social inanities in *Told by an Idiot*, *Crewe Train*, *Staying with Relations* and the rest. It certainly did not affect the popular enthusiasm which greeted *The World My Wilderness*, a Book Society Choice of 1950 which is undoubtedly the author's most successful novel to date, and one whose very considerable sales, thirty years after the publication of *Potterism*, set the seal on a long and distinguished literary career. *Potterism* was still selling strongly thirty years after publication.

The year 1921 in particular brought a notable harvest. Romer Wilson's *The Death of Society* was the first novel to win the Hawthornden Prize. In *Fruits of Victory* Sir Norman Angell added a scholarly sequel to his gloomy forecast of war's consequences *The Great Illusion*. Eleanor Farjeon brought her delightful fantasy *Martin Pippin in the Apple Orchard*, Admiral Evans *South with Scott*, of which more than 100,000 copies were to be sold, Rose Macaulay *Dangerous Ages*, and Henry Williamson *The Beautiful Years* (his first book). Poetry, too, was represented by *The Island of Youth* by Edward Shanks, the first winner of the Hawthornden Prize on its foundation in 1919.

Shanks' poems from the outset reflected the house's own instinctive approach to poetry. Essentially a coinage struck in the so-called " Georgian " mint which Edward Marsh, J. C. Squire and Harold Monro had fostered so devotedly, his verse was among the first to temper the harsh memories of war with a "conspiracy of release," and a new emphasis on the natural beauty which had inspired the work of the post-war Georgians. This apart, the house believed in "poetic language " and form: hence its willingness in the early post-war years to publish the poetry of Francis Brett Young and Gerald Gould.

Looking again at the books of 1921 one finds among them works by two writers of genius—Walter de la Mare and H. G. Wells. As a novelist of world repute, Wells was able to command very large advances and the highest royalties on his new books. As a row of his first editions would show, he had also had many publishers, which may explain the "truism " in the book trade that it was difficult to make money by publishing his works.

The House of Collins certainly did not disprove this when it issued, in 1922, the only Wells work of which it was the original publisher—*Washington and the Hope of Peace*, a topical piece of reportage. None the less, in a different setting, its happy and mutually profitable relationship with Wells resulted in the sale of some 2,500,000 copies of twenty-four of his titles in cheap editions, the rights in which were acquired in 1921 by Sir Godfrey, who once again showed his skill and judgment in negotiating a big literary ' deal.'

To go from H. G. Wells to Walter de la Mare is a weird journey from a teeming world of flesh, blood and urgent prophecy into an enchanted twilight. That many of de la Mare's poems with their unique quality will still be read centuries hence seems as certain as that anything will be read at all. But his prose, too, will endure; for it springs from the same brooding on beauty and "secret laughter" which inspire his exquisite metrical arabesques, and sometimes from that deep pool of darkened reverie which prompted Frank Swinnerton's remark that he would as soon have Walter de la Mare's guidance through a graveyard as anybody's.

In 1921 Pall Mall published de la Mare's novel *Memoirs of a Midget*—the moving life-story of a dwarf who peered through chair legs on her own level (or down the arched throat of a greyhound), and who because of her pygmy size could only be a remote participant in the loves and stresses of every-day life. Not many writers could have handled such a theme; for as a sensitive critic, Richard Church has said since, it looked at life from a point of view that had hitherto baffled human imagination.[1]

After his imposing success with *Memoirs of a Midget*, de la Mare turned to short stories—hence *The Connoisseur* (1926)—and in the meantime Sir Godfrey Collins arranged to reprint *The Return*, a fantasy in which the spirit of an old French adventurer takes possession of the body of a simple modern man, and *Henry*

---

[1] *Crossings*, the author's first play in verse, was published in 1924 together with Armstrong Gibbs' delightful musical score.

Brocken. Much later Walter de la Mare was persuaded to compile *Tom Tiddler's Ground* (1932), a delightful annotated anthology of verse for children.

II

About the time Walter de la Mare came to the house, and for some time after, popular reaction to the evils of the war had taken extravagant forms—extremism in politics, bitter realism in some forms of literature and cynical luxury-loving in social life. It was not a pleasant period, but it produced in Michael Arlen a writer who hit the contemporary social mood so successfully that he quickly became one of the best-selling authors in the early post-war years. /

Arlen, naturalised son of Armenian parents, had gone to study medicine at the University of Edinburgh, where, like the great Charles Darwin before him, he apparently found it more congenial to study botany in the fields and hills outside the city than in the lecture room. He then went to London to cultivate his literary tastes, lived for a time in a single room in Shepherd Market, and began to write the novels which were to bring him fame. By 1924 three of these had been published from Pall Mall without any appreciable stir. Then came *The Green Hat*—a vivid, amusing novel which appeared shortly before Sir Godfrey Collins contested Greenock at the "Zinovieff Letter" election (1924). The book's destiny is perhaps best described by following Sir Godfrey to Greenock. On the morning of polling day, when his political future was supposedly at stake, his election agent enthusiastically declared: "You will be glad to hear, Sir Godfrey, that the Sixth Ward is polling strongly." The only reply he got was an ecstatic murmur: "Think of it! Seventy thousand copies! Never been known before! What a winner!" And winner it certainly was. Within three years 200,000 copies of *The Green Hat* were sold. Since then its sales have exceeded half a million.

Bridewell Place, London, December 31st, 1940

In these many ways, then, the character of the literary list was fashioned in the 'twenties. As with all publishers there had been ill-fortune with some publications now and then, but most of the fortune was good. It was certainly so in April 1929 when Helen Beauclerk's *The Love of the Foolish Angel*, a novel with decorations by Edmund Dulac, contributed to publishing history as the first Choice of the newly established Book Society. Since then the firm has had more than thirty-five such choices.

III

Two other important developments took shape in the later 'twenties. One was a general growth of the firm's markets and its organisation, the other the sudden phenomenal success of its detective stories.

To cope with the first development, Sir Godfrey decided to reorganise and expand the Pall Mall office so that he could centralise in the same building his three essential publishing departments—editorial, sales and publicity. For his executives he resolved to give youth its opportunity, and at the same time confirmed his strong belief in the efficacy of the training which the hard school of Scottish publishing traditionally imparted by transferring some of his young men from the north. Thus in January 1926 F. T. Smith, who had succeeded Herbert Hayens as Editor in Glasgow, came south as Chief Editor, a post which he has now occupied for twenty-six years. For the responsible position of Sales Manager Sydney J. Goldsack was an obvious choice. Still in his twenties, he had already rendered the firm notable service. When the New York office was opened in 1923 he was the first resident manager there, and later made two trips round the world, visiting the West Indies, Canada, Japan, China, Malaya, India, Ceylon and the Middle East. His return at Christmas 1925 was opportune, and the following month he entered upon his new duties at Pall Mall. Incidentally, he was the last representative to make the complete round-the-world trip on behalf of the firm, for so large had the overseas business grown that henceforth special representatives were appointed for the American and Far Eastern journeys.

The Publicity Department was to play an increasingly important part in promoting sales and under the vigorous direction of R. J. Politzer has set new standards in the difficult but essential art of book promotion, which more and more in these modern times has become of paramount importance in the conduct of a successful publishing business. Soon, too, the Production Departments, which were naturally centred in Cathedral Street, were re-organised. General fiction and non-fiction came under Thomas Greig; John Geddes took over the production of children's books; and G. F. Maine was made responsible for the Pocket Classics, dictionaries and other books of reference.

Crime fiction was already quite old when in 1919 the House of Collins published its first detective novel. Three-quarters of a century earlier Edgar Allan Poe's *Rue de la Morgue* had been the first of all detective stories; and since then Wilkie Collins, Conan Doyle, Austin Freeman and others had firmly established the detective story *genre*. By the nineteen-twenties there was, in fact, such an eager "detective" readership that bishops in London clubs were no longer concealing their interest in blood-stained putty knives and the sleuthing of their favourite detectives behind the expansive camouflage of *The Times* newspaper. But here we meet the old conundrum: why should detective stories be so popular in such unexpected quarters? Some of the answers to the riddle are obvious enough. Philip Guedalla, appreciating that the great need an occasional withdrawal from their very greatness, once described the detective story as the "normal recreation of noble minds." In a less rarefied atmosphere, to ask any housewife or hotel receptionist why the criminal romance is so often her favourite reading, is usually to discover that this form of fictional adventure brings glimpses of a new world far removed from the hum-drum affairs of life. Sheer curiosity, one of mankind's strongest instincts, provides another reason:

a detective is a curious searcher for clues, and his follower, the reader is as curious to know the result. Perhaps, too, the very fact that the detective is a hunter wakes a subconscious elemental instinct, for if only a few of us understand the technique of hunting animals, we can fully sympathise with both hunter and hunted when both are human beings. But of course in the end detective novels succeed for the same reason as any other novel. If they are skilfully constructed, if above all their characters achieve an independent existence, they will be read again and again. The best detective stories live because their characters live.

None the less, it is unlikely that these academic considerations were in the mind of Sir Godfrey Collins and his staff when they modestly announced Bernard Capes' *The Skeleton Key*—"a story dealing with a crime committed in the grounds of a country house, and the subsequent efforts of a clever young detective to discover the perpetrator." This, the first of a long, long series of detective novels to be published by the house, appeared in the spring of 1919; and within a few months of its publication, a flood of unsolicited crime-story manuscripts poured into the Pall Mall office. Among these was *The Cask* by Freeman Wills Crofts, a forty-year-old Belfast engineer who during a long illness, had amused himself by writing a detective story. Wills Crofts' ingenuity in breaking down the criminal's unbreakable alibi and his masterly handling of technical problems at once suggested a find, although, by his own confession, he was not quite master yet of his new craft. A number of revisions were therefore suggested: these he cheerfully accepted; and the result was a "masterpiece of practical crime detection" which by this time has sold a vast number of copies. Freeman Wills Crofts quickly attracted notice again with a new detective—Inspector French, who appeared for the first time in *Inspector French's Greatest Case* (1925). Meanwhile, the list of detective stories by other authors had been growing so fast that by 1926 it included such familiar names as Lynn Brock (creator of Colonel Gore), J. S. Fletcher (whose detective stories were a solace to Woodrow Wilson in his last illness), and G. D. H. and Margaret Cole, that erudite pair who were once described as "an educational movement in themselves," but whose academic erudition failed to stifle their crime-writing output. There was also Agatha Christie (creator of Hercule Poirot), who but for the advice of her mother and Eden Phillpotts might have been an opera singer.

Agatha Christie's first Collins novel, *The Murder of Roger Ackroyd* (1926) was soon recognised as a crime classic and as a splendid example of her virtuosity. After this boundary hit in her first over—a metaphor which will soon appear appropriate—Mrs. Christie has never ceased to score all round the wicket of public favour: it was, as the blurb-writer said of a later book, "certainly are remarkable witness to her unfailing verve, that when she is nearing her half-century, she should still be able to knock on slap over the top of the pavilion to the fervent applause of her crowd of admirers." When her fiftieth novel appeared in 1950 it was the then Prime Minister, Mr. Attlee, himself who declared:

> "Fifty books! Many of them have beguiled and made agreeable my leisure. I admire and delight in the ingenuity of Agatha Christie's mind and in her capacity to keep a secret until she is ready to divulge it. And I admire, also, another of her qualities, one that is not always possessed by those who produce detective stories; her ability clearly and simply to write the English language. I am looking forward to the next fifty books."

In the ensuing years so many serious rivals arose to challenge the *Observer's* verdict on Agatha Christie as "the acknowledged queen of crime fiction the world over," that in 1930 the Crime Club was formed. This organisation was an entirely new medium for crime writers, and one which proved that a publisher by such means could successfully run a special kind of story independent of his general imprint. The Crime Club plan, a combined editorial sales and publicity offensive, was simple but effective. Its mailing list of members received advance information about each month's detective stories; and these were chosen by an expert body of selectors, described by Torquemada in the *Observer* as "a gang of five headed by Dr. Alington," well-remembered as a distinguished headmaster of Eton and later Dean of Durham, who yielded to none in his admiration for the art of the detective story. The "gang's" first choice was Philip MacDonald's *The Noose*, a book which quickly proved the efficacy of the new idea. For not only were the author's sales quadrupled, but soon after publication the *Evening Standard* snapped up the serial rights of *The Noose* and sent its vans round London with suitable advertising banners. Within twelve months the Crime Club had acquired 20,000 members, and the judges were making their monthly choices from some three hundred manuscripts. But here, in defiance of chronology, we might conveniently list a few of the writers published over this well-established and popular imprint—Anthony Gilbert, Elizabeth Ferrars, John Rhode, Richard Hull, Shelley Smith, E. C. R. Lorac, M. G. Eberhart, J. Jefferson Farjeon, Ethel Lina White (whose famous story *The Wheel Spins* became even more popular through its subsequent film, *The Lady Vanishes*), Raymond Postgate (a brother of Margaret Cole), and Rex Stout (creator of the celebrated Nero Wolfe). There was also the mysterious Nicholas Blake of whom the 1935 Spring list asked: "Who is this ' Nicholas Blake ' who is bringing into the detective story a quality of writing that is usually associated with masterpieces in other fields of literature?" It took some years to answer the question. But the quality became less surprising when it transpired that this was the *nom de plume* of the distinguished poet, Cecil Day Lewis, who now occupies the Chair of Poetry at Oxford.

There was also Ngaio Marsh, a New Zealander who seems to have gravitated naturally to Collins, so long established on her native soil. Together with Agatha Christie, Dorothy L. Sayers and Margery Allingham she makes one of a feminine quartette which finds itself so much at home amid scenes of murder and carnage as to establish a near-supremacy in detective fiction. In the 'twenties Ngaio Marsh (whose Christian name, pronounced "Nyo," is Maori for a flowering tree) had played Shakespearian rôles for a theatrical company in this country. In New Zealand she is an enthusiastic leader of the repertory theatre movement.

But by good fortune, and despite the footlights' call, she turned to detective-story writing with such success that one reviewer who knew his Chief Inspector Alleyn remarked with gentle wit: "Dorothy Sayers had better be sure her crown's on straight." By equal good fortune she became a Collins author in 1939 (*Overture to Death*); ten years later the firm's imprint was on half a dozen other volumes; and Penguins were publishing a million copies of ten of her best-known titles.

Apart from the orthodox detective story sponsored by the Crime Club, which relies for its appeal on the ingenuity of the problem set the reader, there was also a noticeable increase in the popularity of the thriller-adventure type of story, the best of which followed the John Buchan tradition. Secret agents, foreign agents, F.B.I. agents rushed through the pages of these fast-moving stories—not as single spies but in battalions, or so it seemed. Successful exponents of this school are Charles Franklin, Berkeley Gray, Allan MacKinnon, Laurence Meynell, Lester Powell and J. M. Walsh. And lest such books might be deemed to favour unduly the masculine reader, the house also began to publish for these women readers who enjoy light romances such popular writers as Renée Shann, Pamela Wynne, Mary Howard, Helena Grose, Maysie Greig, Anne Maybury, Marjorie Warby and a host of others.

Western stories of cowboy life presented another fruitful but curious market to be examined. "Westerns" have long been an established feature of most lists of popular fiction—and, as most of us would agree, why not? All may not reach the distinction of Zane Grey, but in fact the standard of competent story-telling among the more popular Western authors is extremely high. Certainly, there is something in their books that appeals to the eternal boy in every male inclined to sigh reminiscently over the days when they conned "Ballantyne the brave and Cooper of the wood and wave." But also, since they demand less concentration than detective stories, while appealing like the latter to all classes, they form the escape literature *par excellence*. It is said indeed, that when Mr. Lloyd George wished to relax from affairs of State over a week-end, his reading ration was often half a dozen stirring stories of the Far West, many of them written by the Collins team of Western "spell-binders."

IV

These tidal waves of fiction during the 'twenties and early 'thirties did not undermine the rock-bottom of the firm's business —its Bibles, schoolbooks, works of reference, children's books and stationery. The overseas trade in Bibles, William IV's special province, was particularly flourishing, not least in the United States where the New York branch had greatly increased its trade under the energetic guidance of David Campbell. Home sales were equally encouraging, so that by 1931 the sale of Bibles, New Testaments, Prayer Books and Hymn Books exceeded 600,000 copies. But in view of the firm's long Scriptural tradition, this could hardly have been otherwise. By the same token, it would have been surprising if schoolbooks had stagnated during the restless 'twenties when the air was brisk with educational theory.

In fact, Sir Godfrey and William IV, at the end of the war, had launched a new schoolbook policy which meant the discarding of many good old texts which had done duty since Victorian days. In their place came a whole series of specially commissioned works by outstanding scholars. The late Professor de Selincourt, a scholar of note, edited a series of reading books for elementary schools; Kenneth Bell the Balliol don performed a similar service for school histories; T. W. F. Parkinson of Manchester set on foot the *Reason Why* Geographies, a series quickly followed by the geographies of Dr. Marion Newbiggin; while John Drinkwater edited and "introduced" a number of reading books and a series of Single-Play Shakespeares. But the new policy went even farther. "I think," wrote an old member of the firm to the present author, "that we were quick to take advantage of the Fisher Act, and actually planned a series of books for the Day Continuation Schools proposed to be set up under that Act, but unfortunately axed by Sir Eric Geddes. This series included a book on Simple Economics by Mrs. Lettice Fisher, wife of H. A. L. Fisher himself, and history books by Professor Raymond Beazley and Andrew Browning. These books firmly laid the foundation of our new programme after the 1914 war, and paved the way to a further expansion and reconstruction under a new educational manager at Cathedral Street, John Crossland." John Crossland's chief contributions were the *Laurel and Gold* schoolbooks, including his own anthology of verse of which more than half a million copies have been sold, and, later, the *Silver Torch* series for very young children.

Anthologies received particular attention in this new drive. The first of these notable collections was John Drinkwater's *The Way of Poetry*, an almost perfect little anthology for children, with an introductory essay sensitively designed to make young readers wake to the full glory of English poetry. The sales of *The Way of Poetry* were spectacular; for not only was the book's own merit at once recognised but its appearance happily coincided with the great success of Drinkwater's chronicle play *Abraham Lincoln*. It is pleasing to discover that in view of the anthology's popularity, Sir Godfrey voluntarily and gladly revised the terms of the original contract.

Another successful anthology was *The School of Poetry*, a collection compiled for "golden lads and girls" by Alice Meynell in her own silver old age, and opening, since she had a sure instinct for the child love of bright imagery, with:

> *The King sits in Dunfermline toun,*
> *Drinking the blude-red wine.*

Alice Meynell briefly annotated many of the poems she had chosen. Unhappily, she died before the book had gone through the press; and as its best tribute to her distinguished muse the house included her own poem *The Shepherdess*. The other anthologies included J. C. Squire's *The Comic Muse*; *The Laurence Binyon Anthology* which the house had invited the poet to make from his own works; and E. B. Osborn's *Anthology of Sporting Verse.*

There were also of course, in these post-war years, modern out-of-school books with subjects ranging from the open air to railways, motor-cars, ships and aircraft. To look further ahead —to 1934—the firm set a seal on the progress of the 'twenties by acquiring the British Walt Disney rights (in company with Messrs. Dean), and publishing the famous *Silly Symphony* and *Donald Duck's* Annuals, and *Snow White.* Within five years the sales of the Disney books exceeded 6,000,000 copies. For the very young came such delightful fantasies as the *Little Grey Rabbit* books by Alison Uttley and Margaret Tempest, and *The Adventures of Mr. Horace Hedgehog* (a Royal Family Christmas gift book). But we have gone far ahead.

Returning to the early 'twenties and the rest of the firm's traditional output, stationery made sufficient headway to belie its name, but the cheap reprint business brought complexities.

Costs of production, to name only one, soared quickly in the post-war years to thrice their pre-war level. Thus the novel which formerly sold at 6s. was forced up to 7s. in the autumn of 1919 and to 9s. in 1920. In the following year it dropped to 7s. 6d., but by this time the permanently increased cost of raw materials was playing havoc with the price structure of the cheap reprint libraries. Faced with this problem in a sphere particularly their own, the directors were forced to recast their policy, but they did not on that account debase their product. Ever since the reign of William Collins III they had striven to produce as many books as possible for as many people as possible at the lowest possible price. Now, as they looked at the post-war scene, it appeared that an army of potential readers was kept out of the ordinary bookshops by the barrier of price. The directors argued therefore, like several other publishers, that it might be possible to get sales so large (and profitable) as to bring down the price of cheap books still further; and this they succeeded in doing with two new series—the *Novel Library* and the *Shilling Novels* (1928). The *Novel Library* varied from thrillers to Galsworthy's

Forsyte novels and various books by Somerset Maugham (two Heinemann authors); yet each volume, bound in linette cloth, cost only sixpence and the firm still made a profit. The equally popular *Shilling Novels* had a sale of one million copies within a year, though not without severe challenge from other publishers. To meet this the house characteristically advanced its fighting line by announcing " The World's Best Shilling Novel " (in cloth and pictorial jacket), and sold another million copies within twelve months.

How then was this done? The answer is enterprise, organisation and luck; and in none of these ingredients of success at this time can the most careful historian find the house deficient. Taking luck first, the year which saw the *Novel Library* also saw the first general distribution of the "talkies"—a sensational development in itself, but one also which gave "books of the film " remarkable sales and proved beyond doubt the screen's influence on the book trade. Good organisation, since we have been in and out of the editorial offices and printing works for more than a century, can perhaps be taken for granted. Enterprise can never be. In this instance, since sales had to rise far above the " Plimsoll " mark of costs, and the friendliest booksellers were a little reluctant to sell sixpenny books (even by Somerset Maugham), the *Novel Library* was diverted into chain stores, bookstalls and other public emporia.

Less successful was the firm's later attempt to restore the *Sevenpennies* (1934). Experience by this time had proved the public's desire for cheap novels, but except for the chain stores most booksellers still refused to handle anything lower than a cased book at sevenpence. Some of the same prejudice now rose against the new *Sevenpennies*. The booksellers, who contended as they had done before, that the *Sevenpennies* would destroy the market for higher-priced books, built up such a formidable opposition that both Collins and one of their competitors had to withdraw them altogether. But the house had still another card to play. It introduced the sixpenny *White Circle* novels, so called because of the white circle on the jacket design in which the author's name and title were displayed, and these, were soon in tremendous demand.

But again we have looked far beyond the vital, formative phase between 1917 and 1932. Clearly, the book side of the business was making considerable progress. But so, too, was stationery, a branch which got fresh impetus in 1927 from the appointment of W. A. G. Morgan, first apprenticed to the firm in 1910, as London manager at Bridewell Place. Abroad, in the meantime, the house was as diligently recultivating its Commonwealth markets.

Thus in 1929 a new Australian stationery factory was opened near Sydney in New South Wales.[1] In Canada, as we know, roving Collins representatives had given an impetus to the firm's trade there for many years. But by 1926, when a resident representative, William Bonellie, was appointed, it became obvious that a permanent office, even a small one, had advantages. Bonellie's appointment was, however, short-lived as in 1930 he resigned to start his own business. A year later Franklin F. Appleton, a former President of the Association of Canadian Bookmen, was appointed in his stead. A year later still when it was decided to open a branch office at 70 Bond Street, Toronto, where stocks could be held, Wm. Collins Sons & Co. (Canada) Ltd. was incorporated.

[1] Soon after the Second World War, this factory was sold when the firm's Australian book and stationery interests were separated.

CHAPTER XV

Altering Course

1932-1939

I

ON THE 1st October 1932, at the age of fifty-seven, Sir Godfrey Collins joined the Cabinet and was made a Privy Councillor. The Parliamentary lobbies were not surprised by his appointment, but Sir Godfrey spoke later of his "utter amazement" when the Prime Minister, Ramsay MacDonald, invited him by telephone to become Secretary of State for Scotland. He also confessed to a feeling of dismay at having to relinquish his formal publishing functions in accordance with constitutional practice. In the ensuing years, however, there is little doubt that his keen gaze often swivelled round from Whitehall to Pall Mall where the younger generation, already seeing bright new vistas, were about to have greater authority.

His years of office were fruitful. Godfrey Collins was not one of those politicians who stride the political stage with gusto amid a constant shower of fireworks. Disliking violent controversy and the "Roman candle" phrases of rhetoric, he never shone in the House of Commons as an orator, though his speeches there were as clear and businesslike as his remarks in the boardroom. On the public platform he always tried to be honest with hecklers and dealt forthrightly with an issue in much the same way as he governed Pall Mall. He was also patient and good humoured, had a knack of reconciling views in conflict, was quite unsentimental when public money was at stake (like his grandfather, William II), and examined his officials' schemes with Pepysian thoroughness. Similarly, although during his term of office he had to deal with more than thirty Government Bills on Scottish affairs, he never allowed himself, as some Ministers do, to lose sight of main objectives under a smothering mass of detail.

During the new Secretary's tenure of office the desirability of returning to Scotland the major part of her administrative machinery was early given serious consideration. He did not live to see the establishment of St. Andrews House—Scotland's "Whitehall" in Edinburgh—as an enduring monument to the patriotism and vision of himself and his immediate successors, but he had many other achievements to his credit. Hearing that children spent too large a part of their holidays in nervous anxiety about their future, he greatly reduced the time for publishing the results of school-leaving certificate examinations. After a typically careful study of the financial minutiæ of land settlement he created several hundred land holdings of from five to nine acres, each with a house and small steading, for use as market gardens or pig and poultry farms. He first applied to Scotland the principle of minimum wage-rates for land workers. He introduced a Scottish Housing Act to relieve overcrowding and ordered the first comprehensive house-to-house survey to discover its full extent. He set up the Herring Industry Board and carried through an Illegal Trawling Act to help inshore fishermen. Thus by 1935, when he fought his last Parliamentary election in Greenock after representing that constituency for a quarter of a century, he had justified his tenure of office, though some of his more extreme opponents thought so much to the contrary that his election campaign was one of the rowdiest since the Reform Act. In the Town Hall once, the audience drowned not only the organ which was endeavouring to cast an Orphean spell on the tumult, but even the voice of the Minister of Labour, the Rt. Hon. Ernest Brown who owned the most robust vocal chords in Great Britain. But this of course was the sort of challenge to whet his stubborn fighting quality. If he could not be heard in the Town Hall he would try to get a hearing in the back courts and greens of the town; which he did by arming his family with a bell and addressing the bell-summoned audience at the open windows of their tenements. In the end he polled the biggest number of votes in Greenock's history.

Sir Godfrey by ill-fortune did not long survive this heartening vote of confidence. In 1936, while holidaying in Switzerland, he was taken seriously ill. An operation was performed at Zurich in vain; and he died there on the 13th of October.

Numerous tributes were paid him. Speaking for the authors, Rose Macaulay said:

> "Never did any publisher realise more fully than he the identity of interest of publisher and author. . . . The more of a nuisance one was the more gracious was he, and the more he made one feel that his rights were one's own."

In the House of Commons the Prime Minister, Mr. Baldwin, ended a moving tribute by quoting Sir Godfrey's last words to him:

> "I want to tell you how I enjoy my work, how I love working for Scotland, and with what pleasure I work with all of you."

II

The younger generation of the family meantime had begun to translate their ideas and idealism into action. By 1932 I. G. Collins, William IV's second son, was industriously mastering the technicalities of Bible and schoolbook production and the export trade. Occasionally he was missing from the Cathedral Street office on special missions—defeating Cochet in the Men's Singles at Wimbledon, playing in the final of the Men's Doubles, representing Great Britain in the Davis Cup, playing for Scotland at tennis and cricket (against Australia), and riding in point-to-point races. Sir Godfrey's son William Hope Collins had served with the Royal Artillery as a professional soldier but he, too, had succumbed like his ancestors to the lure of printer's ink. And in the meantime the future Chairman, W. A. R. Collins (William V) had more and more taken over the publishing duties of his uncle in the latter's enforced absence at the Scottish Office. He came with the determination to extend the firm's output and still further improve its quality. It was of course true that the firm's light fiction and reprints, its Bibles, schoolbooks, children's stories, atlases, diaries and all the rest of Cathedral Street's traditional stock-in-trade were flourishing; and without doubt the book sales organisation, with Sydney Goldsack as Sales Manager, had constantly and greatly improved. But one thing was lacking—as in every publishing house there was always room for the recruitment of authors of quality.

A significant new name on the list was that of Winifred Holtby. She had already served her apprenticeship in fields other than literature. Being a young woman of wide enthusiasms, she had crusaded buoyantly for the League of Nations, justice for the black races and equality of rights for women, with a burning sense of mission which was saved from tedious fanaticism by her humour and sense of fun. But despite all these activities she had never lost the vision of writing as her main career, and had already published a book or two elsewhere. Though immature, these works and her occasional journalism had already attracted Pall Mall when she brought ideas for future books to be published under the Collins imprint. Frequent meetings did not lessen this attraction; and so, in January 1933, appeared *Mandoa! Mandoa!* a novel unfortunately overshadowed by Evelyn Waugh's brilliant *Black Mischief* which dealt with the same theme (Abyssinia) and was made the choice of the Book Society. Her next book was a collection of short stories. And then came her masterpiece, written with the certainty of death already upon her. This was *South Riding*. To complete it she returned to her native Yorkshire at the beginning of 1935, rented a grey cottage on the sea-front at Withernsea, and wrote with heroic endurance until by August the book was finished. A month later she was dead—at the age of thirty-seven. But six months later when *South Riding* was published, it was seen by most critics to be the work of a ripened, sensitive intellect. Sir Herbert Grierson, Professor of English Literature at Edinburgh, awarded it the James Tait Black Memorial Prize for the best novel of the year. It was the choice of the Book Society. And since then its sales not only in the English language but in Dutch, Danish, Swedish, Czech and German have become phenomenal.

Within a short time three other gifted women writers of Winifred Holtby's generation had joined the company of Collins authors. These were Rosamond Lehmann, Margery Sharp and Marguerite Steen.

Member of a family well-known in the world of the arts— her father was R. C. Lehmann, the *Punch* humorist; her sister Beatrix is an actress of renown and her brother John a poet and publisher—Rosamond Lehmann owns a technical brilliance and sensitivity, combined with an intuitive knowledge of women which makes her feminine characters outstanding creations. *The Weather in the Streets* (1936), a novel subtle, limpid, often exquisite in style, was a particularly noticeable example of her powers: it was to be followed by the even more sensitively told *The Ballad and the Source* (1944).

Margery Sharp is a writer whose gaiety and wit have been deservedly rewarded by large sales on both sides of the Atlantic. Deservedly, because her versatility is exceptional. In her time she has contributed to both *Punch* and the *Encyclopædia Britannica*; and in her books she moves easily from sparkling comedy to gripping drama. It is this unusual range which makes readers await each new book with pleasurable anticipation, and which has made *The Nutmeg Tree*, *Cluny Brown*, *Britannia Mews*, and *Lise Lillywhite* such big successes in their very different ways.

Marguerite Steen during her picturesque career has played many rôles, as kindergarten teacher, dancer and actress. Clearly, therefore, she has the best of all qualifications for the successful novelist, experience of life. Thus in the 'thirties she scored

14, St. James's Place, London

immediate successes with novels of contemporary modes and manners, though her greatest fame was to come later with the publication of that vast panoramic novel, *The Sun is My Undoing*, and its sequels *Twilight on The Floods* and *Phœnix Rising*.

There were other women writers with a public of their own in those years: Doreen Wallace who wrote about the East Anglian countryside; Helen Ashton who was to write widely-read biographical novels on the Wordsworths and Jane Austen; and Faith Compton Mackenzie, one of whose delightful volumes of memoirs left the impression, said her famous husband, that he was an amiable lunatic, but he liked it!

Among the masculine discoveries of the period was Howard Spring whose life story is itself a romance. Born in Cardiff, one of a family of nine in very poor circumstances, Spring left school before he was twelve and became a messenger boy in a local newspaper office. While still young he secured a place on the reporting staff, later served for some time on the *Yorkshire Observer* in Bradford, and then joined that nursery of distinguished writers, the *Manchester Guardian*. An article for the last newspaper attracted Lord Beaverbrook's attention and brought an invitation to come to London where, as literary critic of the *Evening Standard*, he added lustre to the position which Arnold Bennett had made so important in the book-reviewing world. But it was the very nature of his duties which altered his destiny. Coping as he so often did with the usual flood of fiction that finds its way to reviewers' desks, he began to think that he could do at least as well himself as a creative writer. So he wrote *Shabby Tiger*, his first novel (1934), a book soon to be followed by that outstanding success *My Son*, *My Son* and other bestsellers on both sides of the Atlantic.

Then there was the phenomenal Peter Cheyney, a writer who himself experienced many of the thrills of which he wrote: he once ran a detective agency and bureau of special investigation which led him into extraordinary adventures; he was wounded as a young captain on the Somme during the First World War; he was an expert fencer of championship class; and despite English ancestry, his novels—with alluring French titles such as *Le Valet Prend la Dame*, *Sinistre Rendez-vous*, *Un Whisky de plus* and *Les Femmes ne sont pas des Anges*—had made him in fact France's most popular author. In this country, also, there is no writer who has commanded such spectacular sales since his first novel, *This Man is Dangerous* appeared with the Collins imprint in the autumn of 1936. Thereafter continuously and gigantically these increased until on his death in the summer of 1951 his books constituted one of the most valuable literary properties handled by the firm. Many, many times must the creator of Lemmy Caution in these years of success have looked back quizzically to other less settled days when he worked in a solicitor's office, on the stage, as a crime investigator, and as the writer of songs and sketches for Nellie Wallace and other music-hall artistes.

The year 1936 also introduced into the catalogue the unconventional genius of T. H. White. The work there announced was *England Have My Bones*, a book so beautiful in the very passion of its patriotism that it caught the attention of many readers. Of the further development of the relationship between himself and the house T. H. White has himself written:

"I did not want to be a schoolmaster. I wanted to be an author. Unfortunately it takes time to earn one's living as an author, so I supported myself by teaching, and wrote novels in the holidays. I wrote nine books like this, all uniformly unsuccessful.

"Then a day came when I had taught everything I knew. I noticed that I was thirty years of age and realised that, if one did not escape now, all opportunity of escape would be gone forever. I had saved about a hundred pounds, and my English publisher was Collins, the kindest and bravest publisher in England. I went to him and asked him for help. He said he would advance £300 a year for two years, and leave the rest to me."

"Leaving the rest" to White meant the end of his schoolmastering. He rented a gamekeeper's cottage, where by his own confession, he started off with several bottles of Madeira, plenty of ink and paper, and a copy of Malory. The outcome was *The Sword in the Stone*, an Arthurian fantasy for children (and grown-ups) so unusual that it must be read to be explained, and so anachronistic as to evoke from *Twentieth Century Authors* the comment: "The strange rustle he must sometimes hear as he writes his versions of Arthur and Guinevere and Lancelot is probably Alfred, Lord Tennyson turning restlessly in his grave." Of this extraordinary book many impressions have been printed.

Within a year of T. H. White's advent came a South African novelist, Stuart Cloete (pronounced Clooty). As a youth he had failed for Sandhurst, but joined up in the Coldstream Guards during the First World War, was severely wounded several times, and, being supposedly unfit for a sedentary life, started to farm in South Africa. There he wrote *Turning Wheels*, an heroic novel of the great Boer trek, which became both a Book Society Choice here and the Book-of-the-Month in the United States—the first occasion any first novel had achieved the double honour. Since then it has been translated into a dozen languages, and the house has published the rest of Stuart Cloete's picturesque and powerful romances.

During the last two pre-war years, the fiction list seems to have lost little in colour and variety. It included, for example, that uncommonly original and stimulating writer Claude Houghton, John Brophy whose striking *Gentleman of Stratford* has often been reprinted, and Leo Walmsley, who widened the list's range with novels of the narrow seas. It might also be said that Walmsley added unusual colour to the chronicle of the firm's authors—as an ex-flying officer in the First World War, former member of a scientific expedition to Central Africa, inventor of a patent lobster-pot, maker of his own furniture from planks of wood washed up on the Cornish coast, and builder of his own house !

This broadening of the fiction list's range during the 'thirties was not entirely due to British writers. From 1934 onwards, there was a steady inflow of manuscripts from the United States, which in themselves provide an interesting illustration of the unexpected ways which so often lead a publisher to authors of distinction.

In the early autumn of 1934, William V and his wife set out on their first visit to Canada and the United States. One purpose of this visit was to inspect the office of the firm's new Canadian company; the other was to call on New York publishers in the hope of finding new books suitable for the Collins list. "In the Macmillan office," William V has since recalled, "we were very impressed by the striking jacket of Mary Ellen Chase's novel *Mary Peters*. When I asked if *Mary Peters* was free for Great Britain, I got the reply that it was on offer, but as no reply had been received, I was welcome to read it. I did so that very night, and made an offer the next day. It was at once accepted, and that was the beginning of the big list of American novels we were to build up during the next ten years."

A similar visit took place four years later; and again chance took a hand when Mrs. Collins espied the bulky proofs of Taylor Caldwell's *Dynasty of Death* in Charles Scribner's pocket at lunch one day. This proved to be a best-seller and the forerunner of others.

In the meantime, the firm had secured the British rights of a number of important American novels. Among these were two famous books—*All This and Heaven Too* by Rachel Field, a writer who like Winifred Holtby was reaching the zenith of her power when she died tragically young, and *Northwest Passage* by Kenneth Roberts, America's foremost living historical novelist. Kenneth Roberts, an encyclopædic historian, particularly in the byways which more academic writers have left unexplored, was an important acquisition. Being also an ardent lover of his native Maine, he found in that state and in New England not only a deep well of inspiration for his stirring stories of early American history, but support for his belief that history can be most effectively told in the form of fiction; and indeed it would be difficult to detect the slightest errors of historical detail, either in *Northwest Passage* or in his later novels—*Rabble in Arms*, *Oliver Wiswell* and *Lydia Bailey*.

Unfortunately, there is no room here to describe in detail the long list of American authors with Collins associations,

but some of their names are familiar enough; Agnes Sligh
Turnbull for example, and Ethel Vance, Christine Weston,
Marcia Davenport, Walter Edmonds and James Ramsey Ullman.

To turn aside from fiction for the moment is to find the Poet
Laureate's name on two pre-war volumes of verse—*The Country
Scene* (1937) and *A Tribute to Ballet* (1938). Both of Mr. Masefield's
volumes were finely illustrated by Edward Seago the artist.

At the same time more of the list than ever before was
devoted to history, biography and belles-lettres. Hence—to quote
an outstanding example—Robert Gore-Browne's *Bothwell*, an
excellent contribution to Scottish history and the forerunner of
many other interesting biographies.

Douglas Jerrold's *Georgian Adventure* appeared in 1937. Thereafter for the next dozen years, amid all the turmoil of war and
the vicissitudes of conducting his own considerable publishing
business, he was preparing his vast and important work *An
Introduction to the History of England*, the first volume of which
appeared in 1949.

Peter Quennell, who is also a poet, is probably best known for
his discerning literary criticism expressed in a style which bears
comparison with his subjects. But it was as a biographer that
he first came to Pall Mall—with *Caroline of England*, a rich subject
for his sympathy and a gift of delicate satire capable of describing
King George II as a monarch to whom "adultery was a duty and
marriage a pleasure." In *Byron in Italy* Quennell appeared as both
historian and critic, a rôle which he maintained in *Four Portraits*
—a collection of biographical studies which views the eighteenth
century through the lives of Boswell, Gibbon, Sterne and Wilkes
—and in his 1949 work *John Ruskin*.

Another new-comer in the late thirties was Lord Elton,
academically impeccable, and one of the pre-war leaders of the
movement to rescue the Oxford school of history from the
dry-as-dust relics of Stubbs and restore to it a sense of
perspective, that power, to quote Douglas Jerrold, of "surveying
the whole field." Among his most popular works have been *St.
George or the Dragon*, an eloquent appeal for an appreciation of

the spiritual value imperilled by the war (1942); and *Imperial Commonwealth*.

III

As the list gathered this considerable momentum in the early 'thirties, a new and formidable question arose in Cathedral Street: could the existing printing plant meet the firm's expanding needs? A careful study was therefore made of the latest types of machinery. Just as his father Sir Godfrey had visited Germany thirty years earlier, William Hope Collins in 1932 visited the United States to examine American equipment and works design. As the result of his visit and a similar examination in this country, orders were placed for over £100,000 worth of printing presses and modern binding machines.

The pace of this interior reorganisation was matched in 1936 by an outside extension in Taylor Street (abutting on Cathedral Street), which has a notable sentimental interest. The added new buildings had belonged to the famous publishing house of Blackie, and their acquisition was a big transaction involving the construction of a tunnel between the two streets, and one happily celebrated by the following letter from Walter W. Blackie to William IV:

> "This is just to express my sense of satisfaction that the vacated premises of our old works should have passed into the hands of William Collins and Company and not to any outsider. The premises were originally those of Andrew and J. M. Duncan, Printers to the University, and were purchased by my grandfather in 1829. Moreover your great-grandfather and my father were, in those early days, closely associated in many philanthropic and other objects. . . . Then my father and your grandfather, Sir William, were friends through life. So altogether I feel that you are the ideal custodians of the ancient printing premises."

Though primarily designed for the book-producing side of the business, the new building was no less important to the stationery side, Collins being so essentially a firm of interlocked interests that at times when book sales have dropped, the stationery branch has usually provided a countervailing gain and enabled the firm as a whole to preserve a solid basis of prosperity. The manufacture of stationery in the same buildings —by a fine lineage of skilled craftsmen—has also given variety to the business, and the strength which comes from a highly developed community sense.

Casting up their accounts in the mid-'thirties William IV and his co-directors, in the light of all these developments, must have seen that the house was larger and busier than at any time in its history. But inevitably, during a period of such rapid growth, something had been lost. There were those in the firm who could remember a *Punch* reviewer praising a Collins book away back in 1917 for "the beauty I have already grown to associate with the imprint of its publisher." But a lack was felt in the quality of production, despite the commissioning of Rex Whistler, an artist of genius, to design book wrappers, Clare Leighton's *The Farmer's Year*, generally acknowledged as a fine piece of book production, and attractive books on hunting, the countryside and painting. But as this did not go far enough, the directors decided to attack the problem from its type foundation. They could not have chosen a better moment. By this time the devoted labours of Francis Meynell, St. John Hornby, Stanley Morison and other typographers had succeeded in creating a new consciousness of the beauty (and the practical importance) of good print. Moreover, in 1932 this new article of literary faith had been blessed by the cardinals of Printing House Square, whose public were delighted one morning when *The Times* came out in a completely new type face, *Times* Roman. But even before this the firm had toyed with the idea of creating a new type face for its own use. Eventually, it was decided to bring Dr. Hans Mardersteig from Italy to Glasgow for this purpose in view of his typographical experience and brilliance of eye.

Dr. Mardersteig soon found a new source of inspiration—the lucid Roman and Italic which the Foulis brothers of Glasgow had made famous throughout Europe in the eighteenth century.

From this classical spring of pure design Dr. Mardersteig drew the ideas which he canalised into " Fontana "—the type in which this book is printed (eleven point), and one which enabled the house in 1936 to announce itself as the first great firm of publisher-printers to create its own "face" for use through the entire range of its productions. The beauty of that type and the clarity on which the beauty rests is well illustrated by the following example in 18 point:

> You only, O Books, are liberal and independent. You give to all who ask, and enfranchise all who serve you assiduously.

Though the interior of a Collins book was now pleasant to look at, the firm decided to add a final touch. The late Eric Gill, then at the height of his fame as an artist, was invited to design a new house colophon: the result was the austere fountain which decorates the title page of this book.

Unfortunately, this intensely creative phase of the 'thirties was approaching its end as World War II came near its beginning, though there does not seem to have been any slackening of energy. With only one year of peace to run, William Hope Collins was honoured by an invitation to take on the Presidency of the ancient Stationers' Company of Glasgow as the first two Williams had done before him.[1] A new four-storey building, adjacent to Cathedral Street, was completed in St. James's Road. And finally, the long term machinery plan reached its triumphant end, just before the outbreak of war in September 1939.

[1] Nine years later he was also elected President of the British Federation of Master Printers.

CHAPTER XVI

Through the Storm

1939-1945

I

THE HOUSE'S wartime task was seen to be immense from the outset. Its transoceanic interests had to be maintained in the path of enemy submarines and aircraft. Paper and other raw materials were likely to be in as short supply as skilled employees, of whom almost five hundred served in uniform, and another five hundred in munition factories.

Yet in spite of the war's fierce impact on normal publishing, the early prospects were only unpromising on the surface. The very tension of war seemed to refine the public taste for art, music and literature, to heighten the demand for poetry and the classics, and to sweep the great Victorians back to favour. The most popular, exciting kind of novel still found, of course, a ready sale within the limits of the restricted paper supply, but serious fiction was bought eagerly by a public reluctant to live its hours of ease in mere excitement. How, then, was this new situation met?

The catalogues soon dwindled in size, though the spring list of 1940 (prepared some time in advance) still had such a prosperous look that its editor blithely quoted, "cheerfulness will keep breaking through," adding his own wise corollary that

265

good books, more than ever, were becoming part of the nation's daily needs.

Then came the storm—Dunkirk, the collapse of our allies, the swift conquest of Europe by Hitler's armies, and the transformation of Britain into a lonely fortress. It was a time of peril, yet also one of pride. The nation, uncertain no longer, suddenly became united, conscious of its heritage, and in the mood to seek inspiration and encouragement in the past. It was in this memorable hour that the house announced *English Saga* by Arthur Bryant.

Arthur Bryant was new to the Collins list. His previous books on Charles II and Pepys had been published elsewhere, and his reputation rested on his knowledge of the seventeenth century. But his first Collins book indicated the new path he had henceforth mapped out for himself, namely the more recent English history which has had the most direct influence on our own times. No path more congenial could have been found, for Dr. Bryant has always had as passionate an interest in the making of his own age as in his country's past.

English Saga—at first published jointly with Eyre & Spottiswoode but now entirely the firm's property—is a grand review of the hundred years concluding with the outbreak of the last war, and was at once recognised by scholars and the public alike as a work of high importance and interest in its field. On its appearance in 1940 it was a Book Society Choice, and its sales still go on at the rate of many thousand copies annually. With *The Years of Endurance* (November 1942) Dr. Bryant began his study of the Napoleonic Wars from the British point of view, continued it in *Years of Victory* (December 1944), and concluded it with *The Age of Elegance* (November 1950). As this last volume ends in 1822 and *English Saga* begins in 1840, he proposes to link up the intervening years in his forthcoming biography of Disraëli. In the meantime a signal success has greeted Dr. Bryant's first three volumes of the life of Samuel Pepys, which were originally published by the Cambridge University Press in the 'thirties and subsequently re-issued with the Collins imprint.

In the firm's own saga the year 1940 will long be remembered. During the fierce air raid of 29th December, Bridewell Place—storehouse of both books and stationery—which had weathered so many storms over seventy years, succumbed to the most violent of all. William IV as chairman at once offered the staff the option of leaving for a safer area or of removing to Glasgow. Unanimously they voted to remain in London, and a swift move, organised by W. A. G. Morgan with great resourcefulness, was made to new premises at Bow Street.

Meanwhile, at the height of the hurricane, the firm was launching in conjunction with Messrs. Adprint, *Britain in Pictures*, an enterprise in which the house took especial pride. Originally designed to temper the war tension by reminding Britons of their cultural heritage, *Britain in Pictures* was an immediate success when the first volumes appeared on 21st March 1941. Seeing them in a bookshop window on the deserted front of a scarred and battered South Coast town, the Chief Editor F. T. Smith asked himself at the time whether they were not in fact "the bright banners on the battlements of our island fortress or, more modestly perhaps, the defiant cockades that a nation of shop-keepers might justifiably flaunt in the faces of their book-burning foes?"

The reflection is eloquent, but *Britain in Pictures* only reached its battlefield bookshops after long and careful planning. Its sponsors aimed at reflecting the British way of life in all its varied colour. Each volume was adorned with coloured illustrations and fine prose. The late W. J. Turner, a gifted poet and critic, acted as editor. The tributes were glowing.

"Not three months after that bad night when Hitler's bombers lit the second fire of London and destroyed the centre of the English book world," wrote Viola Garvin in the *Observer*, "the old and famous house of Collins shakes its head, steps out of the ashes, and comes forward with as timely and bold a bit of publishing as was ever planned. . . . These books manage to distil ' the glories of our blood and state' and with neither vanity nor pomp to make clear to ourselves, as well as the rest of the world, the full and serious nobility of our heritage."

At the same time several writers, new to the list, were also reminding readers that there was more in life than Bren guns and black-outs. Bernard Darwin by 1942 had brought *Life is Sweet, Brother* and *Pack Clouds Away*, two delightful examples from the pen of an essayist in the tradition extending from Addison and Steele to Robert Lynd, Max Beerbohm, Harold Nicolson and Ivor Brown. The biographical tradition was maintained by Hesketh Pearson's *Bernard Shaw* (1942), a biography written in close co-operation with Shaw himself, who gave every possible help to his biographer, allowing him to quote whatever he wished from published and unpublished correspondence, answering every question put to him and revealing a great deal of information about his own life that had not been available hitherto. In the result the book was universally recognised as a very fine life of a great man. The victorious years from 1943 to 1945 brought certain distinguished authors who were new to the list. Among these was Edmund Blunden.

Being not only a distinguished poet but a leading authority on the Romantic Revival, Edmund Blunden was already a name when in 1943 the house published his *Cricket Country*, a book rich with the undertones of peace and well worthy of a contemporary tribute—"a beautiful mind brought to a beautiful game." But a more important Blunden book was to follow in three years' time. This was *Shelley*, a contribution to literary history recognised as the most discerning appreciation yet written of that "poet's poet." Incidentally, Edmund Blunden was not left alone with his period. In 1945 the house published Professor Jack Simmons' excellent *Southey*.

There were also the historians. One was Milton Waldman, an eminent Elizabethan historian who joined the firm in 1938 as a literary adviser and whose best known work *Elizabeth and Leicester* was to be followed by his study of Elizabeth in the *Brief Lives* series. This also included brilliant contributions by C. V. Wedgwood, J. A. Williamson, Roger Fulford and Herbert Agar.

Sir Reginald Coupland's *Wilberforce*, previously published by the Oxford University Press, had been the best of all books about the great reformer, and its subject had been intimately linked with the house's early fortunes. It was therefore gladly reprinted by Collins shortly before the war ended. Then came his two original works—*Livingstone's Last Journey* and that perfect little account of a military action, *Zulu Battle Piece*. Later still Professor Herbert Butterfield brought two distinguished works, *History and Human Relations* and *Christianity in European History*.

Fiction, in some form or other and at all times, is the friend of everyone—from the patient in the sick-bed to the trapeze artist or the metaphysician. As with other kinds of book the demand for fiction was sharpened in the war years. Troops for example, especially those serving abroad, sought the lighter type of fiction first and foremost; while people at home wanted a " good story " quite as eagerly as their sons abroad. The only trouble was that the demand could not be fully supplied, as the firm knew to its cost. However, soon after the outbreak of war it was fortunate enough to recruit a new lineage of novelists in much the same way as it had enriched its list of historians and biographers during the years of peace. These included Thomas Armstrong, Nigel Balchin, Norman Collins, Hammond Innes and Noel Streatfeild.

Thomas Armstrong's first novel was *The Crowthers of Bankdam*, a book, later to be filmed, which reached its eighth impression by the end of the war. He also wrote *King Cotton*, a spectacularly large post-war novel (longer even than *Gone With the Wind*) of which more copies were sold in the year of its publication than any other British novel, and *Adam Brunskill* (1952), a book in which he returned to the nineteenth century Yorkshire scene which he knows so well.

Hammond Innes had written in his peace-time leisure four thrillers. During the war he turned his hand to sterner tasks. As an officer in the Eighth Army he took part in the Sicily landings, and finished his military career as a major. But war had given him more than a taste of adventure and foreign travel. When it ended, he saw new opportunities, at once took up writing as a whole-time career, and soon emerged as an outstanding writer of thriller-adventure stories so successful that his book *The White South* earned for him a Book Society Choice, an honour also awarded to *Campbell's Kingdom*. But then he believes in writing from experience and travels widely in search of copy.

High in the list of popular favourites among the newcomers was Norman Collins (not a kinsman of his publishers), who apart from being a busy B.B.C. executive by day found time by night to write his best-selling novels—*London Belongs to Me*, for instance, and his exciting adventure story for children *Black Ivory*. Later his *Children of the Archbishop* became a world-wide favourite.

Nigel Balchin's rise to fame is a most interesting success story. In 1936 he had modestly appeared on the Collins list as the author of *Lightbody on Liberty*, a delightful skit on bureaucracy which the firm's reader, advising acceptance, called a "gorgeous frolic." The "frolic," however, kindled no great fire: about eight hundred and seventy copies were sold, which probably was a normal sale for a first novel at the time; five copies were sold on the Continent. Somewhat greater success attended his *Darkness Falls from the Air*. But it was not until the appearance of *The Small Back Room* (1943) and *Mine Own Executioner* (1945) that both critics and public discovered a writer in whom great narrative power was combined with a remarkable control of his own subject-matter; a control gained by a thorough professional experience of scientific and psychological technique.

Noel Streatfeild, a lady who had once played opposite such celebrated actors as John Gielgud, forsook the stage for writing. None of her peace-time novels and children's stories were published from Pall Mall, but early in the war her *The Winter is Past*—written at a time when she was acting as a night canteen worker in Deptford's air-raid shelters—made Noel Streatfeild a regular and welcome Collins author.

A less pleasant interlude in the wartime story occurred in

1944 when the Pall Mall office was destroyed. Ever since the earlier destruction of the Bridewell Place warehouse, Pall Mall had enjoyed a charmed life, but in the early hours of 23rd February several high explosive bombs fell round St. James's and No. 48 was demolished. In the resultant confusion several events were unforgettable. Harold Raymond, chairman of Chatto and Windus, came round to Pall Mall, picked his way among the debris of the building, saw the lady members of the staff nobly trying to collect manuscripts and scattered files, and generously offered the immediate tenancy of a flat in his own King William IV Street offices. No less heartening was the unexpected arrival of Mr. Winston Churchill on a tour of inspection of the ravages of the previous night, as if to remind the staff by his presence that while literature is ultimately imperishable, so, too, is the spirit which creates and defends it.

But the war's horizons were wider than Pall Mall. While the firm was rising again from the ruins of London, Bernard Fergusson, a Scottish professional soldier, was writing work of singular merit in the torrid jungles of Burma. There he must have reflected wistfully sometimes on his ancestral Ayrshire home at Kilkerran, whence for many centuries the Fergussons had built up a splendid tradition of service to the State and to scholarship. One of his ancestors was, indeed, Lord Hermand, that genial judge of the eighteenth and early nineteenth century, whose all-night cups prompted Lord Cockburn's *mot*: " Commonplace topers think drinking a pleasure; but with Hermand it was a virtue." Still, good claret was far from being the chief end of Hermand's life. His love of literature, especially for Sir Walter Scott, once prompted him to produce *Guy Mannering* in court and read a number of passages aloud with gusto to his protesting fellow judges. A hundred and thirty years later, another Fergusson was not only fighting in Burma deep behind the Japanese lines but unbeknown to any publisher at home was writing a book in his less combative moments, which Lord Hermand could have read aloud with still unstinted pleasure. This book, and how it came to have the Collins imprint is another interesting illustration of the strange ways in which a publisher often secures a distinguished manuscript.

Somewhere around 1943 an article by Bernard Fergusson about the first Chindit expedition appeared in *Blackwood's Magazine*. By a fortunate chance at this point, Ian Collins appeared on the scene from one of his secret adventures with the Special Air Service, said he knew him, and there and then cabled Fergusson requesting the MS. of a book if he decided to write one. The answer came virtually in the form of the tattered MS. of *Beyond the Chindwin*. *The Wild Green Earth*, its sequel, followed, and then *Lowland Soldier*, a volume of war-time verse with nostalgic memories of Kilkerran:

> *Call on the cattle clearly!*
> *In the evening home seems near:*
> *God knows that I love it dearly*
> *And perhaps I shall hear;*
> *Perhaps in bivouac or battle*
> *Some evening it may befall*
> *I shall hear you calling on the cattle,*
> *Carrick voices calling on the cattle,*
> *And come to the call.*

In 1950 the house published Bernard Fergusson's fine tribute to his own famous regiment, *The Black Watch and the King's Enemies*.

II

Cathedral Street, more fortunate than Pall Mall and Bridewell Place emerged unscathed from the Glasgow air raids. That the Empire's second city, as it then could claim to be, would inevitably become an enemy target had been in the mind of William IV from the beginning of the war. For the Clyde being one of Britain's lifelines, its huge industrial potential was quickly harnessed for shipbuilding and munition-making; and even the new Collins four-storey building, completed on the very eve of the war, was offered and accepted as a munition shadow factory.

W. A. R. Collins

Among the early precautions taken at the height of the 1940 blitz was the removal of master sets of Bible plates, some to the stables at William IV's Ayrshire home, and some to Canada.[1] Though proved unnecessary by events, this wise move led to the printing of the Bible in Canada for the first time. Meantime the long-established transatlantic Bible shipments continued—despite dwindling labour resources and German submarines. The latter in particular caused many anxious moments, not least in the New York office when it was known that certain consignments were crossing the Atlantic in convoy. If they arrived safely there were smiling faces. With equal certainty there was gloom when the manager was heard to refuse a telephoned request for, say, half a million Testaments; or once, when a long overdue consignment of Bibles urgently wanted for a Christmas season arrived without the necessary landing documents. On that occasion, the longer the delay in the docks the more Stygian grew the office atmosphere, till suddenly came the good news of its release, whereupon the entire staff was mobilised as a packing unit to ensure that the Bibles would reach the Middle West and the Far West in time.

The Scriptures were also wanted in other parts of the world. Scotland's National Bible Society was supplied with half a million Bibles during the war in different bindings—khaki for the Army, dark blue for the Royal Navy and light blue for the Royal Air Force. If a shipment of Bibles was sunk—as happened once when a merchant vessel carrying a mixed cargo of Collins Bibles and whisky was torpedoed—every effort was made to replace the loss. In the end the firm produced more than two million Bibles and Testaments for the British and American forces alone—one of the many feats for which the Glasgow Bible manager, the late James More, and the Bible craftsmen at Cathedral Street deserve credit. In return of course came dollars, and, even in wartime, the firm's never-ending African correspondence on Scriptural matters. For example, there was one letter from a small native

[1] 1,082,850 Bibles, New Testaments and Prayer Books were printed at Cathedral Street in 1940—a total more than double that in 1895.

child, which asked " Mr. Collins " for a Bible with great politeness
and added the equally charming postscript: " Please ask God to
make me pass my examination this year."

Credit for the wartime achievements is not, however, confined
to any one quarter of the firm, nor for that matter to the present
generation. Many, many times during the war the directors
must have been stirred by a sense of profound gratitude that their
ancestors had planted so sturdy an imperial tree. For inevitably,
had the Commonwealth branches failed, the house would have
emerged at the war's end seriously weakened. As it was, many
Dominion branches started to publish and print on their own
territories for the first time. Thus 11,000,000 copies of the famous
White Circle novels were produced during the war in Australia,
Canada, South Africa, India and Ceylon.[1]   This achievement
merits a closer look.

When it became clear that the supply of books to Australia
was endangered, the Sydney branch with the aid of a number of
leading printers in New South Wales and Victoria, began to
publish the firm's books on its own, starting off with Australia's
own distinguished novelist Eleanor Dark (*The Timeless Land*),
and even printing ready reckoners, diaries, dictionaries and
atlases.   The Australian manager was then Alec B. Glen, who
was succeeded by F. O. Howe, who went out from London in
1946.   In Auckland H. J. Preston, head of Collins, New Zealand
since 1932 and a member of the firm since 1907, also organised
his own production and maintained a steady rate of publication
despite the absence of many of his staff on active service and
the usual shortage of publishing raw materials.

In South Africa Mrs. C. A. Roy not only became the firm's
representative after her husband joined the South African forces
—he was taken prisoner by the Germans—but looked after Collins
interests with such vigour that after the war Roy wrote to
Cathedral Street: " For nearly six years you had a woman
representative, one Mrs. C. A. Roy, who showed her husband a

---

[1] By 1945 the total sales of the *White Circle* novels since their inception exceeded
30,000,000 copies.

few points in the matter of adding prestige and popularity to the representation of the House." Roy was later succeeded by John Donaldson, with whom was presently joined—for the territory is now far too large for one man—R. J. Hardingham, who had served in the R.A.F. and been awarded the Distinguished Flying Cross for his attacks on the *Scharnhorst*.

The chief representative in India was K. Jackson Marshall, a member of the firm who for some years had travelled some forty thousand miles annually by air in the East and the Far East. By invoking the aid of Indian printers, Jackson Marshall produced almost 1,900,000 wartime books with the Collins imprint.

There remains Collins, Canada. Early in the war, when the Atlantic crossing was hazardous, many of the firm's books were printed in Canada from imported plates. But this was only a first step. By 1946 Collins, Canada, had produced no less than 11,000,000 books including many by Canadian authors. After the war R. Ross Taylor, repatriated from prison camp in Germany, was sent to Toronto where he is now in control of the Canadian Branch.

This, then, was the Commonwealth achievement. To William IV especially, since he had himself made five Commonwealth tours, the overseas frontiers of the business he controlled must in truth have looked far-flung, settled, and rich in promise. It was certainly to appear so to William V in 1948, when he flew 30,000 miles round the world in eighty-eight days, eight more than Jules Verne's hero took; but then that adventurer had neither branches of a business nor bookshops nor clamorously hospitable authors to visit.

III

For most of the world 1945 was a year of great, if transient, glory. By summer, tumultuous crowds were celebrating the war's end with thanksgiving in public places. In the privacy of the Collins board-room, too, there was relief though much of its property had been destroyed by enemy action, valued members of the firm had been lost, many authors—like the firm itself—had suffered a compulsory and inevitable cut in book sales, and the future looked uncertain. Yet life never lacks the compensation of good for its ill moments. The firm's old Empire chain had become a Commonwealth comradeship, the literary list founded in the First World War had been enriched in the Second and further enrichment was promised. Suddenly, this heartening outlook was darkened by the death of William IV.[1]

Before the war he had occasionally remarked that he might soon transfer even more of his responsibilities to the younger family members—a process which he had in fact begun as early as 1931. His sons and his nephew were already in full and unimpeded charge of their several spheres of the business. But the war removed not only two of the sons but many of the senior staff, and the chairman felt himself called, in those difficult circumstances, to prolong his labours. In addition he took over in the early days the care of many West of Scotland clubs run for servicemen from overseas, and latterly became responsible for similar clubs in the whole of Scotland. For this and other war activities he was awarded the C.B.E. in 1943. Yet despite all these many calls upon his time, and despite the impossibility of one man controlling directly the manifold details of the vast organisation over which he had so long presided, every employee down to the humblest sensed his personal interest in their work with the certain knowledge that the chairman, whenever referred to, would understand and help to overcome their particular problems. It was this quality, perhaps more than any other, which spread a sense of such deep personal loss through the entire firm when it was known that the friendly, distinguished presence would never again appear amongst them, smiling and indefatigable. He died on 3rd September 1945 at the age of seventy-two.

[1]His cousin and co-director for many years, William Collins Dickson, who had been living in retirement since 1929, also died in 1945.

CHAPTER XVII

Fanfare

1945 and after

I

DESPITE THE many difficulties the firm seems to have swung quickly into its peace-time stride. Though materials were still in short supply the demand for the firm's products continued brisk as ever; and the vacancies on the staff soon began to be filled as the absent members streamed back. Among these was the vice-chairman, I. G. Collins, who had returned with many battle honours (the Legion of Honour, two awards of the Croix de Guerre and the O.B.E.).

Since the Pall Mall offices were no more, the present offices at 13-14 St. James's Place—purchased during the war—were brought into full use: and certainly for an old publishing firm no more suitable premises could have been found. The two eighteenth century houses which comprised it—one of mellow brick, the other painted cream—were adjacent. They had the panelled rooms of their period, and graceful winding stairs; both were haunted by strange memories of the past. In this one building, as the two houses soon became, a William Wilberforce, (*not* the anti-slaver) had lived for a time, and, later still, it is said to have housed Mrs. Robinson, the beautiful "Perdita" to whom George IV, when Prince Regent, played no unimpassioned

Florizel. But the whole of St. James's Place, short street though it be, is thronged with the oddly contrasted ghosts of famous former residents—among them, appropriately enough, two literary figures: Oscar Wilde and Samuel Rogers, that almost forgotten Poet Laureate who confessed so charmingly to young Alfred Tennyson that he felt sure of his own poetry's immortality.

The coming of peace reminded many people of the oldest and most enduring of simple pleasures, the countryside. For the benefit of the countrysiders, so long cut off by barbed wire and defence regulations from their haunts, the list was extended, though for some years it had already been noted for works devoted to natural history, horticulture and ornithology. Now, a very distinguished venture in this field was launched in the form of *The New Naturalist Series*.

This ambitious collection had gone through the chrysalis stage of planning during a grim period of the war. It was first discussed in 1942 by W. A. R. Collins, Julian Huxley the biologist, James Fisher the ornithologist, and a director of Adprint Ltd. The project they discussed was the present chairman's own. For a long time he had pondered a new series of illustrated nature books which would be not merely a popular addition to the literature of natural history, but a series of definitive texts judged by the strictest scientific standards. It was therefore resolved to conduct a complete new survey of Britain's natural history with at least fifty titles, each written by a specialist and all edited by a committee of four—James Fisher, Julian Huxley, John Gilmour the botanist and Dudley Stamp the geologist: Eric Hosking was to be photographic editor.

There were tremendous difficulties to be overcome. Many scientists were on military or government service and photographic materials were hard to find. It says much for the firm's inbred obstinacy that despite the hindrances, the first two titles in the series—*Butterflies* by Dr. E. B. Ford and *London's Natural History* by R. S. R. Fitter—were on the market within three months of the end of the war. Since then, more than twenty titles have been issued.

Collins Magazine for Boys and Girls, which first appeared in January 1948, was also designed to meet an obvious need. The very young had their "comics," and adolescents turned often to adult literature; yet there seemed a gap between the two which books perhaps could only partially fill. Moreover, the house, which had run a successful children's magazine in the decades of the nineteenth century, was anxious to revive an old tradition. But again there were obstacles in the way. Because of paper shortage, to cite only one, no new periodical could be launched in this country, which explains why the *Magazine* was at first printed in Canada and shipped monthly to this country. Fortunately all these and many other difficulties were eased when the lifting of periodical paper control in 1950 enabled the *Magazine* to go full steam ahead.

While these varied new enterprises were making their peacetime way, a number of outstanding new names were added to the catalogues. An early newcomer was John Moore, a Gloucestershire writer whose service in the Fleet Air Arm had not obliterated from his memory the pleasant paths, rural humanity and wise good humour of his native county. John Moore brought a captivating trilogy: *Portrait of Elmbury*, *Brensham Village*, and *The Blue Field*. Of these, two were Book Society Choices; but apart from this accolade we can imagine all three still being read many years hence for their romantic picture of a good life which neither bombs nor the blinder forms of bureaucracy can destroy. Robert Henriques, also from Gloucestershire, found in the Cotswolds an attractive setting for his powerful novel *Through the Valley*. Another country writer, H. J. Massingham wrote with wisdom and knowledge of English rural arts. Christopher Sykes, a writer of style, contributed several volumes, notably his biographical *Four Studies in Loyalty*. Gerald Bullett brought one of the best studies yet written of George Eliot. Francis Steegmuller's *Flaubert and Madame Bovary* (an important study first published in 1939 but rather lost sight of in the first flurry of war) was wisely reprinted: it was also the precursor of a new and equally striking Steegmuller work, *Maupassant* (1950). In *Autobiography* and *Second Innings*, Neville Cardus, long famous as a writer on cricket and music, proved once again that the best journalism and literature are indistinguishable.

War books, however, still held their interest, somewhat surprisingly considering the general distaste for such literature in the years immediately following 1918. During the period of hostilities the firm had published a few chronicles of personal experience such as Gerald Hanley's *Monsoon Victory*, laid in Burma like Bernard Fergusson's two war-time volumes. But the success of these was surpassed by three titles which followed one another in fairly swift order, Roy Farran's *Winged Dagger*, Eric Williams' *The Wooden Horse* and Brigadier Desmond Young's *Rommel*—the first a personal account of remarkable experiences behind the enemy lines, the second a great escape story, the third the biography of one of the most brilliant and certainly the most fascinating of our enemies. The success of these books was astonishing. As these lines are written, the sale in this country of *Winged Dagger* is approaching 70,000, *Rommel* 210,000 and *The Wooden Horse* 440,000. In addition to these three bestsellers, quite substantial success was obtained by two personal memoirs written by distinguished war figures—Sir Arthur Harris' story of the *Bomber Offensive* which he directed, and Lord Templewood's account of his exceedingly delicate four years' task in Spain as *Ambassador on Special Mission*.

While these books were being written—and published—one author was constantly at work on the research necessary for a major history of the war and its consequences. Early in 1952 appeared Chester Wilmot's *The Struggle for Europe*, a book that was immediately hailed as one of the most important contributions to both military and political history; a book, moreover, whose great popularity was to bring its reward to author and publisher alike.

Carrying on the now well-established tradition of publishing a really finely produced book that by reason of the
high cost of production must appeal mainly to the connoisseur
rather than to the general reader, the firm brought out in the
autumn of 1951 a magnificent edition of Thornton's *Temple of
Flora*, perhaps the most coveted flower book of all time. For
an original edition several hundred pounds may be paid. In
comparison, the prices charged for this reprint—fifteen guineas
for the limited edition and eight guineas for the standard edition
—seem a modest exactment for such imperishable beauty.

This brings us towards the end of the London story. But
before the curtain rings down on St. James's Place, a noteworthy
event must be recorded—the start of the *St. James's Library* in
1950. By this means many books of merit which had already
found favour with reviewers and readers have been kept in print
at a moderate price. Nor is this library confined to any one kind
of book. With quality as the only test, it includes biography and
autobiography, literary criticism, history, belles-lettres, books of
adventure, and fiction including detective stories. In general, and
this seems to be the chief virtue of the project, the *St. James's
Library* consists of books which the discriminating reader wishes
he had read, or having read, and perhaps given away, wishes he
had kept on his bookshelves. Amongst the first titles selected for
publication were works by Rose Macaulay, T. H. White, Winifred
Holtby, Peter Quennell, Rosamond Lehmann and Milton
Waldman.

But the curtain is beginning to fall; and the last to appear
on our stage at St. James's Place is, curiously, a theatre critic
and, appropriately, a Scottish writer. Ivor Brown, an Aberdeen-
shire man, who was born in one Scottish colony (Malaya) and
educated in another (Balliol), is journalist, essayist, literary and
dramatic critic, novelist and philologist. *Winter in London* and
Summer in Scotland are full of the magic of place, but it was
highly fitting that he should have distilled into one fascinating
book his chief enthusiasms—the magic of words and the spell
of the theatre—and that almost inevitably the book's title was

Shakespeare, the "onlie begetter" on whom no curtain can ever fall.

II

At a greater distance of time, when someone uncovers the complete mosaic of Scottish writing in this century, it may well seem a striking achievement. A hundred years ago the literati of Scotland were remembering with reverence the not-so-distant Robert Burns, the Augustan Age of David Hume and his fellows, and the Romantic Age of Sir Walter. But they themselves seemed to be poised as it were in a sabbatical pause, until a new flowering began with Robert Louis Stevenson—not less a Scots writer because most of his work was written furth of Scotland than Eric Linklater who lives and writes on his native heath. Since Robert Louis there has been no break in the pageant. Nor, half-way through the present century, is there any sign of decreased vitality: more than ever Scotland has become a friendly soil for literature in all its forms.

During this prolonged renaissance the house of Collins has played its part. For many years it published the novels of Frederick Niven, a Glasgow librarian who eventually went to Canada, where he cultivated such interest in the American Indians that the Blackfeet of Alberta gave him the honorary title of Apasto—reputed to mean "one who uses the sign-language in converse." In common with Bernard Fergusson, George Blake has attracted an English as well as a Scots audience—a tribute not only to his fame as a broadcaster on many national occasions, but to the narrative power he has developed in novels about his native Clydeside, several of which have been Book Society choices. There have also been the vivid Scottish novels by James Barke—a Collins "discovery" of the early 'thirties— who achieved a world-wide success with his series of novels based on the life of Robert Burns.

But these writers carry a spear. The distaff side of the house's

Scottish literature has been no less active. Jane Oliver, with an acute historical sense, writes her novels of Scotland's past among historic Border hills. D. E. Stevenson, a widely read novelist whose stories are popular both at home and abroad, is a native of Edinburgh. March Cost is the author of a remarkable novel, *A Man Named Luke*, which has run into many editions and with her later work has gained her a considerable reputation abroad, especially in France. And what could be more sentimentally Scottish than that great success, *Geordie* by David Walker? But this brings us to Cathedral Street—for the last time.

III

If, while these words are being written, William I could revisit the business created by his burning energy he would probably blink with bewilderment at the fierce energy around him. Presently the bustle of men and the noise of machines, the hundreds of girls with gaily-turbaned heads, the hurrying executives, and the scores of different mechanical processes would appear as the long multiple rhythm of all those smaller rhythms which change gleaming white paper into millions of printed books. His recollection of his own struggles would be profoundly stirred. In those days, his little handful of men, huddled round his Stanhope lever presses in the Candleriggs, set up every letter by hand, using at first only home-made printer's ink until, as a great advance, he advertised his future use of the "best London-made." He would remember, too, how he worried about the quality of his paper; and why was the letter "z" in his first fount of type slightly blurred? To-day he would see some 2,500 people at work in the various buildings which comprise "144 Cathedral Street." Drifting through thirteen acres of floor space he would mingle not only with the members of the staff who handle authors' manuscripts in the early stages, but with the many kinds of skilled workers who make them ready for the bookshops—the compositors, machinemen, electro- and stereotypers, lithographers, binders, marblers, cutters, sewers, pagers, machinists, bundlers, chemists, engineers, and a score of other skilled trades. Among them he would also find men and women whose ancestors had served himself and his son. It is quite remarkable how long the firm has been served not only by successive generations of the Collins family but by successive generations of the staff in most branches of the business.

As a good printer himself, William I would no doubt wish to start his tour with the paper stocks, since paper is the primary raw material of the whole business. He would see it arriving in huge rolls and packages for temporary storage in long catacombs under the buildings. Nearby he would see the chemists' laboratory —a department perpetually busy testing inks, paper, cloth, and even glue, since household glue is regarded by tropical insects as such a luxury that the chemists must provide a special fixative which these distant enemies will find unpalatable.

Higher up in the buildings, meanwhile, the never-ending process of actual book production is in full swing. In the caserooms highly skilled monotype or linotype operators are sitting at their keyboards, punching out authors' words at astonishingly high speed. In other departments the size of manuscripts not yet ready for the compositors and printers is being estimated; type and lay-out is being chosen, hieroglyphic instructions pencilled for the caseroom and the printers.

The founder's biggest surprise would probably come among the printers in the machine rooms. For here, if they were all running at once, the machines could together produce at least 15,000 finished copies of a 256-page book within an hour. His astral ears might find it difficult to take in such figures, but certainly his astral eyes would be dazzled by what he saw. The new rotaries—printing on both sides of the sheet and throwing off 128 pages at a single revolution—would perhaps remind him of a river in spate as the unending sheets of white paper flowed swiftly down from the top of the machine. The illusion would change, as, standing in front of a lithographic machine printing children's books or say, the Collins *Graphic*

Atlas[1] he saw the colours being impressed on the paper as it rolled round the cylinders—like a whirling rainbow.

But perhaps the founder would feel more at home among the Bible-printing machines and their skilled printers, compositors, gilders and binders. For this is the trade of a century. There are gilders in Cathedral Street who remember the days when their fathers, working with gold leaf, used to rub their fingers over their hair and their beards, and sell both for the gold they held. There are no beards now. Nor, any longer, are fresh eggs necessary to make the albumen which, in its turn, makes gold adhere to the edges of a page or a Bible cover. But if a little of the old glory has departed, there is still romance to be found in the printing of the Scriptures, judging by the following message received in April 1948 from the Massachusetts Bible Society:

> "Although we had to stretch the size of the building to get them all in, we were most happy to receive 4½ tons of Bibles from Collins. I do not remember a shipment as large as that—it is a landmark in the Bible Society's history."

It was a landmark familiar to Cathedral Street. The Ruby Bible alone sells about a quarter of a million copies annually; and at a time when American currency is urgently needed by the nation's sorely-strained economy, hundreds of thousands of dollars accrue each year from the sale of Collins Bibles. Most impressive figure of all, in the hundred and ten years devoted to this work the house of Collins had produced (by 1950) some 70,000,000 copies of the Liturgy and the Scriptures.

Such sales of the "Guid Book" would rouse all William I's religious enthusiasm. His commercial zest might be equally excited by the development of the stationery business which he himself founded long before he had printed his first Psalm. He might even feel that this department of Cathedral Street justified his own fine-flavoured trade announcement:

[1]On 1st January, 1938, Collins and Longman made a joint atlas sales agreement to pool their resources except in areas where one or the other had a special sphere of influence.

CHALMERS & COLLINS beg to submit a SCALE of their Prices, for LEDGERS, JOURNALS, CASH BOOKS, &c. which, on examination, they trust, will be found charged on very moderate terms. They have calculated them all at the Money Prices; but if they are placed to account, a percentage, proportioned to the Credit, or the mode of settlement, will be added.

The Books will all be made of the best English Papers, except the Post and Foolscap, which will be of the best Scottish Makers.

From the variety of MERCANTILE BOOKS, they are unable to specify all the varieties; but each will be furnished on the same Scale. They are likewise enabled to furnish every description of SUPERFINE and COMMON WRITING PAPERS, and STATIONERY ARTICLES, in the same proportion.

    15, WILSON STREET, GLASGOW, ⎫
        1st March, 1824.   ⎬
                       ⎭

A century and a quarter later William I would still see the manufacture of account books, diaries of every imaginable kind from a Gardener's to the Royal and Merchant Navy Diary, cricket scoring books, writing-pads, more than 180,000,000 envelopes a year, many different branded lines of notepaper, even special notepaper for children. No one, indeed, should imagine that this department lacks its own brand of inventiveness and enterprise. Certainly William I had never thought so himself when he saw his stationery sales develop steadily year after year, even although the cost of sending a letter from Glasgow to London was thirteenpence. He got of course a fresh impetus from the introduction of the penny post in 1840. But the full benefit of this was reaped by William II who greatly expanded the trade, leaving William III to bring in a wide variety of new notepapers with names as attractive as many a fine old tavern-sign —Crown Parchment, Oxonian Blue, Old Kent Mill, and Royal English Linen. In our own time the founder would hear that despite the difficulties of tariffs and other hindrances to trade, the firm was still supplying markets all over the world with commercial and personal stationery; that in London the Bow Street and Long Acre warehouses, showrooms and offices were handling it all in addition to Cathedral Street's literary works; and that true to the past these London offices were situated in an area of historical interest and importance—beside the Covent Garden Royal Opera House and the famous Bow Street Police

Station. He would hear, too, that in Bow Street and Long Acre as well as in Cathedral Street there were faithful members of the firm with half a century of service behind them.

The Glasgow department known as Stock Control (comprising the whole of the old Blackie printing works) would be the next to engage his eager eyes; for during five days out of seven—the firm works a $43\frac{1}{2}$-hour week—all finished products arrive continuously in the stock-rooms. It may be any sort of book: whatever it is, it disappears into Stock Control where seldom less than 10,000,000 books of all kinds are ready for dispatch to booksellers. Children's books, now the firm's biggest export, have a floor to themselves. But on all floors the wanderer would see large packages of books with their titles for legend on the wrapping-paper. He would also see on the wall of each room an index, perhaps even someone consulting it as one consults a gazetteer, to find the exact location in the building of certain books just ordered by booksellers in Ashby-de-la-Zouche or Zanzibar.

It sounds simple enough. But this department mirrors one of the publisher's chief difficulties—the uncertainty of a book's fate. It is a difficulty which the present Chairman and his colleagues face to-day just as William I did when he, too, had his best-sellers. There must have been many occasions when his faithful old printers worked late into the night to meet urgent orders brought from London by stage coach. To-day, there is, and inevitably must be, the same uncertainty about initial printings.

A similar question mark hangs over the overseas markets. But these perhaps are more subject to historical trends than temporary popularities—trends like the growth of nationalism, or the desire to produce locally for economic as well as sentimental reasons. These were bound to affect the firm's trade in India and Pakistan, for instance. But elsewhere, nationalism has taken the familiar form of trade restrictions on imports, though books have fortunately been less subjected to this interference than the products of many other industries; and, where existent, it has generally taken the form of exchange quota restrictions rather than import duties or purchase tax. On the other hand, in almost any country, once a series of books or a particular author is established the demand continues. It is difficult to imagine Arthur Bryant's books falling out of favour in the Commonwealth, or the firm losing its trade in exercise books and other stationery lines in East, Central and West Africa. In all, Cathedral Street's exports reached a record value of about £750,000 in 1949, which is excellent business not only for the firm but for the nation, and a distinct contribution to international understanding. More than ever, books and correspondence in a confused, disordered world are good ambassadors.

There is a certain pride in this at Cathedral Street—from the board-room downwards. But one of the outstanding things about that roof-tree is its camaraderie. Modern analysts of the new craft of management make great play with their discovery that a business is a community. It is not new by the nineteenth-century test of Robert Owen (early) and William Collins II (late). In the Glasgow works, assuredly, family tradition is not confined to those whose name appears at the bottom of a Collins title page, for in most branches of the business William V has colleagues whose grandfathers worked with his; and such a continuity has naturally created a sense of mutual responsibility.

Every employee shares in the profits of the business, and has within recent years drawn an annual dividend equivalent to five weeks' wages. But this is only one part of a Welfare Scheme— run by an enlightened doctor with a staff of thirty—whose capacious wing covers every form of communal activity from concerts and a library to dental, optical and chiropody treatment. Additional to the National Health Service there is a sick benefit scheme, a contributory pension scheme, and Holmwood, a convalescent home on the Ayrshire coast established after the war as the firm's joint memorial to William IV and Sir Godfrey Collins. Even catering in the works canteen comes under this comprehensively-named "Welfare Scheme," and the Collins Institute which Sir William Collins founded so long ago in

W. Hope Collins

I. G. Collins

Collins Street. It is perhaps not surprising that since 1945, when conditions were inevitably unsettled, absenteeism has dropped from about twenty per cent to only four, and the hours lost through minor accidents or ailments over a twelve-month period from eight thousand to less than a hundred.

On such a note of social friendliness and communal aim this story might well have ended. It would, however, be incomplete without a record of the board of directors in 1949-1950,[1] when the firm was one hundred and thirty years old, and of a final memorable event in the firm's history.

It occurred at 10 a.m. on Wednesday, 14th December 1949, and with it the curtain again falls—on the last Cathedral Street scene. That it should fall on a meeting of the directors is fitting, for they have the day-to-day responsibility of guarding the far-flung interests of the business.

But this was an unusual meeting. For some time the directors had wished to bring the nominal capital of the firm closer to the real value of the business; they also wanted fresh working capital, and a free market on the Stock Exchange for Collins shares; lastly, they wished the firm's friends to participate in its prosperity. With this end in view they floated—on 14th December 1949—the first public issue of shares in the firm's history, heard in the board-room at Cathedral Street that it was oversubscribed four times within a few minutes, and then went on to plan for the future.

[1] The Board at this time consisted of W. A. R. Collins (Chairman and Managing Director); I. G. Collins (Vice-Chairman and Managing Director); W. Hope Collins (Managing Director); W. A. G. Morgan (Director, a member of the firm for forty-one years and latterly until his death in 1952 in charge of the stationery side of the business, having also been Chairman of the Diary Publishers' Association (1943-5) and of the Executive Board of the Stationers' Association (1944-5); Sydney J. Goldsack (Director, with thirty-nine years' service with the firm, first Chairman of the National Book League (1944-45); and R. A. Jamieson (Director, a member of the firm for twenty-five years and previously chief accountant of the Palestine Government Railways).

Kenneth Collins retired from the board about this time, as did Harry B. Lang, an accountant who had seen fifty-six years' service in the firm under four William Collinses, and Duncan McGibbon, another faithful member of the firm with forty years' experience of bindery management. It should be further noted that in 1951 two additional Directors were appointed: H. F. Philips, for many years in charge of the printing and binding factory, and, as Special Director, F. T. Smith, Chief Editor since 1926.

It was an impressive vote of confidence not only in the firm's financial stability but in its management and its vision for the future. To the historian the success of the flotation seems the crowning—in a few dramatic moments—of long imaginative toil. For inevitably as our story ends, memory roves back to William Collins I slaving with passion and genius in his tiny Candleriggs printing office; William II amid his Bibles and school texts, thrusting out the imperial tentacles on which one day his house's fortune was to rest; William III not only impetuously widening his overseas frontiers but adding flying buttresses at home; and William IV and Godfrey Collins providing books for the million and founding a new list of original literature. Of William V's skilful pilotage some future historian must speak. But certainly in the meantime his son William VI might well say with the Psalmist, " Yea, I have a goodly heritage."

Bibliography

IN VIEW of the extent to which I have drawn on the Chalmers MS. Collection in Edinburgh, it seemed unnecessary, when dealing with Dr. Chalmers, to give many footnote references. Students of the man and his profound influence on Scottish life will recognise Dr. Hanna's standard *Memoirs* as the source of facts long familiar. When Chalmers' own *Private Journal* (also in the MS. Collection and never published in full) is the source, due acknowledgment is made in the text. All new information about him is taken either from this Collection or, in a much lesser degree, from those records of the house of Collins which survived a twentieth-century bombing in London and at least one spring-cleaning orgy in Glasgow between 1819 and 1919.

As this book deals with the events of more than 160 years, the lengthy historical research involved has placed me deeply in the debt of many authorities.

In Edinburgh they were Mr. William Beattie, Keeper of Printed Books, National Library of Scotland; Dr. C. A. Malcolm, Signet Library; Mr. C. T. McInnes, Curator of Historical Records, Register House; the late Rev. Millar Patrick, D.D.; Miss Balfour of the Public Library's Edinburgh Room; Sir David Milne, K.C.B. and Mr. W. M. Ballantine of the Scottish Office; Messrs. William Blackwood and Son; Messrs. Oliver and Boyd; and especially the Rev. J. B. Primrose and Miss Leslie of the New College Library.

In Glasgow I am greatly indebted to Mr. John Dunlop of the Mitchell Library; Mr. William M. Hutcheson, Library of the Royal Faculty of Procurators; Mr. J. B. Boyd, Curator of the

"Old Glasgow" Museum; Mr. William Kerr, Town Clerk of Glasgow; Rev. Hassal Hanmer, Scottish Temperance Alliance; members of the house of Collins too numerous to mention; and Mrs. W. A. Collins.

In London I was helped by Mr. Walter de la Mare, C.H.; Mr. Robert Wilberforce; Mr. J. G. Wilson; Mr. M. Samuels, *News Chronicle* Library; and the staff of the London Library.

I must also warmly thank my brother, the Rev. Thomas H. Keir of Melrose and Mr. Cyril Ramsay Jones, two consistent well-springs of literary, historical and ecclesiastical knowledge. One final tribute I should like to have paid to an old member of the house of Collins in his presence. Unfortunately the late James McKenna of Glasgow died before this book was published, and could not therefore see the full fruits of his own devoted research into the firm's records and his enthusiastic help while it was being written.

It only remains to add that at this distance of time any vision of the firm's progress during the last twenty years must necessarily be imperfect: it is too foreshortened for historical perspective; and in any event, it would be quite impossible within the confines of this book to achieve a considered estimate of all in the great company of the firm's contemporary authors.

EIGHTEENTH AND NINETEENTH CENTURY SCOTLAND

Social

Social Life of Scotland in the Eighteenth Century by Henry Grey Graham (1900); *Peter's Letters to His Kinsfolk*, written anonymously by J. G. Lockhart (1819); *Memorials of His Time* by Lord Cockburn (Foulis, 1910); *Old Church Life in Scotland* by Andrew Edgar (1885); *The Social and Industrial History of Scotland from the Union* by Professor James MacKinnon (Longmans, Green, 1921); *History of the Ten Years' Conflict* by Robert Buchanan (1868); *Annals of the Disruption* by Thomas Brown (1893 edition);

Scottish Democracy, 1815-1840 by Laurance J. Saunders (Oliver and Boyd, 1950).

Literary

Scottish Men of Letters in the Eighteenth Century by Henry Grey Graham (1908); *A Literary History of Scotland* by J. H. Millar (1903); *The Glasgow University Press 1638-1931 with some notes on Scottish printing in the last Three Hundred Years* by James Maclehose (1931).

GLASGOW AND EASTWOOD

Glasgow

Annals of Glasgow by James Cleland (1816); *The Rise and Progress of the City of Glasgow* by James Cleland (1820); *Glasgow Past and Present* (1851); *Old Glasgow Essays* by John Oswald Mitchell (1905); *The Second City* by C. A. Oakley (Blackie and Son, Ltd., 1946); *Glasgow in 1901* by J. H. Muir (1901); *The Lord Provosts of Glasgow* (1883).

Eastwood

Sir John Sinclair's *Old Statistical Account of Scotland* (1791-1799); *Pollokshaws 1600-1912* by Andrew McCallum (Alexander Gardner, Paisley, 1925); *Eastwood* by Rev. George Campbell (1902).

WILLIAM COLLINS I

Robert Buchanan, D.D. by Norman L. Walker (1877); *Reminiscences* by Thomas Carlyle (1881); *Early Heroes of the Temperance Movement* by William Logan (1874); *Disruption Worthies* (1876); and most books on Dr. Thomas Chalmers.

Dr. Chalmers

Memoirs of the Life and Writings of Thomas Chalmers by William Hanna, four volumes (1849 ff.); *The Published Writings of Dr. Thomas Chalmers*, compiled by Professor Hugh Watt, D.D.

(Privately Printed 1943); *Thomas Chalmers and the Disruption* by Professor Hugh Watt (Thomas Nelson and Sons, Ltd., 1943); *Heritage, A Study of the Disruption* by Professor G. D. Henderson (Oliver and Boyd, 1943); *Letters and Journals of Anne Chalmers* (Privately Printed, 1922); *Miscellanies Literary and Historical*, Volume I, by Lord Rosebery (Hodder and Stoughton, 1921); *Germany, England and Scotland* by Merle D'Aubigné (1848).

COLLINS NINETEENTH-CENTURY AUTHORS AND PUBLICATIONS

(*excluding standard literary reference works*)

Life of William Wilberforce by R. J. and S. Wilberforce (1838); *Wilberforce* by Sir Reginald Coupland (Collins edition, 1945); *The Life of Edward Irving* by Mrs. Oliphant (1862); *The House of Smith Elder* (Privately Printed, 1923); *Letters to His Family* by Nathaniel Paterson, D.D. (1874); *Memoirs of the Life and Writings of James Montgomery* by John Holland and James Everett (1854); *Memoirs of the Life of Rev. Charles Simeon* by William Carus (third edition, 1848); *Memoir of Christopher North* by Mrs. Gordon (1879); *Foster's Life and Correspondence*, edited by J. E. Ryland, (1846); and the files of all nineteenth-century Glasgow newspapers.

COLLINS TWENTIETH-CENTURY AUTHORS AND PUBLICATIONS

The Georgian Literary Scene by Frank Swinnerton (Everyman's edition, J. M. Dent and Sons, Ltd., 1946); *British Authors, A Twentieth-Century Gallery* by Richard Church (Longmans, 1948 edition); *Twentieth-Century Authors* (The H. W. Wilson Company, New York, 1942); *Testament of Friendship* by Vera Brittain, a biography of Winifred Holtby (Macmillan, 1939); *Walter de la Mare* by Forrest Reid (Faber and Faber, Ltd., 1929); *Masters of Mystery* by H. Douglas Thomson (Collins, 1931); *Murder for Pleasure* by Howard Haycraft (Peter Davies, 1942).

Index

8416